With the SAS
and Other Animals

Dedication

For Nicola.

To David and Sarah

With best wishes

With the SAS and Other Animals

A Vet's War – The story of a young Veterinary Officer, seconded to the Special Air Service Regiment for six months during covert operations in the Arabian Gulf in 1974

Andrew   20. 5. 12

ANDREW HIGGINS

Pen & Sword
MILITARY

First published in Great Britain in 2011 by
PEN & SWORD MILITARY
An imprint of
Pen & Sword Books Ltd
47 Church Street
Barnsley
South Yorkshire
S70 2AS

ISBN 978-1-84884-486-5

Typeset by Concept, Huddersfield, West Yorkshire.
Printed and bound in England by CPI, UK.

Pen & Sword Books Ltd incorporates the imprints of Pen & Sword Aviation,
Pen & Sword Maritime, Pen & Sword Military, Wharncliffe Local History,
Pen & Sword Select, Pen & Sword Military Classics, Leo Cooper,
Remember When, Seaforth Publishing and Frontline Publishing.

For a complete list of Pen & Sword titles please contact
PEN & SWORD BOOKS LIMITED
47 Church Street, Barnsley, South Yorkshire, S70 2AS, England
E-mail: enquiries@pen-and-sword.co.uk
Website: www.pen-and-sword.co.uk

Contents

Preface vi

Foreword viii

Maps xi

Prologue – From Ulster With Love 1

1. The Kennel Club 4

2. *Bir Bint Ahmed* 10

3. BATTman 17

4. The *Wali* of Sudh 25

5. The Flying Scotsman 35

6. Flotsam and Jetsam 44

7. A Good Audience 55

8. An Iron in the Fire 64

9. Up the Hill 74

10. The Royal Connection 81

11. The Winged Dagger 96

12. The Muscateer 104

13. A Close Run Thing 119

14. His Majesty's Zoo 128

15. White City 141

16. Court and Social 148

17. The Animals Come First 159

18. The Coming of the Irish 167

19. A Load of Bull 176

20. A Sleepless Night 187

21. *Ma'a as-salaama* 194

Glossary and Abbreviations 201

Further Reading 205

Index 206

Preface

This book has been waiting in note form for over thirty-five years. The encouragement of my patient wife Nicola and my impatient children, Ben, Amelia, Joanna and Venetia, made me finally start writing an account of my experiences in Oman in 1974, based on a journal that I had the sense to keep at the time. Once the manuscript was in first draft, the book seemed to take on a life of its own and reopened friendships that had long since faded. Sadly, some of the people mentioned in the book have died. Several of them had a major impact on my life at the time – Oliver Graham-Jones, Roy and Elizabeth Ansell, Mac Maclean, John Clarke, Tony Brunton, Philip and Laura Romans, Brigadier Jack Fletcher, Brigadier Harry Orr, General Sir John Akehurst and General Sir Tim Creasey. I hope in a way this book can serve as a small tribute to them.

Encouraging yet down to earth comments on the manuscript came from Paddy King-Fretts, my Squadron Commander in Dhofar and a published author himself. Scott Moffat and Chuck Pringle had many constructive views that helped me a lot. Thanks too to those friends and family members who offered to read the text and made valuable suggestions. All remaining errors are my fault alone, so please can I say sorry in advance where I have got it wrong?

My aim in writing the book was threefold: firstly to try and craft an interesting story about a remarkable part of my life as a young and rather impressionable man endeavouring to adapt to highly unusual and certainly very unexpected circumstances; secondly, I wanted to recount something of the veterinary profession's contribution to a serious conflict in the ever sensitive Middle East; finally, I thought it would be interesting to look at the SAS in the 1970s through the eyes of an outsider privileged to work with the most professional, dedicated and skilled soldiers in the world. During their five month Dhofar tour in 1974, 'A' Squadron lost two men killed in action (Captain Simon Garthwaite and Lance-Corporal 'Curly' Kent) and several were wounded. There were also decorations – one Distinguished Campaign Medal, two Military Medals and three were Mentioned in Dispatches. They were an amazing group of men to be with.

I would also like to acknowledge the work of my six predecessors as Operation Storm's BATT Vets: Tony Horne, Brian Thompson, Geoffrey Durrant, John Clemenger, Bill McLaren and of course the redoubtable Scott Moffat, my predecessor, mentor and guide. All were serving RAVC Veterinary Officers and I trod carefully in their footsteps benefitting from the solid foundations they had laid in the previous four years.

To my delight, Richard Dannatt agreed to write the Foreword – the importance of 'heart and minds' has always been close to his own heart, not least during his challenging years as Chief of the General Staff. Lord Dannatt, who is now Constable of the Tower of London, is a Founder Patron of Help for Heroes (www.helpforheroes.org.uk), the charity that ensures injured servicemen never feel neglected or rejected by the people of the United Kingdom. The charity will benefit by the sale of every copy of this book.

Finally, I offer my thanks to David Thurlow for critically reading the draft and for his editing talents, and to Blair Wallace for his help with the photographs and for skilfully extracting some of them from ancient Super-8 film. I am greatly indebted to the superb team at Pen & Sword, particularly Pamela Covey, Matt Jones, Jon Wilkinson and Noel Sadler, for their help at all stages of the production process, and to Henry Wilson not only for his faith in the book but also for the inspired title and for his unfailing courtesy, humour, patience and guidance.

I have tried to limit the amount of abbreviations, but they seem to be an inescapable part of the British army's way of life. Hopefully the glossary will help and also provide a few often used Arabic expressions.

I do hope you enjoy this gentle stroll through a small, but unique period of history.

Andrew Higgins
Bury St Edmunds, Suffolk
June 2011

Foreword

By General The Lord Dannatt
GCB, CBE, MC, DL
Chief of the General Staff 2006–2009

The key to winning any counter-insurgency campaign is the support of the local population and, to me, 'Hearts and Minds' describes how to gain the trust, confidence and respect of people caught up in a conflict by pragmatic and psychological means. Without local support, insurgents will become increasingly isolated as supplies, shelter and secrecy diminish. The process is usually a long one, and not without risk as the rebels may inflict appalling brutality in their struggle to regain influence and control over a previously compliant community.

The concept is not new. General Sir Gerald Templar, when Director of Operations during the Malaya Emergency, said in 1952: 'The answer lies not in pouring more troops into the jungle, but in the hearts and minds of the Malayan people.' Even earlier, President John Quincy Adams in 1818 writing about the American Revolution commented:

The Revolution was effected before the War commenced ... (and) was in the minds and hearts of the people; a change in their religious sentiments of their duties and obligations. This radical change in the principles, opinions, sentiments and affections of the people, was the real American Revolution.

In warfare, the aim of all psychological operations (or PSYOPS) is to influence the perceptions, attitudes and behaviour of targeted groups in order to gain political or military objectives. Today the main vehicle is the media – television, radio, newspapers – but on the ground, often in areas where communications are limited, other more basic methods are needed. These might include the scattering of leaflets by air, use of posters, and the deployment of extension teams trained to penetrate the population in order to demonstrate tangible and sustainable benefits and to influence basic perceptions. Depending on the circumstances, the desired outcome may be any number of needs, such as the provision of food, water, housing, medicine, religious freedom and, of course, weapons. However, the overriding necessity in any successful Hearts and Minds campaign is the establishment of ongoing political stability and reliability.

The British model of PSYOPS was honed in the Second World War and has been used widely in many campaigns including Northern Ireland, Kosovo, Iraq and Afghanistan. It succeeds only as long as it does not alienate populations that are already confused, often frightened, deprived of basic necessities and unstable. Most are looking for little more than peace, political stability, order and a better future for themselves and their families. Kicking the door in uninvited, as the Multinational Force did in Iraq, does not pave the way to winning the 'minds and hearts of the people'.

Operation Storm was a covert operation, which was fought between 1970 and 1975 for the hearts and minds of the *jebali*, or hill tribes of Dhofar in Southern Oman. Soldiers of 22 Special Air Service Regiment were deployed to help the Sultan's Armed Forces destroy communist insurgents operating from bases in the neighbouring People's Democratic Republic of Yemen. The objective was to recruit local tribesmen, turn them, train them to fight, and show the people that what was offered by the government of the newly-installed Sultan Qaboos was infinitely better than that of the failed regime of his father, or a future under the communist-driven policies of the insurgents and their backers.

The lives of the *jebalis* were largely focused on cattle as well as camels and goats. Their wealth was vested in their herds and flocks. As part of the Hearts and Minds approach to Operation Storm it was shrewdly decided to target the needs not only of the tribesmen, but also of their animals. Wells were drilled and water troughs built at key locations, which were used for education and other purposes. Veterinary care was included by attaching a British army Veterinary Officer to the SAS squadron as part of the British Army Training Team. The BATT Vet, as he was known, helped the civilian authorities to establish basic animal healthcare policies and supported military units on the *jebali*, often by providing a rapid response to disease outbreaks or other animal health problems. Not easy in a war zone.

Andrew Higgins was the last of the BATT Vets to serve in Dhofar. He has provided an entertaining insight into a specialised but significant part of Operation Storm during a critical period in 1974. There are many books on the military aspects of this important conflict, which successfully stopped the potential expansion of Marxist influence along the Arabian

Gulf. This is, however, the first account of the role played by the Royal Army Veterinary Corps in supporting the Hearts and Minds programme. It deserves recording as part of the history of defeating a rebellion.

Richard Dannatt
The Tower of London
Tower Hill
London EC3

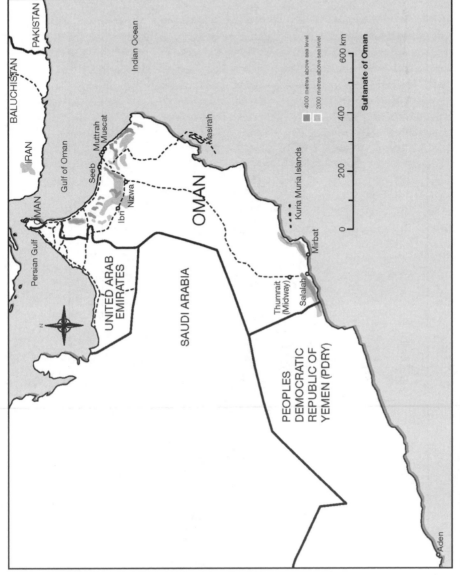

Oman and the Arabian Gulf.

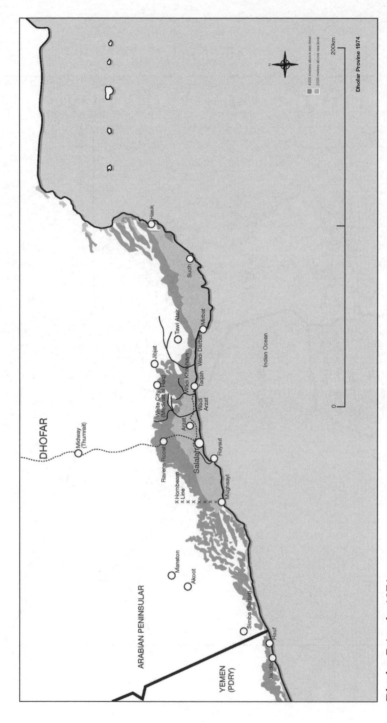

Dhofar Brigade 1974.

Prologue

From Ulster With Love

It is January 1974, and I am Acting Captain in Her Majesty's Royal Army Veterinary Corps, posted at short notice to Dhofar on the Arabian Gulf, on an attachment classified as Secret, to 'A' Squadron of 22 Special Air Service.

Christmas 1973 inside Long Kesh prison camp in Northern Ireland had been unutterably gloomy and there seemed no prospect of a new posting for at least a further eighteen months. There was an establishment of three RAVC officers in the Province in charge of 1 Army Dog Unit (1ADU) with its 170 army dogs and handlers. Since the troubles restarted in the late 1960s, infantry battalions had become drearily familiar with repeated four-month tours of duty, but because of the nature of their duties and the skilled training involved in pairing a soldier with an arms/explosive search dog, it was considered uneconomical to post dog-handlers to Ireland for less than two years. This was tough on the soldiers, their families – and their officers.

I had been in Kesh for six months, having been posted to Ireland within months of graduating as a veterinary surgeon from the University of London's Royal Veterinary College in March 1973. It now looked as though I would be spending most of the remainder of my three-year Short Service Commission based in that bleak bog, recently re-named the Maze Prison. Admittedly, the job did have its bright moments. To visit some of the twenty-five units with dogs I could sometimes task a helicopter, which was exhilarating and felt far safer than using a routine unmarked Q car. My job was to visit the units regularly, examine the dogs and talk to the men, posted away from their families for far too long as their infantry colleagues came and went. The physical and mental fitness and capability of both dogs and their handlers were vital. People's lives could and often did depend on a 'sniffer' dog detecting whether or not a barn door, or a car, or a milk churn was clean or had been booby-trapped with explosives.

Active service changes people philosophically and emotionally and Ireland had changed me. I had grown up very quickly during my posting to 1ADU. I was a recent graduate, with a conventional middle-class, Catholic upbringing and no concept of the hatred that existed in the prison, in the towns and throughout much of the Province. How could it have happened that a green vet, clutching his barely dry certificate of membership of the Royal College of Veterinary Surgeons, had been sent to a war zone in Ireland with virtually no military training? The answer was that the escalation of the troubles in Ulster and operational commitments elsewhere meant the RAVC had become so severely stretched that there had simply been no time for training at Mons or Sandhurst, and my introduction to army life had comprised a crash course in basic military instruction from the Corps RSM at the HQ in Melton Mowbray, dog-handling and riding courses, and a few hours on the ranges. I had to hit the ground running in Northern Ireland and it had been up to me to learn how to deal with totally new and difficult problems including, during my six-month tour there, the deaths of two of the Unit's soldiers and the maiming of two others.

Major Gerry Quigley, a Scot, had been Regimental Sergeant-Major of the RAVC before he received his commission. He was in his forties and was now Officer Commanding 1ADU. Gerry had gone on leave for Christmas and I had been left, at least nominally, in temporary charge. He got back to the Unit on 27 December and started to deal with his backlog of mail and signals. After briefing him with tales of my non-festive season, I returned to the relative peace of my office and pharmacy on the Camp perimeter.

Later in the day as I was dealing with the mangled tail of an irascible German Shepherd guard dog the telephone rang and the pharmacy NCO, Lance-Corporal Johnson, told me I was wanted by the OC as soon as possible. This was not unusual, as Gerry often wanted me to cover for him while he went to Headquarters at nearby Lisburn. So, having put in the last stitch and settled the sleepy but still grumpy animal on a blanket to recover from the anaesthetic, I drove up to the main Camp. Gerry was in his office talking to the Unit Staff Sergeant, George Yeandle. George was the man who had almost single-handedly made up for my lack of military training and taught me more about the army and how to be an officer than anyone else. A large, formidable-looking man with a bristling black handlebar moustache and a booming West Country voice that worked to good effect on his men, George was indispensable to the soldiers to whom he was nanny, teacher, counsellor and close to God. I had no illusions about him being my guardian too and he often saved me from making a fool of myself. At heart he was a gamekeeper and he bred German short-haired pointers quietly in the Long Kesh kennels. The Camp, on a disused airfield, was ideal for dog-training and through George's generosity and encouragement, I started my own lifelong affair with those lovely dogs.

The OC's office was small. I knocked, went in and saluted. Gerry told me to sit down, so I took off my beret and waited with curiosity mixed with apprehension as he picked up a piece of paper from a closed file marked with red stamps declaring its contents were 'Secret', 'Eyes Only' and 'Urgent'. Secret signals had not really come into my life, and I associated them with another part of the army rather distant from my work with amputated tails, sore pads and vaccination certificates. He told me the signal was from the MOD and concerned me. I could feel my increased heart rate as my mind raced trying to work out what could be coming next. The telex print-out advised that my two-year posting had been altered due to what was referred to as 'the contingencies of the service' and I would be leaving Northern Ireland at the end of the week and would be posted to the British Army Training Team in BFPO 66; Dhofar, Oman. Full briefing details would follow. In the meantime, I was to return at once to the RAVC Depot.

I knew that for a few years the RAVC had seconded a Veterinary Officer to 22 SAS operating in Oman. Although the posting was classified, some good stories had been told by the officers, all Majors up to now, who had been posted there. However, the posting had been scheduled to end with the present incumbent, Major Scott Moffat, an amiable Glasgow veterinary graduate about twenty years older than me. I hadn't given a single thought to the possibility that I might be posted there. It just wasn't an option. And where was Oman anyway?

Now I was being told on a gloomy December afternoon that I was on my way to the Middle East. It was unbelievably bloody marvellous! Gerry Quigley remained expressionless. He told me matter-of-factly that I was to be given the Acting rank of Captain until becoming substantive, which was due anyway in four months' time. He then reminded me that 'Secret' meant what it said and that I was to tell no one about the posting. As far as the world was concerned, I would be in BFPO 66. The prospect of telling friends and family that I was being sent to an unknown destination overseas, only identified by its British Forces Post Box number, was going to create a bit of a stir – but hell, it was exciting.

Chapter 1

The Kennel Club

Queasy was not the word for it. Confused. Sozzled. Pissed as a newt. I knew I had drunk too many beers in the boisterous sweltering wooden hut that was the dog-handlers' Mess, but it had been a very long day and the effects of the alcohol were aggravated by jet-lag and tiredness. I managed to stagger to my feet, sway over to the President of the Mess Committee, a wizened Flight Sergeant, who looked long and hard at me as I slurred out some words of thanks before raising an uncertain hand in farewell and weaving my way out of the door. It seemed a ridiculous introduction to RAF Salalah, that unlikely and bleak outpost of the British military in Arabia.

I leaned against the hut. God, it was hot; a sultry, oppressive Arabian night. The sweat poured down my face and I wondered how I would find my way back to my room in this sprawling, brown, dusty camp. There was a full moon and the stars twinkled with an intense brightness in the cloudless sky. A chorus of frogs croaked and cicadas called shrilly and fitfully to each other across the sandy tracks winding between the silent, blacked-out buildings. I shook my fuddled head.

A gale of laughter sounded from the shack. I noticed a dilapidated sign hanging limply from the sun-bleached timber lintel announcing in faded red letters that this was *The Kennel Club*. The dog-handlers were NCOs in the RAF Regiment (affectionately known as Rock-apes), which was responsible for guarding this small piece of the United Kingdom. *The Kennel Club* was their oasis in a war zone where the operational and living conditions were difficult and off-duty drinking was serious. I smiled despite my weariness as I had thoroughly enjoyed my evening sharing dog and vet stories with these professionals. However, the day was drawing rapidly to a close and I aimed myself unsteadily in what I hoped was the general direction of the prefabricated wing where passing British diplomats and oddments like me were housed when no room could be found in the overcrowded Officers' Mess.

I was lucky to have a room to myself. It was large, but sparsely furnished with a creaking and worryingly wobbly ceiling fan, which might once have been white and had several exposed wires that looked as if they would be best avoided. There were also mosquitoes, squadrons of them; they had no difficulty snubbing the torn tin mesh grilles that half-heartedly lined the window and outer door. The bed had been made up with a single pillow and two greyish sheets and I rapidly undressed and lay on it staring nauseously at the slowly revolving fan. This was to be home for the next few days until I took over as Veterinary Officer to the British Army Training Team, and my predecessor had taken his six-month-old suntan back to the RAVC Depot in a wintry Melton Mowbray.

I was surprised to find that my head was gradually clearing, helped by the squirts of adrenaline that periodically shot round my body in response to the unfamiliar deep booms which resonated around the base, as defensive 25-pounders positioned around the RAF Camp fired their warning shells into the hills, collectively known as the *jebal*, that surrounded Salalah.

Salalah. The garden town, and capital of Dhofar Province, that war-torn region of south-east Arabia bathed by the Indian Ocean and part of the Sultanate of Oman. There had been a sizeable influx of British military assistance into Oman since a coup in July 1970 had overthrown the old Sultan, Said bin Taimur, and his son, the 29-year-old Sandhurst-trained Qaboos bin Said, had assumed power. Up till then insurgents, mainly a revolutionary force called the Popular Front for the Liberation of the Occupied Arabian Gulf, known by the awkward acronym PFLOAG, had almost succeeded in taking over this under-developed but potentially oil- and mineral-rich territory. Now, under Qaboos, the country was slowly beginning to emerge from decades of neglect. PFLOAG, which had evolved from a group of Dhofar dissidents, promoted and nurtured by the Russians and Chinese, operated from bases in Oman's southern neighbour, the communist People's Democratic Republic of Yemen, or PDRY.

By January 1974, three and a half years after the coup, the well-armed and determined enemy forces had been pushed further back from the plains into the surrounding Qara Mountains, from where they still harried the Sultan's forces and their British support. Only a few months before, a *Katyusha* 122mm rocket fired from the *jebal* had landed outside the RAF Officers' Mess injuring nine people. So nobody took any chances and the 25-pounders continued to pound into the night.

I was excited. There was no doubt of that. It felt surreal to be lying on a bed in a Foreign Office hut some 5,500 kilometres from home, under a creaking fan and listening to the infuriating high-pitched whine of invisible Omani mosquitoes. Every so often, the room lit up as a Verey light exploded on the *jebal*, its incandescence penetrating the sun-faded, ill-fitting, unlined cotton curtains and filling the room eerily with colours.

The sound of the Hercules transporter aircraft in which I had spent sixteen long, cold, hungry and extremely noisy hours still reverberated

5

round my weary brain. More experienced soldiers found a space straight after take-off, got into their sleeping bags, covered their heads and slept until we touched down at RAF Akrotiri in Cyprus. The rest of us on our bum-aching webbed seating along the sides of the rattling dimly-lit drone looked glumly at each other, realising that conversation, sleep and reading were out of the question. The only entertainment was to watch the wires and controls of the aircraft move erratically above our heads until, after several uncomfortable hours, a Loadmaster arrived with a cardboard box containing a few tired sandwiches, a bit of fruit and a bottle of Coke.

Old Oman hands tended to avoid the Brize Norton-Akrotiri-Salalah C-130 route. They booked on the long-haul VC10 service to Singapore, which stopped to refuel at RAF Masirah, an island off the north-east coast of Oman. The VC10 Squadron was also used to ferry Ministers and VIPs and had more conventional passenger comforts. After a good night's sleep on Masirah, it was possible to catch a shuttle to Salalah. Yet, as so often in life, it's funny how nobody tells you these little nuggets until it is too late.

The Hercules had eventually bounced into RAF Salalah and I had staggered down the rear ramp into the blinding desert sun to meet the outgoing Veterinary Officer, Scott Moffat, and his chief assistant, Veterinary Dresser Number 1, Saleh bin Hassan Al Yafai. I cannot imagine what Saleh must have thought of this young, sleep-deprived wreck that emerged out of the murky interior of the Herc, stuttering out some words of greeting in Arabic, inadequately learned on a crash course at the Royal Army Education Corps Centre in Beaconsfield the previous week. Still, he was very polite and carried my bag enthusiastically to Scott's battered grey Land Rover pick-up.

The British Army Training Team, or BATT, had been in Salalah since 1970 and for most of the time its presence was virtually unknown to the British public. The Omanis wanted to focus on modernisation and had no wish to attract world attention to the assistance they were receiving from outsiders. The British government had played a careful balancing act, reflecting the strategic importance of Oman at the entrance to the vital oilfields of the Gulf and the need to avoid any charge of imperialist meddling at a time when Britain was taking positive steps to withdraw from the region. The Special Air Service was ideally suited for such a low-key role.

I had been briefed at the headquarters of 22 SAS at Bradbury Lines in Hereford by Lieutenant-Colonel Peter de la Billière, a soldier from the Durham Light Infantry who later was to become a household name as Commander-in-Chief of the British forces in the 1990 Gulf War. In 1974 he commanded 22 SAS. When he talked, his vivid and penetrating blue eyes darted constantly and he paced his office like a caged tiger talking with infectious enthusiasm and boundless energy, illustrating his points by jabbing at maps and wall charts. He was dressed in an army pullover and SAS belt and there was a packed Bergen rucksack near the door as if to demonstrate his readiness for any action anywhere and at any time.

Peter de la Billière was friendly and welcoming, and reassuring about the value of the BATT Vet post over the previous four years. It was, he said, one of the four pillars of Operation Storm, the codename for the Dhofar campaign, which he considered to be of such strategic importance that it would go down in history as a significant battle for Western supremacy and the fight against communism. The counter-insurgency effort was being developed hand in hand with psychological warfare designed to demonstrate to the battered population the merits of Sultan Qaboos' rule and the shortcomings of PFLOAG's communist alternative. Agricultural development and animal health were a vital strategic part of the civilian reorganisation of Dhofar's rural economy.

I was handed over to a stocky sergeant, who had completed three tours in Oman. On one tour, he reassuringly told me, he had survived a helicopter crash by rolling himself into a tight ball as the aircraft plummeted to the ground. He explained the province's geography and climate, and how the fighting was made more difficult by the annual monsoon, which, unusually for Arabia, hit Dhofar between June and September each year with mist and drizzle, known as the *khareef*, that markedly restricted operations. The war, I learned, was progressing satisfactorily but slowly, painstakingly so at times. Sultan Qaboos was, said the sergeant, remarkably British in many of his cultural attitudes. This wasn't surprising as his father, who had a great affection for Britain, had read, written and spoken English perfectly. He had, however, brought up his only son in a narrow, traditional and simple style with few privileges. After this repressive childhood, Qaboos had been sent to England in the care of the Reverend Philip Romans, a tutor, who with his wife Laura had endeavoured to educate and prepare him for his future life. He had learned English, studied British local government administration and, finally, gained admission to the Royal Military Academy, Sandhurst.

Qaboos had graduated from Sandhurst in 1962 and was commissioned into the Cameronians (Scottish Rifles). This was followed by a year with the battalion in Germany before his father recalled him to Salalah. When he returned to Oman his freedom was severely restricted, reflecting the old man's irrational insistence that his son should have no favours or live any better than other Omanis. As a result, the young Qaboos was placed under virtual house arrest in the Old Palace in Salalah, where he must have lived a frustrating and restless existence. However, although he was given no responsibility, he was allowed visits from selected British friends and in this way he was able to plan the eventual overthrow of his father with the help of his contemporary at Sandhurst, Tim Landon, then a junior intelligence officer in Dhofar.

The RAF Regiment and artillery were sent to secure the airfield in Salalah and were soon joined by other British support. The SAS had originally been sent to Oman to protect the new Sultan. Then BATT had been set up to train the tough, battle-scarred tribesmen, known as *firqats* who had come over to Sultan Qaboos' side after his accession. Training and taming this local militia was no easy task, but their role would be fundamental in winning the war and overcoming the communist-inspired indoctrination of the *jebali* or hill people. The *firqats* knew their enemy, the *adoo*, better than anyone else, as they had been part of them. They knew the location of the *adoo* bases and arms caches, their plans, arms sources and command chains, and were a priceless source of intelligence information.

Despite his youth and inexperience, Sultan Qaboos had set to work at once, offering an amnesty and promising much. Some *firqats* came over immediately; others chose to wait and see how the pendulum might swing. To join the government side, however, did have its dangers. The *jebali* people of the Qara hills were fiercely tribal and were largely indifferent to life and death. Vengeance could be wreaked in many ways and disloyalty to the tribe or tribal leader could have profound and fatal effects on other family members.

The new Sultan shrewdly went for their hearts and minds to show that he could offer more than guns and atheism to these poor, often confused and deeply religious people. What was needed was action, not words. So Sultan Qaboos started building settlements at strategic points on the hill. Wells were drilled to enormous depths, and at huge expense, to provide clean and pure water. Storage tanks were made available, as were drinking troughs for the nomadic *jebalis* to bring their cattle, goats and camels.

These settlements allowed the government to interact with the people, but it was made clear that if enemy action resumed, the new life-supporting water supplies and assistance would be cut off. Under the aegis of the Dhofar Development Department, Civil Aid Teams moved in to supplement the water with essential food requirements, basic schooling and medical services. A mosque (often a prefabricated hut) was put up and a programme of agricultural improvement started. Because the new settlements were vulnerable to attack, BATT detachments had been posted at key locations to train the *firqats* how to guard their new-found rewards.

Nomadic people's wealth is often vested in their animals. The Qara people's lives were centred on their cattle and a man with thirty or forty cows was rich. To put it into perspective, the dowry for a beautiful young wife might be fifty cows. In 1974, a *jebali* goat might have been worth £80 (perhaps five or six times as much in today's terms), a cow £250 and a good camel £500 or more. It was an enormous investment and so it was not surprising that a sick animal was sometimes viewed with greater concern even than a sick child. Sultan Qaboos' decision to include a veterinarian in the Hearts and Minds campaign was a clever way of demonstrating in practical terms that he really understood his *jebali* people and was doing what he could to help address their practical needs.

In the longer term, it had been planned that the DDD would take over the veterinary responsibilities and employ civilian veterinarians to do the job. Scott Moffat was supposed to be the last British army Veterinary Officer in Oman, but it was not yet safe enough for a civilian to work on the *jebal* where the success of the Hearts and Minds drive was crucial. So the decision was made to have just one more military vet. Me.

The Verey lights continued to shine, the artillery continued to pound, the squeaking fan continued to turn and the effects of my exhausting journey finally sent me to sleep on my little bed in Salalah. The mosquitoes sharpened their fangs and prepared for dinner.

Chapter 2

Bir Bint Ahmed

At 7.30 the next morning I was awakened by a swarthy unshaven Pakistani Mess attendant bearing a mug of British army tea, made with condensed milk and half a pound of sugar. This was Mohammed. He was wearing a none-too-clean shirt, pyjama-type trousers and blue flip-flops. Mohammed muttered a few deferential words in some language halfway between Urdu and English, as I blearily watched him open the thin cotton curtains and politely pick up and remove my travel-worn clothes, which had been flung haphazardly into a dusty corner the previous evening.

Twenty minutes later, Scott collected me for breakfast. Over a hundred British serving officers and Sultan's Armed Forces (SAF) mercenary or contract officers from a variety of countries, but mainly the UK, lived in the Mess and ate together in the large dining room. Breakfast was as silent as an enclosed convent, with the quiet broken only by a gentle rustling of tatty, dog-eared pages of week-old newspapers. The food was pretty awful. Reconstituted milk did not taste good on stale cornflakes. The vintage eggs from Lebanon were served without any bacon out of respect for the country's religion. The bread was impressive only for the number of dead weevils per slice. Scott warned me off the coffee and suggested lemon tea, with generous spoonfuls of sugar, which was good advice. The atmosphere dampened my excitement so I sat down and flicked unenthusiastically through an ancient *Sunday Times* magazine and absently scratched my mosquito bites as I pondered the day ahead.

After breakfast we made a brief courtesy call on the RAF Camp Commander, a Wing Commander who clearly relished his position. He proudly surveyed his territory through his office window and explained that the immediate protection of the airfield was provided by the RAF Regiment with artillery support from Cracker Battery, home to the 25-pounders that had greeted me the previous night. There were also things called Hedgehogs, which were observation posts on the Camp's perimeter; defensive trenches made of lumps of concrete, oil-drums, ammunition boxes, sandbags and razor wire. Outside the window the Camp was a hive of activity and in addition to the usual airfield bustle and noise, aircraft were beginning to warm up and take off.

Courtesies over, and with Scott at the wheel of the Vet Land Rover, we careered out of the Camp and along the road towards the Dhofar Development Department's Farm Project at *Bir Bint Ahmed*, literally Ahmed's well, a couple of kilometres or so to the west of the town, where the Veterinary Officer had his office and pharmacy.

Tarmac roads were a fairly new introduction to Oman. The previous Sultan had been apprehensive of modern ways and the threat he felt that roads and cars posed to the traditional, Islamic way of life meant that he had successfully kept the country's transport system in an almost medieval time warp. The same applied to social services. There had been virtually no schools and no higher education. Apart from one American missionary hospital at Ruwi, just outside Muscat, run by a few dedicated non-conformists, there were only a handful of medical dispensaries scattered around the country. The first hospital in Dhofar, with just twenty-two beds, had opened in 1961. There had been very little mains electricity, or sewage disposal or mains water, no television and hardly any telephones. Jeans were prohibited as was cigarette-smoking, and of course alcohol was banned. Outside visitors were rare and it was said that the old Sultan personally issued all visas for foreigners entering Oman. Nobody was allowed to move about the country without permission.

Sultan Qaboos was slowly and progressively reversing his father's obsessions and was intent on liberating his people. The Omanis responded well to this new permissiveness, as health and education began to leap the centuries in giant steps. A few roads had been built, including a loop around Salalah town and a road to the port, Raysut, about 20 kilometres to the west beyond *Bir Bint Ahmed*. The new Ruler moved at a pace he could control and finance. Oil revenue was increasing and offered considerable opportunity, but the reserves in Oman were nothing like those of its oil-rich neighbours in Saudi Arabia or the United Arab Emirates.

Bir Bint Ahmed was part of the Dhofar Development Department's Agriculture Branch, which was run by an ex-cavalry officer called Mike Butler. Mike was responsible to the Director of DDD, a British mandarin called Robin Young who steered the overall development of the Province and worked closely with the local Governor, or *Wali*, Sheikh Braik bin Hamoud, Sultan Qaboos' personal representative in Dhofar. Braik had played a key role in helping Qaboos to overthrow his father, who was quietly retired to the Dorchester Hotel in London's Park Lane where he had died in 1972.

The people of Oman considered themselves to be either 'Omanis' or 'Dhofaris'. The birth of Qaboos in 1940 had bridged this divide as his mother was a much-loved Dhofari woman, Princess Mizoon bint Ahmed Al-Mashani, affectionately known as Bibi. In 1974, Bibi spent much of her time at a small residence and farm at Shabiat, on the outskirts of Salalah. Although Qaboos had been shut up in his father's high, windowless

11

fortress on the waterfront in Salalah, as Sultan he built a small palace at Robat, just outside the town and not far from the RAF Camp. He took a keen personal interest in all aspects of development in the Province as well as in the counter-insurgency campaign and was said to be very close to Sheikh Braik, who provided him with much of the Dhofar intelligence.

As Scott filled me in on the background, we reached *Bir Bint Ahmed*, a surprising oasis of greenery. Salalah and those bits of Dhofar that annually caught the tip of the monsoon were well supplied with water, and along the coast where the monsoon struck there were palm trees and some lush plantations. On the *jebal* itself, thick vegetation grew in the rainy season; this was glorious to look at, but from a military perspective the growth often seriously restricted operations and provided excellent cover for the *adoo*.

We turned through crumbling gates and went along a drive through fertile gardens to a whitewashed single-storey building. Scott parked the Land Rover, and as the engine died I could hear the gentle throbbing of a diesel pump as it pushed water from a well along an impressive *falaj* or open aqueduct system feeding small alfalfa fields and vegetable patches around the farm. It seemed extraordinarily tranquil.

Two wiry, scruffy but traditionally dressed Arabs clambered to their feet as we turned towards the entrance to the building. These, explained Scott, were our *askars*, a sort of Home Guard, who survived as a relic from the old days when there had been no police force and the *askari* had carried out whatever policing duties were needed. The two *askars*, who had been appointed by the *Wali* for our protection, stood to attention as we got out of the Land Rover. One had no teeth and looked about eighty with a worn, deeply-etched brown face and a straggling grey beard. He was dressed in a filthy grey *jalabiya*, or dishdash (the long robe traditionally worn by the men), and a headdress of uncertain colour. His companion on the other hand was about thirteen, and his ancient Martini-Henry rifle was longer than he was. He looked very much the junior version of his partner and had a cigarette dangling from his lips. This he removed and they both gave us cheery grins and murmurs of polite greetings as they waved us into their protectorate.

Scott showed me round. The building was thoughtfully designed. There were two offices, a store-room, washroom and a small room for the *askars* with a couple of mattresses, a primus stove and a few cooking things. Next to a sparsely equipped laboratory, manned by a spare-looking, Pakistani technician called Abdur Rahim ('utterly useless!' muttered Scott) was a multi-purpose examination room, where minor surgery could be performed. This room opened on to a yard at the back, where there were four loose boxes, in one of which was a sick calf. A scribbled card pinned to the door explained that it was a doubtful reactor to a tuberculosis test and was waiting to be re-checked.

A few metres away were two bull-pens – good, solid structures made of concrete and steel piping and each containing a large, overweight and very sleepy bull. Scott explained that Mike Butler had brought the bulls from R'as al Khaymah, one of the Emirates further up the Gulf. He hoped to use them to upgrade and improve the poor productivity of the local *jebali* cattle. One was a Friesian-Hereford cross-bred whose weight I thought must have brought tears to the eyes of the tiny *jebali* cows. The bulls had been flown in by the RAF and caused mayhem and panic on the aircraft by struggling heroically to break out of their crates.

Scott and I were leaning on the bull-pen musing on veterinary problems when a noisy scooter skidded to a halt behind us. Two Arabs dismounted.

'*Salaam alay koom,*' said the shorter and fatter of the two, beaming at us with a broad and friendly grin.

'*Way alay koom salaam,*' Scott replied in Arabic, and we all shook hands.

I recognised the chief Veterinary Assistant, Saleh, who had come to the airport to meet me. Saleh was about 40 and had been with all the BATT Vets – a point he emphasised in his halting but understandable English by listing them one by one.

The second man was Hafeedth bin Ahmed Al Theeb, officially the Base Number 2 Assistant. He was younger and wore a lime green trouser suit with black shoes and sunglasses topped off with a traditional Moslem cap or *tagiyah*. I was pleased to discover that he also spoke reasonable English.

We walked back to the office where Saleh conjured up tea with the expediency of any British squaddie anywhere. This was my first exposure to the hot, sweet, milk-free brew served in small glasses that the Omanis enjoyed as tea. I soon learned that Arabs are instinctively welcoming and sociable and take great pleasure in looking after guests. Scott warned that I would need a digestive system like a sponge to cope with all the tea, coffee and canned fruit juice that would be coming my way.

Like most Dhofaris, Saleh had spent most of his life in the Province. His wife came from a village called Taqah, 35 kilometres east of Salalah and once an important centre for the frankincense trade. Since the fighting began, the graded road between Salalah and Taqah had become unsafe due to indiscriminate laying of mines by the *adoo*. Now, he told me, the drive to Taqah was along the beach in a fast Land Rover.

Scott worked hard to brief me and explain how the system worked. When at base, he came to *Bir Bint Ahmed* first thing every morning and Saleh told him what visits were requested in the town and surrounding villages. It became clear that the position of BATT Vet was multi-faceted and that my parish was divided essentially into three sections. First there were the coastal plains around Salalah itself – a strip of land of about

13

90 square kilometres bounded to the south by the Arabian Sea and to the north by a few kilometres' thickness of fertile *jebal*. People often brought their animals to *Bir Bint Ahmed* either on foot or trussed in the back of a pick-up truck, and routine visits were made within the town and to the villages and settlements in the immediate area inside 'the Wire', a perimeter fence some 6 kilometres either side of the town centre. Outside the Wire, there were trips to other villages on the plain, like Taqah for example, or to the quarantine station at Raysut to deal with the huge numbers of imported food animals.

Secondly, there was the work with the BATT units providing animal health support on the *jebal* itself. The Qara hills comprised green foothills and a plateau, all only a few kilometres deep, before they merged into the *Negd* desert wilderness. These trips were usually organised a few days in advance and generally required the use of either a helicopter or Skyvan. The work involved close liaison with the BATT teams in the operational area and could be dangerous. I would be a target.

Thirdly, there was the veterinary care of the Sultan's animals. Needless to say, this was a sensitive duty and one that had to be handled with care. Scott told me that the Sultan kept horses, camels, cattle, goats and dogs. And his mother, Bibi, had a farm and a large cat. Most of the royal horses were kept in the north at a place called Wutayyah, just outside Muscat. The Stable Manager was a British ex-army officer, Major John Clarke, who was a veteran of the 1958–59 *Jebal Akhdar*, or Green Mountain, campaign in Northern Oman, in which the SAS had played a highly significant role in overcoming an earlier internal revolt against Sultan Said bin Taimur. The Major was competent in dealing with most minor veterinary problems, but if something serious arose, he would signal BATT and the vet would be sent north on the first available flight. On one occasion, Scott told me he had been summoned by John to deal with a severe colic in one of His Majesty's favourite mares and they had flown him up in a two-seater Strikemaster getting him to Muscat in a little over an hour, by which time the mare had fully recovered.

The Royal Stables had a branch in Salalah and Scott advised me to look in regularly. John Clarke visited every few weeks to check that the *syces*, or grooms, were doing their job properly. When the Sultan was in residence, John tended to base himself in Salalah, as the Ruler liked to ride out, often at very short notice. Fortunately, most of the horses were hardy, Arab-bred animals, with hooves as tough as flint and digestive systems to match.

We finished our tea and turned our attention to the day's list, which was always drawn up by Saleh. There was a camel to see (a sick camel? I suddenly felt concerned), a herd of goats, a lame donkey and some cows with mastitis, all within the town. Cases to see and descriptions of ailments

14

reached Saleh by vague circuitous routes involving neighbours, shop-keepers, sisters, cousins and aunts and as a result, Scott warned me, descriptions of symptoms were generally rather non-specific and frequently challenging.

'In fact,' chuckled Scott, 'you'll frequently find that by the time you arrive to see the case, either the owner is a Bedouin who has packed his tent and moved on, or he has got too impatient and slaughtered the animal for dinner.'

We started with a visit to the quarantine unit to check on some recent arrivals of sheep and goats from Somalia. As he drove me to Raysut, Scott described how the Quarantine Station had evolved. Meat in Dhofar was an exorbitant price, he said, with a locally-bred goat costing about the same as, or more than, a man's monthly wages. As a result, the government encouraged the importation of meat-on-the-hoof from Africa. This posed two immediate problems. Firstly, there was the risk of importing exotic diseases into what had been an isolated part of Arabia, and secondly, the welfare issues were considerable as the animals were transported from the east coast of Africa to Oman in small, wooden dhows, with up to 1,500 sheep at a time.

Scott and his predecessors had worked hard to persuade the authorities that the importation of live animals into Dhofar and their random distribution into the province to mix with local animals could prove disastrous. Foot-and-mouth disease, anthrax, rinderpest, bluetongue and many other formidable and contagious diseases, often rampant in parts of Africa but not yet seen in Oman, could become established and decimate the local animal population. Eventually, the *Wali* had agreed to a three-week quarantine period for all imported live animals. Quarantined animals had to be killed at the Quarantine Station and no live beasts would be permitted through the Wire until they had completed their period of isolation. The *askari* had been told to deal severely with any infringements.

We sped along the coast road with the stunning Qara hills rising like an impregnable barrier between sea and desert, with no hint of the ruthless ideological struggle under way within their folds. Nestling in the foothills was a series of shanty dwellings which seemed to have been put together from a jumble of builders' debris and rusting oil-drums, called *burmails* after the Burmah Oil Company. Scott told me these were transit camps for tribesmen wishing to escape from the fighting and relocate their families to the relative security of the plains. They came bringing all they owned and built these improvised homes where they lived with their cattle, goats and families. One hut was made of wood and stood out from the rest. That, said Scott, was where the headman lived.

The gate through the perimeter wire was closed when we returned. An *askar*, with his rifle gripped purposefully in his left hand, approached the vehicle and raised his right hand in greeting. Scott acknowledged and explained he was the *'tabeeb'* or doctor. The *askar* gravely nodded, the gate opened and we swept into the town precincts.

'Never rush them,' advised Scott, adding cheerily, 'they always have a round up the breech and some of them can be a bit trigger-happy.' I assured him I would never rush them.

By the time we got back to *Bir Bint Ahmed* the working day was over. Government offices closed promptly at one o'clock. Saleh and Hafeedth said goodbye, climbed onto their bike and roared away. As the dust slowly settled in the wake of Hafeedth's Honda, I thought the Dhofari day seemed well organised into a morning's work, a good lunch, and then a sleep, after which many would start their second job, often one with an entrepreneurial slant. Still, it was very tough raising a family in war-torn Dhofar and my assistants were more privileged than most, with a steady job, overtime when needed to travel up the hill or to a remote village, reasonably good working conditions and excellent prospects for the future. They worked hard and, as long as they could leave by one o'clock, they rarely complained. I could see I was going to enjoy working with them.

Chapter 3

BATTman

The British Army Training Team was housed in *Umm al Gwarrif* Camp, a few kilometres east of RAF Salalah. *Umm al Gwarrif* (literally meaning Gwarrif's mother) was known as *UAG* and was the headquarters of Dhofar Brigade as well as the base camp of the Muscat Regiment, or MR. There were four Omani infantry battalions in the Sultan's Armed Forces, two of which would be in Dhofar on nine-month tours at any one time. In addition to MR, there were the Jebal Regiment, the Northern Frontier Regiment and the Desert Regiment.

SAF also had two Baluchi battalions, both permanently based in Dhofar. These were the Frontier Force and the Southern Regiment, or *Kateebat Janoobiya*, known as *KJ*. Baluchistan is a mountainous region in South-West Pakistan, and its principal town, Quetta, was acquired by the British in 1876, becoming the capital of the British Province of Baluchistan until it was absorbed into Pakistan in 1947. Gwadar, a town and port on the sandy Nuh coastal headland that juts into the Arabian Sea just opposite Muscat, became part of what was then called the Sultanate of Muscat and Oman in 1797, and remained Omani until the Pakistani government bought it back in 1958. This enclave on the Makran coast that straddles Pakistan and Iran has for hundreds of years been one of the main routes of communication between the Middle East and the Indo-Pakistan subcontinent. It is a very poor region made up largely of barren desert and with low employment prospects. Oman still had a political agreement that the Sultan could continue to recruit from there for his armed forces.

Sultan Said bin Taimur relied heavily on his Baluchi regiments, but Sultan Qaboos had expanded the Omani troops. Although they were still under British contract or seconded command, the first few Omani nationals were already passing through Sandhurst in 1974 with others in the pipeline. Brigadier John Akehurst, who commanded Dhofar Brigade in 1974–75, described the Omani soldiers, who mostly came from Northern Oman, as generally well-experienced, well-disciplined and cheerful men, some of whom were very brave indeed, but prone to a sharp drop in morale and motivation if things were not going well.

SAF also had the Oman Artillery, an Armoured Car Squadron and the Oman Gendarmerie, which mainly manned garrisons in the north. Then there were battle groups from other countries, in particular Iran (still ruled by the Shah, a close ally of Sultan Qaboos) and Jordan, whose King Hussein had done much to help and advise the new Sultan. These were two important supporters at a time when Arab leaders were not universally backing the Sultan's pro-Western tactics in the Dhofar War.

UAG was a large, fortified camp surrounded by barbed wire, with watchtowers manned by SAF soldiers armed with GPMGs or 7.62 FN rifles. The red, white and green Omani flag fluttered proudly from the main building in the centre of the camp.

As we approached the gate, Scott yelled 'BATT' to the SAF gate guard who waved us through without asking for ID as if the word was an impeccable credential, which perhaps it was. We zigzagged around a network of huts and tents until we reached a smallish compound at the rear, separated from the remainder of the camp by barbed and razor wire. This was BATT HQ.

Scott parked the Land Rover nose-out, telling me this was a standard operating procedure to facilitate a rapid departure. At first glance there seemed to be nothing very special about the BATT unit: a series of khaki tents, basic huts marked 'Stores', 'Medical Room', 'Cookhouse' and so on. There was a heavy concrete bunker with an impressively solid metal door, which was clearly the armoury. My eyes were drawn to a small hut marked 'Bar', from where loud singing rushed out when the door opened. 'Lads down on R and R,' remarked Scott as we passed.

Rest and Recuperation was essential therapy in any theatre but a lifesaver in this dry, barren desert state. There was nothing for British soldiers in Salalah – no female company, no bars, no bright spots. There was the small, rather staid, chronically overbooked Dhofar Hotel, full of visiting VIPs or businessmen, but that was no place for men just down from the hill. Access to alcohol was strictly controlled, apart from in the hotel, the Officers' Messes and private residences, and it was totally banned for locals who, if caught drunk or in possession of liquor, could face the harsh penalties of the Islamic *Sharia* court. Expatriate residents had to apply for a government licence which specified the amount of money (based on salary) that they were permitted to spend monthly on alcohol. It was strictly forbidden to sell alcohol to Omanis – a sure way for a Brit to be expelled rapidly from the country as a *persona non grata*, known as being 'PNG'd'.

We stopped at a large hut at the back facing the *jebal*. To the left was a door labelled 'Ops Room' and next to it was 'Signals', from the depths of which came a chatter of Morse and static and the ceaseless loud hum of air-conditioners. Behind the hut was a forest of aerials with a tangled web of wires linking the operations centre with forward positions and countless other locations. Beyond the masts was a sea of dirty-coloured wasteland which led, a couple of kilometres away, to the foothills of the *jebal*.

At the entrance to the Ops Room was the small office of the Unit's Chief Clerk, a young, thin, pale-faced Corporal, wearing horn-rimmed glasses stuck together with insulating tape, who told me he had been seconded from the Pay Corps. I said hello and he gave me a cheery grin. He said he was thoroughly enjoying his field experience after a colourless career in the UK and it was fun being a 'shiny-arsed desk commando'. This lad knew he was needed to sort out pay, pensions, allowances, family crises and endless other bureaucratic nonsenses that challenge soldiers abroad.

Scott introduced me to the Squadron Sergeant-Major, a WO1 called Fred who was sitting at a paper-strewn desk, and the Ops Officer, Corporal Bronco Lane (who in May 1976 achieved international fame as one of two men to climb Everest by a new route, losing several fingertips through frostbite in the process). The Ops Room was the hub of the BATT command. An impressive collection of captured weapons was displayed on the walls. Machine guns, mortars, rifles and ammunition, mostly of Russian or Chinese origin, and presumably unserviceable, were respected trophies of the war's successes. In the centre of the wall above the desk was an imposing Russian RPG7 anti-tank weapon flanked by a couple of AK47 rapid assault rifles.

Large charts and maps covered in transparent plastic sheets indicated SAF and *adoo* positions in red and blue crayon and were amended as the positions changed. Flags and markers, 'ours' and 'theirs', were pinned to the maps.

'The OC's round at the Q Stores,' said Fred to Scott. 'But before you go, there's a signal here for you somewhere.' He rummaged around on his desk and produced a flimsy sheet of paper. He read out: 'Brigade HQ has asked for the BATT Vet to go to Sudh as soon as possible. There's a report of goats dying by the dozen and the local *Wali*'s getting anxious. We've no contact right now at Sudh so I can't get confirmation. If it's OK with you I'll task a chopper to get you there in the morning.'

I glanced at Scott, who nodded. It would be his last day in Oman. 'I've never been to Sudh,' he said.

Fred pointed to a map. 'It's 70 kilometres north-east of Salalah; a small fishing town of about fifty or sixty houses, pretty run down. We

19

secured it from the *adoo* a couple of years ago. It seems friendly enough and there are a few *firqats* about. The *Wali* is a cunning old sweat so we do keep an eye on him; now the Sultan's flag is flying above his house, we don't want any double-dealing and there was an Intelligence report last week that arms may be filtering through Sudh and up into the hill by camel train.'

'Are the sea routes secure?' I asked.

'Sort of,' said Fred, 'but there are only three Brooke-Marine patrol boats and a few dhows in the whole of the Sultan's navy. They have deterrent value but if the enemy wants to get stuff through badly enough, they can.'

He drew his finger along the map. 'It is a hell of a big coastline and Sudh's is well to the east and off the beaten track for most of the air patrols.' He turned to us, 'I'll let you know your ETD at prayers.'

'Prayers?' I queried as we left the Ops Room.

'Daily situation reports,' said Scott, 'SITREPS are given twice a day to all in camp. You are expected to go to evening prayers when in Salalah. It is the only way to learn what's going on. You'll see tonight.'

We walked round to Stores. The BATT men in camp who were not drinking, sleeping or on duty seemed to be working out using improvised gym equipment. Most wore olive green shorts and loose open shirts, desert boots with rolled down socks and they all looked tanned and fit. One guy wearing only swimming trunks and desert boots was doing rapid step-ups on two ammunition boxes. Another was effortlessly lifting dumb-bells made out of iron rods set in concrete-filled paint cans. At least he had the decency to sweat.

These men had to be fit to survive. The amount of stuff they had to carry was impressive: a 40-kilogram pack, 10 or 11 kilos of General Purpose Machine gun or radio, 10 kilos of ammunition, food and drinking water – often over many kilometres of rugged and steep hillside. I reckoned I would have enough to cope with carrying a rucksack full of drugs.

The Squadron's Quartermaster Sergeant was a large, likeable Cockney called Wally, who had arms thicker than most men's thighs. Probably another addict of the concrete-filled paint tins. He amiably welcomed me to Oman and told me he was on his fourth tour to Dhofar. 'Whenever I go away these days the wife expects me to come home with a suntan,' he said.

We said we were on a hunt for the OC and Wally poked his head around a huge rack containing everything from Bergens to mess tins, all in immaculate order. 'The vets are here, Boss,' said Wally.

'Haven't you got a bloody mosquito net without rips, Wally?' said a voice. Round the corner came the owner of the voice, a short, fit, fair-haired bright man, in his mid-thirties, who gave a broad smile and shook me firmly by the hand. 'Welcome aboard,' he said, temporarily forgetting the mosquito net. I liked him at once.

Major Paddy King-Fretts, who commanded 'A' Squadron, had been an officer in the Devon and Dorset Regiment. He was dressed, like others in the unit, in desert boots and shabby olive green trousers with a shirt showing no badges of rank, regimental belts or insignia. There was no sign of the famous sand-coloured beret with its winged dagger badge and motto 'Who dares wins', the blue stable-belt or the winged shoulder emblem of the SAS.

'Good afternoon, Sir,' I said.

'Forget the "Sir" bit,' he replied, 'we tend to be on first name terms here.'

Unusual in the British army, rank was quietly obscured within BATT, as both anonymity and teamsmanship were regarded as key to the success of the Special Forces. Despite the lack of formality there was no lack of respect. Paddy and the other officers as well as the SSM were always called 'Boss'. Such a relationship could only work with men of the highest professional calibre who could operate in a relaxed way, yet with deadly precision and efficiency.

'Although I'm your OC,' he said, looking directly at me with his alert pale blue eyes, 'I know sod all about vetting and you'll be mainly on your own. We'll pass on messages and get things sorted to get you up the hill in a hurry when necessary. Apart from that, I will always try to help with any problems but chiefly it'll be for you to liaise between here and Mike Butler in DDD. My best advice is just to get on and enjoy the job and make the most of it.'

He nodded at Scott. 'We had better introduce Andrew to Ben Higson, he's a Captain, Royal Signals, on detachment like you, and he's OC PSYOPS. In BATT, psychological operations mean getting the message across to the locals, which is what it is all about. Ben's got photographers, printers and God knows who else working for him to produce leaflets, posters and so on. You know the sort of thing; a picture of one of your Omani assistants injecting a sick goat on the *jebal* might encourage some more wobbly tribesmen to come to one of our hill locations with their beasties.'

Paddy continued. 'There are two other officers in "A" Squadron in Dhofar; John Innes, the Operations Captain – you'll meet him in a moment – and Simon Garthwaite, Royal Irish Rangers, who's up the hill coping with our *firqat* friends. Now,' he said, turning to Wally, 'we'd better get him kitted up; usual gear, but he can take over Scott's Bergen. Get him issued with his own weapon.'

He turned back to me. 'Look in at the Ops Room when you're through.'

With a smile, he was gone.

Scott wandered off to have a cup of tea in the Ops Room as Wally shuffled around his store like QMSs everywhere. Rapidly, kit appeared on the counter in front of me. I carted the pile out to the Land Rover and when I came back I found Wally dangling two small phials wrapped in black tape and suspended from a neck string.

'Your morphine,' he said matter-of-factly. 'All of us carry it in case of injury. I'll also get a dog tag printed off with your army number, blood group and religion and you can thread it onto the necklace.'

I pocketed the phials thoughtfully. In a war zone where medical help might depend on location and availability of air support nothing must be overlooked and an identity disc with pain-killer attached could be important. As if to reinforce my thoughts, Wally gave me my last two items – pressure bandages. 'Strap them to your rifle or tape them to your webbing,' he advised. 'Right,' he said, 'let's go and meet Kev. He's REME attached to us.'

Wally double-locked his store and then fitted a huge padlock. 'Can't be too careful,' he said, '*Dhobi-wallahs*, mess-men, cleaners – they don't miss a trick.'

We walked across the compound to the concrete bunker where he pressed a bell. A flap lifted and an eye peered through the small spy hole before a tanned, thickset man in his late twenties opened the heavy iron-plated door. This was Kev the armourer. He led me into his cool, window-less vault and the door slammed heavily behind me. There was a smell of gunmetal, oil and cordite. Kev, who spent much of his life inside these unyielding, air-conditioned walls, was in the middle of restoring an old Martini-Henry rifle recently captured from an *adoo*. The weapon was in pieces but Kev delightedly explained there were thousands of them in Dhofar, many still in excellent working order and well maintained by their owners who had probably inherited them and passed them on from generation to generation. Martini-Henry rifles were made towards the end of the nineteenth century and became the British army's first service rifle. Kev showed me the falling block action and .45 calibre cartridges. It was clearly a labour of love restoring these old weapons, and they would get a good price from collectors in the UK.

Like much of NATO, the British army had adopted, among others, the Belgian FN 7.62mm self-loading rifle, known as the SLR, and the 9mm

Sterling submachine gun, but in Dhofar the BATT standard issue weapon was the Armalite, the US army's M16 5.56mm machine rifle.

'You imagine lugging a four and a half kilogram SLR up and down these hills,' Kev said. He picked up a gun from the bench in front of him. 'The Americans made a really good job of this,' he added, handing me the M16. 'It only weighs 3 kilos and they've made over 3,000,000 of them. Amazing piece of kit. You can get sand stuffed down the barrel, and it still won't let you down.' He threw an empty magazine over to me. 'Takes up to eighteen rounds in each; semi-automatic or automatic.' He opened a drawer and picked out two full magazines. 'Come on. If you've never fired one before, we'll have a crack on the range.'

In Ulster I had carried a 9mm Browning automatic pistol, a heavy handgun that had provided reassurance on more than one occasion as I drove in my Q car between the dog units, but the Armalite was in a different league. We jumped into one of BATT's open-top, long-wheelbase Land Rovers, which were painted for sand camouflage and were known as 'Pink Panthers'. With Kev driving and me clumsily clutching my new weapon, we sped rapidly across *UAG* to the nearby practice range. This was a strip of sand just outside the camp perimeter, with *burmails* as targets placed at various distances. A crash course on firing the Armalite as a left-hander followed, with Kev's instruction not to use it in the automatic mode unless I had to. He indicated a couple of painted *burmails*.

'They're at about 120 metres,' he said. 'The Armalite's range is around 400, less than the SLR, but it's only likely to be used at shorter distances and the killing range is 250 metres.'

I managed to take out a couple of *burmails* and Kev nodded his approval. I let out a sigh of relief.

Back in the armoury, Kev showed me how to strip the gun down and reassemble it and he suggested I spent a day doing nothing else until I could do it in the dark. 'If the bugger jams under fire, you'll get scant sympathy from anyone else if you can't sort it out.' He gave the gun a quick clean through and told me to collect the weapon and ammunition in the morning before leaving for Sudh.

Wally was waiting outside his Stores, basking in the sunshine as he filled in the paperwork for me to sign. He gave a friendly grin.

'We have a film show two or three times a week,' he said. 'Open air, under the stars. They fly movies down from RAF Masirah and we swap with the RAF and the Taylor-Woodrow Mess. It's the 1970 World Cup report tomorrow and we usually start with a *Tom and Jerry*.'

23

I thanked him and moved on to join Scott and Paddy in the Ops Room. The second in command of 'A' Squadron, the lanky John Innes, came in to join us. We shook hands and exchanged a few words as he passed Paddy a slip of paper.

'Your heli is confirmed for tomorrow,' said Paddy. 'I'm sending Ian along too,' he added, introducing me to a Sergeant in the Intelligence Corps who spoke Arabic. 'If the three of you are armed, you shouldn't need anyone else. I'm afraid it's an Iranian chopper,' he added rather ominously.

Chapter 4

The *Wali* of Sudh

The Sultan of Oman's Air Force, or SOAF, was commanded in Dhofar by a seconded British RAF officer, Wing Commander Ian Worby, affectionately known as War Commander Wingby. Under his command was a Strike Squadron of eight Strikemaster fighter aircraft, several of which sat on the apron of RAF Salalah surrounded by their own sandbagged enclosures. Strikemasters were armed with Sura rockets, machine guns and bombs, and were rapidly scrambled in ones or twos regularly throughout the day providing essential cover and useful deterrence. Apart from the jets, there was a sizeable Helicopter Squadron made up of large Wessex and smaller American Huey aircraft. Then there were the chubby tactical transporter aircraft called Skyvans, which seemed to be able to land and take off on rough ground not much longer than a cricket pitch and on almost any terrain. The Skyvan was Thomas the Tank Engine with wings, and ferried people and supplies up and down the *jebal*. SOAF also operated Beaver reconnaissance aircraft and a number of old propeller-driven Viscounts, which shuttled military personnel or officials daily to and from the capital, Muscat.

As part of the Iranian battle group, the Shah had sent his own transport squadrons including gunship helicopters. Our helicopter to Sudh had been tasked for 0800 hours and at 0715 we reported to Dhofar Brigade Headquarters, an outwardly uninspiring two-storey building facing the main apron. Inside was a buzzing nerve centre from where SOAF Staff Officers calculated logistical needs, troop movements, deployment, resupplies and the endless minutiae of running a war.

With Scott's help, I loaded the Bergen with veterinary drugs and equipment. I wore my OGs and desert boots and when I fitted on the webbing was almost beginning to feel the part. The Brigade Major, Peter Packham, told us to check our latest departure time with the Air Transport Liaison Officer, or ATLO, and report back to him when we returned. Our visit would become part of the daily SITREP circulated throughout the Brigade: 'BATT VET visits Sudh to treat sick goats.' My first experience of 'Hearts and Minds' in action.

Outside, the helicopters were already in action taking off and landing with assorted loads; Minimokes, a sort of roof-less, door-less, Jeep-like vehicle, scurried across the apron carrying pilots and aircrew to and from their aircraft.

We sped up to *UAG* to collect our weapons. The Intelligence Corps Sergeant Ian who was to act as our interpreter joined us and we just had time to drive into the town to collect Saleh from his house.

Back at the air base, we made for the ATLO's desk and walked to the Iranian Helicopter Squadron pilots' room. Each air squadron had its own room and we passed the British Strikemaster squadron and waved to the pilots who were sitting around smoking or reading in armchairs ready to spring into action when they heard the 'Scramble' bell. On the signal, they would run to a Minimoke and race across the apron to their waiting jets.

There were two Iranians in the helicopter room, both slouched in their seats smoking. Neither seemed to speak English and none of us spoke Farsi. So we smiled nervously, looked at our watches and shuffled around until an Iranian Loadmaster suddenly appeared in the doorway and gesticulated for us to go with him. Outside the building, Saleh was on his knees praying but he responded to my shout and ran after us clutching his dishdash, which was flapping about his ankles.

The helicopter with its Iranian markings was close by with rotors already spinning, sending the dust flying in a dense choking cloud around us. We ran to the front of the clattering machine and waited for the thumbs up from the pilot. This SOP was to minimise the risk of people running into the rear rotor blade, a tragedy that could happen only too easily in the noisy excitement and clamour of getting in or out of a helicopter.

The young pilot signalled OK and we followed the Loadmaster towards his aircraft, involuntarily ducking as we ran. Saleh was bundled aboard first with an inelegant heave similar to that given to my Bergen, which rapidly followed. Scott, Ian and I jumped in next and then the Loadmaster, who immediately and adroitly clipped his belt onto a harness point above his head. There were no seats or belts for the passengers, which was slightly alarming, as the door remained wide open. The engines increased their revolutions, vibrations and noise, and we lifted 10 metres above the ground before the aircraft's nose dipped and the pilot pointed us due west. I felt the exhilarating surge of acceleration and we were soon thundering at 70 or 80 knots towards our destination.

Satisfied with our departure, the Loadmaster shut the door, produced a foldaway seat from somewhere and lit a cigarette. There was an exchange of Farsi into his headset every so often with the pilots up front and he totally ignored his passengers. We might as well have been a cargo of dates.

I looked at the flight crew and saw they were both smoking too, so I shrugged and lit up myself. We had no headphones, so communication was limited. Scott did his best to yell above the noise to point out landmarks on the outskirts of Salalah. We crossed the perimeter wire near Arzat and the helicopter followed the deserted unsecured Salalah to Taqah road, passing coconut plantations and a small fortress. The pilot then turned jerkily south-east towards the sparkling blue sea to follow the silvery sands of the coast.

Soon we reached the village of Taqah and now it was Ian shouting in my ear to say that this strip of coast was once part of the Kingdom of Sheba, ruled by that formidable Queen who had reigned 3,000 years ago and tested the wisdom of King Solomon with riddles. The area had once been fertile and, as the world's main frankincense-producing region, the source of Dhofar's historical prosperity. Now, from the air, it all looked barren. Sultan Said bin Taimur, horrified at the prospect of the insurgents closing in on him as he brooded in his medieval palace in Salalah, was said to have ordered the wells to be filled in to remove the enemy's water supply. He must surely only have intended this as a temporary measure, and it was sad to see how arid and sterile was the plain that had once watered the whole of the Mesopotamian army.

We passed over the bay surrounding the fishing village of Mirbat that was the scene of one of the war's most famous battles during the monsoon of July 1972: 200 *adoo* launched an attack at dawn and an SAS team of nine men plus a handful of locals successfully defended the position, which was at that time of considerable strategic importance. A small group of *adoo* had cleverly lured the *firqat* away from the town, leaving it defended only lightly by *askari* and a few soldiers from the Oman Gendarmerie. Over 200 heavily armed *adoo* then marched on Mirbat planning to take the fort, with others firing mortars from the surrounding hills. Strikemasters and the arrival of SAS and SAF reinforcements eventually ended what was a dramatic chapter in the Regiment's history. Tragically, two SAS soldiers died in the grim fight. As we flew over the village, inhabitants came out of their houses, looked up from the dusty streets or from their rooftops waving and watching.

After forty minutes or so we reached Sudh. The small coastal village had no airstrip and only a rough helipad sited halfway between the village and the sea. The pilot decided not to approach the landing pad from the sea, as two land projections surrounded the Bay of Sudh and could be good positions for firing at approaching aircraft. So we came in from the escarpment over the flat-roofed and mud-walled houses. Air currents threw the aircraft about and the engines complained alarmingly as I bounced on the floor of the helicopter, clutching my gun and kit and trying not to show the serious unease that I felt. Beneath us, corrugated iron roofing was lifted into the air, washing flew across the streets fanned by the downward thrust of the rotors, and dust billowed everywhere. Saleh was in communication again with Allah. At last, with a shudder and two cracking bounces we came to rest on the pad. Scott raised his eyebrows and swallowed. Ian shook his head and sighed heavily. 'That'll have gone down well with the ladies. Nothing like having your washing scattered around the village for good hearts and minds.'

The engines gradually ground to a halt and through the small window I could see a hundred or more people eagerly running towards the helicopter. Ian told us to fit a magazine onto our Armalites. The Loadmaster threw open the door and with knees still shaking, I stepped onto Sudh soil.

The village stretched along a *wadi*, or valley, towards the stark backdrop of pre-Cambrian granite, the foothills of the Qara Mountains. I glanced at the group of smiling, chattering faces gathering around the aircraft, and decided that they were friendly. The spontaneous greetings, impulsive handshaking and instinctive warmth made me feel that our clumsy arrival had not jeopardised our mission too much.

Ian was immediately in deep conversation with an old *askar*, a gatekeeper from the *Wali*'s fort who told him that we should wait at the aircraft until the *Wali* arrived to greet us. Soon the crowd parted and a dignified, bearded Arab in white dishdash and elegant headdress approached with a retinue of six or seven elders. The senior members of the entourage did not carry guns but small cane camel sticks and each wore an embroidered belt with the traditional curved Omani dagger, or *khunja*, in its ornate silver scabbard, fastened at the front. *Khunjas* are handsome knives, very sharp and widely worn as a symbol of seniority. The handle of the *khunja* was of horn and it was said that the very best came from the rhino (others claimed giraffe) – perhaps reflecting Oman's long and historical connections with Africa. In turn, we shook the hands of the *Wali* and his party.

'Tea first,' said Scott as an aside to me with a wink.

As if on cue, Ian turned to us and said the *Wali* would like us to go to his house. The *Wali* politely indicated that we should precede him but, reciprocating the politeness, we insisted he led the way. In the event, we all walked in a straight line apart from Saleh who trundled along at the back, happy to be back on firm ground and chatting contentedly to the locals.

The crowd divided; some joined the procession, others stayed to stare at the helicopter, guarded warily by its jumpy crew. As we walked to the fort, three impassive and rather aloof camels passed us, each bearing an impressive burden of building blocks in panniers. A donkey scuttled hurriedly by carrying two excited, shoeless boys towards the helicopter – they gave us beaming smiles and cheery waves as they swiped the poor donkey on to greater speed. A few mangy sheep meandered across the

28

dusty road looking for anything edible. Bantam-like chickens pecked lazily in the dirt, hoping to find titbits among the piles of rusty tin cans that were strewn everywhere. Organised rubbish disposal was a luxury yet to arrive in Sudh.

Like Salalah, the houses all looked as if they were half constructed (or half demolished). They were made chiefly of sandstone and the larger ones had strong wooden doors. The entrance to the *Wali*'s fort had one of the largest sets of doors in the town. The wood had been bleached by the sun but the doors were dignified and solid and of a design typical of Islamic tradition, which gave prominence to the entrance. The wood was imported from East Africa and a lot of money was spent on buying doors and carving them with intricate designs. The *Wali*'s doors were of venerable years and looked as if they might well have defended the fort's occupants against intruders over many centuries.

The Sultanate's flag flew from a flagstaff erected next to a large aerial on the roof, and a petrol generator spluttered intrusively to one side of the house providing the *Wali*'s, or perhaps Sudh's, electricity supply. Outside the fort, two armed *askars* stood impassively as we entered but proved well up to the task of restricting access to the house as the remainder of the village tried to follow.

After the glare of the morning sun, it was gloomy inside and it took me a few minutes to adapt to the darkness. There were no lights but I could just make out a narrow stone staircase winding up into the blackness. Following the *Wali*, we climbed round and round up the spiral steps until we arrived at a landing from which led off several small rooms. The landing was about two storeys above ground level and was lit by narrow fortress gun slits. Wide-eyed, snotty-nosed, swarthy children peered inquisitively from behind the entrances to the various rooms, which I guessed were the domestic quarters for the *Wali*'s family.

We went up a further winding stair and came out on what might originally have been part of the roof, perhaps 15 or 20 metres above the ground. Walls made quite recently of sandstone blocks with wooden struts formed a base for the ceiling of latticework and plaster.

A couple of youths in scruffy dishdashes were kneeling in a corner pumping at an ancient brass primus stove. They were surrounded by tempered metal trays, teapots and small porcelain coffee cups with no handles, and appeared to be in charge of refreshments. Generally speaking, outside the family, the men sat together in one place and the women in another. Where there were no servants it usually fell to the younger males in the family to attend to their elders and there was often quite a structured pecking order. The two boys stopped pumping for a moment and gazed at the new arrivals.

29

The *Wali* led us into an inner room, casually slipping off his sandals as he entered. We struggled manfully to remove our high laced-up desert boots. I discovered that one of my laces had become knotted and wrestled with the wretched thing, watched with interest by the rest of the party – even the youths at the primus stove were staring. Eventually I managed to jerk it off and, smiling weakly, picked up my Armalite and followed the others into the room.

The *Wali*'s receiving room was free of any furniture but was carpeted with large Baluchi rugs. Around the walls were several dozen brightly-coloured cushions provided for back support. The natural courtesy and hospitality of the Arab people are demonstrated in so many ways in every-day life. The deep-seated politeness code extends to an unspoken and, to the uninitiated, confusing order of precedence. I had seen it when we left the helicopter, then on entering the fort and this room. Now who was to sit down first? There were murmurings and gestures of the hands. The *Wali* was king in his land, but we were the visitors to be treated with centuries of tradition and custom. Eventually we all sat down awkwardly but more or less together.

Scott had warned me that it was a sign of disrespect or, at best, ill manners to point the soles of your feet towards anyone. This seemed logical, and in the certain interests of those who had to entertain a group of sock-wearing Europeans after a day's tramp in the hot desert. I tried to follow the rule but my thigh muscles were reluctant to comply and I wriggled and shifted every few minutes trying without much success to get comfortable.

Although there were ten of us in the room, conversation was slow to begin. Ian started with some gentle pleasantries in Arabic and replied on behalf of the rest of us to the *Wali*'s grave but limited inquiries. This was part of the ritual. Take your time, Scott had said, the world moves slowly in the desert. Ian played the game and there were suitable pensive pauses between each new overture. The *Wali* and his advisers nodded sagely as Ian reported that all was well in Salalah and passed on greetings through his Intelligence network. Eventually he explained who we were and that we had come in response to the *Wali*'s request for veterinary help.

In due course a young boy entered carrying a large tray. He slipped off his flip-flops and shyly muttered '*Salaam alay koom*' to the room in general. On his tray were a dozen cans of Egyptian mango juice. The boy went straight to the *Wali* who removed a can and handed it at once to Scott, the oldest member of the visiting party and therefore the most esteemed. Scott held his can to salute the *Wali* and thanked him; the *Wali* nodded and gave a can to Ian and then to me. The boy then took the tray around to the others. Nothing more was said until we had drunk the cool, thick, sweet syrup. The boy with the tray came back and collected the empties.

30

The atmosphere eased a little after the mango juice and the time had come to talk business. Ian translated the *Wali's* concerns and before long we learned something of the background to our urgent summons. The villagers, it seemed, owned between them about a thousand goats, which mostly grazed on the *jebal*. By day, the womenfolk and older children would take the animals into the hills and bring them back at dusk. During the previous week, it seemed, hundreds of goats had been taken ill and many had died. This presented the poor owners with a serious problem and the *Wali* had been asked to get some help from Salalah's *tabeeb baitary*, or animal doctor.

Turning to me, Ian added that there was no way of telling whether 'hundreds' was accurate or an exaggeration to impress us with the importance of the problem. He reckoned that there was certainly a problem but our arrival would have given the *Wali* credibility with the townspeople and demonstrated the government's desire to help.

The general consensus seemed to be that goats were either found dead in the morning or were seen dying. When the carcasses were opened up, the villagers had seen nothing unusual. The animals had been grazed and watered at different places in the surrounding hills and none of the elders could remember seeing anything like it before.

Discussion was interrupted as a stream of boys entered bearing trays of small bananas, a bowl of tinned fruit salad (with a couple of spoons between us) and a large plate of *halwa*, a sticky, very sweet delicacy made from dates. I discovered that *halwa* varied from region to region; the *Wali* of Sudh's *halwa* was a brown, translucent jelly and was generously decorated with flies. The town was said to be well known for its honey, so I guessed that may have been a major ingredient.

We tucked in, respectfully murmuring enthusiastically as each of us was presented with the various offerings. The *Wali* insisted we tried each dish, so I complied until the pressure eased a bit. Another dilemma was what then to do with my very sticky right hand; did I lick my fingers or wipe them on the carpet or my trousers? Patience, as usual in Arabia, paid dividends as soon one of the boys arrived with a small bowl of scented rosewater and a little towel.

We had been sitting there for about three-quarters of an hour and I was becoming restive, but no one made any sign to move. Conversation had again ground to a halt but Ian sat patiently on and we dutifully followed suit. Presently the mango boy came in again. This time he carried four coffee cups stacked together in his left hand and an enormous Arabic coffee pot with a long spout in his right. He went first to the *Wali*, who waved him to Scott. With confident skill, the lad stylishly poured a long stream of hot coffee, Sangria-like, into the top cup. Scott took his cup and slurped noisily. I followed suit and Ian and the *Wali* were given the remaining cups. My cup was only about a quarter full but it smelled fragrant with the spices of cardamom and other faintly medical aromas, perhaps menthol or eucalyptus. It was hot, restorative and delicious.

Like *halwa*, I found out that traditional Arabic coffee, or *qahwa*, varied hugely from the sublime to undrinkable, grainy sludge. The *Wali* of Sudh could be proud of his coffee-makers and things began to look up. Scott had finished his and was being given a second cup. Mango came and stood in front of me and waited patiently for me to drain my cup. He took the cup from me and again with panache he poured me some more.

As I mulled over the flavours, I saw he had come back again and was again hovering in front of me. One can have too much of a good thing, so I gave him the cup and flashed my best 'no thank you' smile. To my slight surprise, it made no difference and I was given another cupful.

Scott must have noticed the little game Mango and I were playing. With an amused look on his face, he turned to me and muttered, 'When you've had enough, shake your empty cup from side to side.'

Now he tells me. The next time he came, I shook my wrist as instructed, and as if the spell had suddenly worked, the cup was at last taken from me, and filled for someone else.

When the coffee things had gone, the *Wali* stood up and the rest of us scrambled to our feet. I was jiggling my leg about to try to get rid of pins and needles. 'Right,' said Ian, 'I think we're off to see the goats.'

We followed the *Wali* back out into the bright hot sunshine. Saleh joined us, as did half the village. Ian was in deep discussion with the senior village men. He was trying not to laugh as he came to report to us that there was a slight glitch. Since the *Wali* had not known when we were coming, or even if we would come, all the goats were out of the village grazing on different parts of the hill and would not be back until dusk. There were no sick goats in the whole of Sudh. Not even a carcass to look at. It all seemed to reinforce Ian's theory about this being political rather than a clinical visit.

I suddenly thought to ask: 'Have any new animals been brought in from outside Sudh recently?'

There was a lively exchange among the men and Ian turned back to me.

'Well, who's a clever boy?' he said. 'As it happens, some geezer brought a load in a dhow direct from Africa last month.'

'Were they the ones that died?' I asked.

'No. The new ones are OK. It's the local goats that copped it.'

'How many died and what were the symptoms?'

After some exchanges, Ian turned to me: 'About a hundred dead. Rapid onset, stop eating, weak, die.' Not a lot to go on.

'Are they still dying?'

More mutterings.

32

'No. Last one died a week ago,' replied Ian, adding with a knowing smile '*Yimkin,*' an Arabic *mañana* word, loosely translatable as 'maybe'.

I said, 'Well, as all the dead animals have been eaten or otherwise got rid of, it would appear to have been a self-limiting problem. Tell him to let us know if others get sick and you might also explain that Africa is full of nasty bugs, which is why we have a quarantine system.'

Quarantine is a hard message to convey. The people of Sudh had probably been importing goats direct from East Africa without a second thought for hundreds of years. Yet, as DDD extended its influence, the Province's quarantine rules would begin to bite and the risks of importing exotic diseases would fall.

Saleh came up and touched me on the elbow. 'One donkey,' he said, 'very bad skin, over here.'

The donkey's back was red raw. The wounds were open and sore. This was a common condition in pack animals and caused by the chafing of a badly-fitting harness compounded by unbalanced and top-heavy loads of bricks or whatever. The sores were covered with flies. It was going to be an uphill struggle to educate owners and to find a means of providing tack that was properly designed and fitted. Yet in such a rapidly developing society as Oman, the days of the pack donkey were surely numbered anyway.

The owner looked at me suspiciously, not least because I was armed but also as I was followed, Pied Piper-like, by a couple of dozen curious children. I greeted him as affably as I could and shook him firmly by the hand. Saleh spoke to him in Arabic and explained I would like to help his donkey. He nodded. I smiled. Then I cleaned and dressed the wounds as best as I could and, through Saleh, tried to explain the need to rest the back and give it time to heal, and then get properly fitting harness and padding. I knew it was probably futile. The man's livelihood depended on the donkey and his attitude was unemotional and economical. He would not be able to afford to rest his animal and would continue to work it. If it died, he would look for a replacement.

I gave him an aerosol of gentian violet antiseptic and antibiotic which was the universal remedy for wounds in the field, and with a dejected pat to the donkey's thin rump I returned to the others.

A huddle of goat owners was now surrounding Scott as he dispensed packets of antibiotics and electrolytes to the *Wali* to give to any owners of sick goats.

'This is quite impossible,' he said. 'With no patients and no clinical evidence apart from vague reports of diarrhoea and death there is nothing else to be done. At least they can drench any new sick ones with this stuff. I've told him if any more die, they must call you at once and keep any sick ones in isolation here in the village.'

When we got back to the helicopter, the Iranian crew showed me a large bag full of oyster shells they had collected from the beach. The mother-of-pearl lining glittered in the sun in contrast to the rough, beige outer shell. Smiling apologetically at our hosts, who had come to see us off, I hurried down to the beach and collected a hatful of these beautiful treasures, wondering whether the pearls were harvested as they had been for generations in other parts of the Arabian Gulf.

With that, we took our leave of the *Wali* of Sudh. He came to the aircraft and as we took off I saw him standing there like a biblical figure; detached, dignified but, I hoped, pleased with the response to his request for help. He was surrounded by his villagers, camel stick in one hand, the other holding firmly on to his headdress, with his dishdash flapping furiously as our downward thrust covered everyone with sand and dust as we lifted off for Salalah.

The direct costs of deploying a helicopter crew, two Veterinary Officers, an Intelligence Officer and Saleh were ludicrous to treat one donkey. Yet, I reflected, at a time when there was minimal communication, the *adoo* were not yet ready to give up the fight, and public relations were considered the key to the people's hearts, what price can be put on the perception that the Ruler is so concerned about his citizens that even their sick animals receive such priority?

Chapter 5

The Flying Scotsman

The fact that Sultan Qaboos was an Anglophile was evident to any Briton arriving in Dhofar. The province seemed full of British nationals, English was widely spoken and road signs were as often in English as Arabic. Some places on the *jebal* were still known by their English nicknames, such as White City or Raven's Roost. The British presence was not that of a colonial power, and I never got the feeling that the people of Dhofar felt they were under British domination or control. Omanis invariably held the top posts, and always remained the public face of government, with their foreign advisers remaining in the background, conscious that their appointments were short or medium term. These advisers had huge responsibilities, but their overriding duty was to help the Dhofaris to become skilled at running their Province for themselves.

One such administrator was Robin Young, the Director of Dhofar Development Department and Adviser to the *Wali*, Sheikh Braik. It was Braik who ran the Province, who had the connections, who knew the real intelligence, who liaised with his officials throughout Dhofar and who briefed Sultan Qaboos.

People like Young, products of the old British Colonial Service were vital to the development of the infrastructure on which the Omanis would have to re-build their country. Few questioned Sheikh Braik's authority, yet Young could quietly juggle the cogs of power and, steeped as he was in the workings of Whitehall and with finely honed diplomatic skills, he could carefully and shrewdly influence events and encourage and support the *Wali* with his knowledge, experience and back-up. The success of DDD in providing the essential infrastructure for this war-torn, disturbed region was probably a measure of the successful tenure in Salalah of men like Robin Young.

Inevitably the presence of expatriate advisers and the military was fuel to the PFLOAG propaganda machine, which put out regular and bitter denunciations supported by outraged statements from collaborating communist governments and other hostile international groups such as the Palestine Liberation Organisation, who readily condemned what they then saw as neo-colonialism in Oman. Of course, from our perspective, the British, along with Oman's allies from Iran and Jordan, were there for perfectly legitimate strategic reasons. The Western approaches to the Arabian Gulf were vulnerable and, in 1974, it was reported that up to 60 per cent of the West's future available oil reserves might be located in the region. Every fifteen minutes or so a supertanker was said to pass along the Gulf of Oman to cross the Indian Ocean to Japan and the Far East or to make either for the Red Sea and the Suez Canal, or for the Cape of Good Hope and the Atlantic.

The tactical sinking of a small number of supertankers across the Straits of Hormuz, where Oman's northern territory projects finger-like towards Iran and the Gulf narrows to a channel barely 40 kilometres wide, could result in the region's oil supplies being effectively cut off. As a measure of the Straits' strategic significance, Iran had seized three small islands in 1971 causing a bitter row with the United Arab Emirates, which claimed them.

Another British administrator was the Sultan's Private Secretary, James Maclean. Maclean had been a Petty Officer writer in the Royal Navy before taking a job as personal assistant to the Managing Director of the company Petroleum Development (Oman), or PDO, based in the north of Oman. Although Sultan Said bin Taimur did not fully exploit the oil potential of his country, PDO, largely owned by Royal Dutch Shell, was the major source of the national wealth and the old Sultan maintained good relations with the company. It was not surprising that when he needed someone to draft letters for him and to present his papers in English, he turned to PDO for help and Maclean was appointed.

I first met Maclean within forty-eight hours of my arrival in Salalah. He had sent a signal to Scott to say he would be arriving on the afternoon SOAF Viscount from Muscat and, as he was bringing down two of HM's dogs, he wanted the vet to meet the aircraft. I asked Scott what Maclean was like:

'A likeable Scotsman, like me,' he grinned, sipping a coffee in the vet's office in *Bir Bint Ahmed*. 'Early fifties, white hair, large build – been out here for years and knows everything that goes on. Everyone calls him Mac. We'll go together to meet the aircraft.'

'Why is he bringing dogs to Salalah?' I asked.

'I suppose it may mean a visit by HM is imminent,' replied Scott. 'The Sultan spends several months each year in Salalah, particularly in the hot weather when Muscat is roasting in the scorching heat of the Arabian summer. But he also comes down for the odd week or two at any time of year and stays in the small palace at Robat. It is important

36

for him to be seen here and to be briefed on the war. Also his mother, Bibi, and his sister still live here.

'HM personally has a couple of black Labradors,' added Scott. 'They are the only black labs allowed in Oman. He used to take them to and from Muscat with him in his Falcon jet but now they are a bit of a handful and stay at Robat Palace, where they are bored and overfed. I'm sure Mac will arrange for you to inspect them. All the royal dogs come from Harrods,' he added with a laugh. 'Mac is very friendly with the woman who runs the Pet Department. She gives a good service and vaccination and pedigree details are always immaculate.'

'What about those coming today?' I asked.

'Bound to be from Harrods too,' said Scott. 'They could be new ones – possibly gifts for a couple of servants.'

Scott explained that Sultan Qaboos had a number of close courtiers, who were known as his 'Servants' or 'Slaves'. They were all of black African descent and several were in their teens or early twenties. The tradition of Oman's Sultans having black slaves was etched in the country's past. In its colonial days Oman had controlled a thriving international slave trade. The robust Omani empire had included Zanzibar and parts of the coast of East Africa at a time when slaves had been the commercial currency of Africa. There was now a sizeable black population in Dhofar, who were descended from early slave stock, but were now well-integrated Omani Arabs.

'Have any of the Servants got dogs already?' I asked.

He nodded. 'There are a couple with Dalmatians and two or three have yellow Labs.' Scott leaned across the desk and lowered his voice. 'The Servants are close to the Sultan but are not very popular with Saleh and Hafeedth,' he said. 'There are strong feelings. The boys are very well looked after – new cars, flashy watches and lots of spending money. Personally, I have always found them to be polite and charming and they all seem to speak some English. They spend most of their time hanging around the palaces or tearing around Salalah in their air-conditioned limos.'

We were interrupted by the entry of Saleh with tea. There was outside, he said, one man with goat. I gulped my tea and went out to see them. The man was a *Bedouin*, thin and wiry with dark leathery skin, brown beard and straggly hair. He wore a long strip of orange material about his waist with the end slung over his left shoulder and carried a rifle in his right hand.

The goat stood at his feet, looking resigned. Its right foreleg was clamped, vice-like, just above the hoof between the man's left big toe and second toe. The man was upset. He was talking loudly in the *jebali* tongue to the two *askars* and gesticulating wildly with his gun. They were grinning which did not seem to be the right response. The diplomatic Saleh endeavoured to calm the man down using his knowledge of the hill languages.

The goat had torn its udder on barbed wire. It was suckling two new-born kids and so it wasn't surprising the owner was worried. It was a nasty rip, right into the teat canal and milk tinged with blood was dripping out through the wound at a steady rate. We carried the startled animal into the clinic and lifted it onto the examination table. Many willing hands restrained the patient as I cleaned up the wound, injected local anaesthetic and sutured it. Absorbable sutures were the only option as it was clear I was unlikely to see the goat again.

I tried to get Saleh to explain that just because the wound was no longer gaping, the affected quarter would have to be rested or the stitches would tear and the wound open again. The man would have to strip out the milk gently by hand and keep the wound covered to prevent the kids sucking. He could feed the stripped milk to the kids using a bottle and top them up with powdered milk or with cow's or camel's milk as necessary.

I put some antibiotics into the udder. If infection did not set in (milk was a glorious medium for bacteria to grow and set up mastitis), the injury should repair OK. Saleh relayed this to the owner and gave the goat a shot of long-acting antibiotic to help it on its way. Saleh wagged his finger at the man to emphasise the instructions.

'*Inshalla*,' was the reply. God willing. This said little for my skills, but at least gave me something of a let-out clause.

Back in the office, Scott was finishing off his final report. 'I've signed the stencil,' he said, 'and the BATT clerk knows the distribution list; just give the report to him and he'll do the rest.'

He glanced at his watch, 'We've got about an hour before Maclean gets in, so we've just got time to go and meet the team at DDD.'

We climbed into the battered Land Rover and drove the kilometre or so into Salalah. Just before reaching the walls there was a crossroads; the only tarmac crossroads in Dhofar. In the middle of the road was a black and white striped pedestal on which, between the hours of 6.00am and 6.00pm, one of Dhofar's eight traffic policemen stood, energetically waving his arms with scant regard to the amount of traffic.

We turned right and through a large gateway, the only break for vehicles in the high stone walls that surrounded the old town. A posse of *askars* nominally guarded the gate, which, until recently, had been closed to traffic at night. Once inside the walled area, I discovered how small the capital of Dhofar really was. There was a large white mosque in the centre of a wide square. To the right, Scott pointed out the *Wali*'s quarters in a large old building adjoining the perimeter wall, and next to it was the Dhofar branch of the British Bank of the Middle East, with its prominently displayed green signs. The Old Palace was sand-coloured, perhaps three storeys high, with shuttered windows and a flat roof; it occupied two sides of the square and was notable by the presence of elite Royal Guard sentries in their red berets who were strategically posted at each entrance to the inner courtyards. It seemed to hide its mysterious history well.

Driving around the square we passed the *souk*, or marketplace, on the left, and the shimmering lapis lazuli blue Indian Ocean on our right with a fringe of wide-leaved palm trees waving gently in the sea breeze. Beyond the market, on the small sea front stood a new government building that housed the Dhofar Development Department. Outside the main door *askars* were gossiping to each other, keeping a casual eye on the healthy bustle of visitors coming and going, although nobody seemed to be stopped or questioned. We walked up the steps and into the hall where there was a crush of people crowding around a besieged young Dhofari in white dishdash and red *musar*, the characteristic loosely-wound turban commonly worn in Oman. He was seated at a desk arranging appointments with the *Wali* or his representatives but was submerged below a sea of men, all jabbering away and waving pieces of paper, trying to persuade him of the pressing nature of their case. He looked up, spotted Scott, smiled broadly and waved a greeting, encouraging us to move on up the stairs. At the top of the first flight, the corridor moved to left and right. To the left were the *Wali's* offices and to the right those of the DDD Administration.

'Come on,' said Scott, 'let's say hello to Robin Young.'

He knocked on a thin door and we walked into a light, cheerful, air-conditioned office. Behind one of two desks sat the DDD Director Robin Young, who was puffing on a pipe as he talked in Arabic on the phone. He waved a chubby arm at us and went on with his conversation. Behind the other desk was an attractive thirty-something woman, called Robin Butler, wife of the Agricultural Development Officer, Mike, and PA to Robin Young.

'Robin won't be a moment – he's got the *Wali* on the phone and they're trying to sort out a problem with Taylor Woodrow,' she said, flashing me a friendly smile. 'But welcome to Dhofar; how are you finding it?'

'An amazing place,' I answered truthfully. 'How long have you been here?'

'Oh, it seems like years,' she replied. 'I think Mike and I are more Dhofari than English by now.' She turned to Scott, 'When are you off?'

'Tomorrow's flight to Masirah,' said Scott, barely concealing a smile, 'then the VC10 to Brize Norton.' No Hercules transport aircraft for this canny major.

'Come and have dinner after Scott leaves tomorrow,' said Robin.

That sounded like a good idea and I happily agreed.

'If you look in when it's less frantic in the morning I'll tell you when and where,' she added.

The telephone on her desk rang and she answered in fluent and rapid Arabic. Scott and I sat down on two rickety wooden chairs and within seconds an Indian clerk brought us sweet, milky coffee in sepia-coloured glasses. I was wondering how to tackle it when Young put the phone down and got up from behind his desk. I slipped the glass under the chair. We shook hands.

'How simply lovely to meet you,' he said. 'You must be, let me see, I think our sixth BATT Vet? You probably know Scott was supposed to be the last but we didn't want to lose momentum before we can recruit a civilian vet to take over. I imagine Scott has filled you in on most things?'

We chatted for a few minutes and I soon realised I was fairly well down the pecking order. He was Mike Butler's boss and would I be good enough to liaise with Mike etc. I got the message.

'See you tomorrow,' said the female Robin as we went out. Young was already back on the phone and airily waved a hand vaguely in our direction as we left.

'Don't worry about Robin Young,' said Scott. 'He is a very experienced administrator and is a huge support to Sheikh Braik. Things work with him in place.'

'Is he married?' I asked.

'No,' replied Scott, 'he lives alone in one of those prefabricated houses on the sea front near *Bir Bint Ahmed*. He doesn't seem to socialise much.' He paused, 'I had dinner with him once.' He made it sound like quite an achievement.

We walked along the corridor and Scott knocked on another door. Inside were two men poring over a map. One was in his thirties, tall, with hair sun-bleached so fair it was almost white and looking very much the ex-cavalry officer. This was Mike Butler. Next to him was a short guy in his early twenties with long straggly hair and a beard. They turned as we entered and Scott introduced me first to Mike and then to Chris Klotz, an American Peace Corps volunteer, assigned to the Agriculture Department because of his knowledge of arid crops.

Mike was very much a hands-on man who I guessed would prefer to be on a tractor or mending a water *falaj* pump than sitting in meetings or behind a desk. He had taken some major initiatives to upgrade the *jebali* cattle, to improve crops and a big part of his work was overseeing the ever-increasing agriculture developments on the hill.

Leaving DDD, we got back into the Land Rover and drove past the busy fish and fruit markets and out of the gates towards the airport. Soon it was time to meet the SOAF Viscount. The policeman on his pedestal waved us energetically across an empty junction and we swerved to avoid a cow, which was being chased by a flustered, veiled woman who was shouting abuse at the stubborn animal and throwing stones at it in an unsuccessful attempt to stop it crossing the road. The policeman ignored the woman and the cow and continued to wave at non-existent cars.

About halfway between the RAF Camp and *Umm al Gwarrif* was a small turning towards the *jebal*, which led to the civil airfield. Large painted white letters proclaimed 'SALALAH INTERNATIONAL AIRPORT' across a wall of rusting *burmails* on the apron. It must have been one of the tiniest passenger airports in the world and certainly one of the most basic. Four unprepossessing wooden huts comprised 'Arrivals', 'Departures', 'Administration' and 'Customs'. The Terminal Buildings leaned optimistically against a high chain link fence, which served to separate us, the visitors, from them, the passengers. On the other side of the fence was a *burusti*, or palm frond, shelter – a bit like a large carport – under which sat thirty or forty soldiers and workmen avoiding the midday sun. On a small bench nearby were three limp-looking European businessmen waiting to escape Salalah for something more akin to civilisation.

Once or twice a day, a SOAF Viscount arrived (*Inshalla*) from Muscat. Twice a week, the airline Gulf Air (owned jointly by several Gulf States with a significant British input and crew), tasked a Fokker Friendship, a twin turboprop aircraft, on the only commercial flight to and from the capital, but again it was somewhat *Inshalla* as to when or if it actually arrived. Every flight was packed to capacity. If you couldn't pull rank, you could be stuck in Salalah for days. For the pioneering businessman, getting in and out of Dhofar was not easy.

Flights to the *jebal* locations by Skyvan or helicopter used the military side of the airport, but all passengers and goods were in the hands of Movements Officers, seconded from the RAF, who gallantly made some sort of order out of extraordinary demands, juggling military and humanitarian requirements with the needs of those wanting to get home on leave. In the 'Administration' hut was one of these officers, immersed under a dozen excited would-be travellers all waving tickets or bits of paper at him. A pilot poked his head through the glassless window and yelled something incoherent. The desk was piled high with papers and signals and the room was stiflingly hot. A large Baluchi sergeant tried to keep the peace and explain to the baying mob that the afternoon Viscount was totally full and the only thing to do was to come back tomorrow.

Suddenly the RAF officer had had enough. He stood up and pointed firmly at the door. There was a millisecond of stunned silence, which enabled him to grasp the initiative. 'Out,' he shouted firmly, then, with confidence growing 'out, out, OUT.' Ushered by the Baluchi sergeant, the grumbling crowd reluctantly left the hut.

'Now,' he said when peace had been restored. He picked up a persistently ringing phone and immediately replaced it on its cradle. Silence. He turned to the pilot at the window, 'Yes, Colin?'

'I was told to pick up a package for Jibjat,' the Skyvan pilot said. The Movements Officer shuffled papers on his desk and handed over a large, sealed manila envelope. 'Just the mail,' he said.

'I think I'll get off while the going's good,' said Colin with a grin and vanished from the window. We heard his Minimoke roar as he sped off to his waiting aircraft.

By now the phone was ringing again. It was ignored.

'To think I volunteered for this posting!' He smiled at us. 'What can I do for you chaps?'

'Any news of the Viscount?' asked Scott.

'It's on time for once,' he said, looking at the manifest. 'I see you have two royal dogs aboard – that's probably why!' He looked at his watch. 'The canine carrier will be here in about ten minutes.'

'You couldn't be a mate and double-check I'm on the Masirah flight tomorrow?' said Scott anxiously. The officer checked a sheet and to Scott's huge relief confirmed his name was down on the crucial list.

We left the steamy hut and strolled out onto the apron, passing unchallenged in our olive greens, through the guarded gate. A luggage trolley in the shadow of the empty Customs shed seemed a sensible place to sit and wait. As we sat, Scott told me there were several RAF Regiment guard dogs on Masirah. It was a bleak island but I should be ready to be called up there to see a sick animal.

'They'll signal if they need you. Strictly speaking, they come under Cyprus,' he said, 'but that is 3,000 kilometres away. I'll give the dogs a quick once-over tomorrow on my way through.'

'What happens to the dogs after their tour?' I asked.

'They'll be re-trained with another handler if possible,' said Scott. 'If not, or if they are at the end of their working lives, they have to be put down. Quarantine isn't a military option.'

'Any rabies in Oman?'

'None of the BATT Vets has seen it,' replied Scott, 'and I've heard no reports from any of the human hospitals.' That was a relief. The prospect that every pi-dog and house dog in Salalah could be a potential carrier of rabies would have been grimly daunting.

There was a loud roar and the SOAF Viscount, with its characteristic red and white markings, careered down the runway in a cloud of dust, gradually slowed, turned and taxied sedately if noisily to the apron. It was waved into place by an RAF corporal in shorts, chocks were put down and steps wheeled to the doors. There was a burst of activity. A fire engine appeared from nowhere, blue light flashing, and positioned itself importantly by the tail of the aircraft. Then a refuelling tanker lumbered up, a luggage lorry, trucks, saloon cars and a score of men scurried busily around the plane.

Mac Maclean was the last to disembark. He was easily identifiable by his Jermyn Street shirt and tie and a shock of white hair. He was carrying one end of a large wooden crate with an easily recognisable Harrods green label. The other end of the crate was held by the Loadmaster. They put the crate down as a Palace car and Land Rover, both with distinctive red, green and white number plates, swept up and two men got out and loaded three crates into the back of the Land Rover.

We meandered up and Scott introduced me to Sultan Qaboos' Private Secretary. He was friendly but preoccupied. I could see snuffling noses and wagging tails through the grills of the cages. The dogs at least seemed cheerful enough.

'Look,' said Maclean to me in a gentle Morningside accent, 'I've a lot on right now. The dogs have all travelled OK, but give me a ring tomorrow and come and give them a proper looking over.' He gave me his phone numbers. 'I've had them in my flat in Muscat for the last three days.'

He turned to Scott. 'I've arranged for you to see the Sultan' (he pronounced it *sultarn*), 'tomorrow afternoon.'

Scott was delighted and his face lit up. 'What time?' he asked.

'Come to the office at 11.30 and ask for me. HM will be down later today and I'll squeeze you in. What time do you leave?' Scott told him. 'OK. I'll see you tomorrow.'

With that, he got into his royal Datsun and was driven away with the three Harrods dogs following behind in the Palace Land Rover.

'Well!' said Scott. 'I may just get that watch yet.'

Chapter 6

Flotsam and Jetsam

The arrival of the Sultan and his court in Salalah for anything other than a brief visit was a major event. Courtiers, administrators, advisers, baggage, servants and dogs were crammed into the Viscounts, playing havoc with routine travel. The usual relatively inactive and unhurried life of the small town tangibly shifted up a couple of gears. Police reinforcements appeared and the presence of soldiers became very noticeable with far more Royal Guard Regiment berets to be seen. The adrenaline levels of the population, Dhofari and expatriate alike, seemed to rise in anticipation and excitement. Eventually, the Ruler himself would arrive in a small Falcon Executive jet, often with little more advance notice than when it was on final approaches. RAF Salalah ground rapidly to a halt and all movements were frozen until the plane had landed and HM had safely disembarked and driven off to the Palace.

Scott Moffat was keyed up at the prospect of an audience with the Sultan and began to consider carefully what he should wear and say.

'We'd better check the stables,' he said eagerly. 'I'd hate a lame horse to spoil my chat with HM.'

I pointed the Land Rover in the general direction of the Royal Stables and we slipped out of Salalah and followed the coast eastwards towards the Wire at Arzat. After a couple of kilometres, we turned right towards the sea along a rough, bumpy track, and into a tidy gravelled yard surrounded by neat white-painted stones. An Omani flag waved in the sea breeze, giving me the impression of arriving at a small military camp in an outpost of Kipling's Empire. Along one side of the yard was a line of basic but attractive wooden stables with roofs made from *burusti* to provide shelter and ventilation for the horses; it all blended sympathetically with the tropical setting of sand and sea, dunes and date palms, coconuts and coral.

The stables were near Al-Balid, the site of ancient Salalah. Now a wasteland, with only the remains of a few ancient buildings, this had once been the thriving centre of the Manjawi civilization from the twelfth to the sixteenth centuries. Famous, not only for its frankincense trade but also, appropriately, for the breeding and export of prime Arabian horses.

The Royal Stables were run by John Clarke and his assistant, Tony Brunton. Both were based in Muscat but came to Salalah regularly. One of them was invariably around when HM was in residence. John had signalled Scott to say he would be down as soon as he could get a seat on a Viscount. The head 'lad' was an elegant old man called Shenoon, with a craggy, mahogany face and deep twinkling eyes. He had been in the service of three Sultans, starting with Taimur bin Faisal, who had abdicated in 1932, and he told me with considerable pride how he had held the present Sultan as a baby in his arms soon after his birth in 1940.

Shenoon had the task of keeping an eye on the Royal Stables in Salalah with a dozen or so Indian or Pakistani *syces*. Our unannounced arrival had caused some confusion and it was comical to see the effect that the noise of our tyres on the gravel had, with *syces* leaping off their mattresses trying to appear busy sweeping or attending to horses.

The animals themselves looked tough and fit. Most were between 14 and 15 hands in height, lightly boned but hardy. There was a lot of Arab blood in them, but they were locally bred and none had seen the inside of a Stud Book. The colours were varied and I counted ten mares and one stallion – perhaps the perfect herd size.

Sultan Qaboos enjoyed riding and I imagined a Sultan would choose an impressive stallion as a mount, so was surprised when Shenoon proudly showed me his employer's favourite – a beautiful slightly-built mare called *Reem el Fellah*. Her long, lank mane hung loosely over her shiny coat. She was a picture of health – graceful, elegant and very pretty, with a sweet, feminine head and clear, bright eye. Loosely translated, her name meant 'gazelle on the open plain'. *Reem* was the perfect mount for a king and her appearance seemed to epitomise the Arabian legend that the horse was created by God from the South Wind.

Shenoon escorted us proudly along the rest of the line. The horses were bedded on sand in their airy *burusti* boxes. They looked at us inquisitively as we passed before returning contentedly to their rations of cut alfalfa. Their tails flicked constantly with the ceaseless irritation of flies.

I stroked one affectionate muzzle and gently opened its mouth, curious to know her age. I was shocked to find I was looking at the mouth from hell with the dentition of a wizened hag from a Grimms' coven. The mare appeared happy enough but all of her teeth were broken, distorted, black and irregular. I had never seen anything like it and my five years at veterinary school had certainly not prepared me for such as this. I looked at the next horse. It was a similar picture.

'Most of them are like that,' said Scott in response to my questioning look. 'Dates,' he said. 'They feed them whole dates. That's why the

45

coats are in such great condition. The damage to the teeth is done by the stones.'

'What's wrong with oats and bran?' I asked.

Nothing. But you tell that to old Shenoon! They've fed dates here for centuries and Shenoon is here by royal decree – or so he reckons. I gave up trying to change these things months ago. You can take a crack at persuading them yourself but I wouldn't hold out much hope.

I glanced at Shenoon, who gave a cheery, gummy grin.
'What does John Clarke make of it?' I asked.
'He's changing things slowly but HM believes in blending the traditional with the modern. They've been breeding horses here for over 800 years and reckon they know a bit about it.'
'So Shenoon is boss when John Clarke isn't here?' I asked.

There is a chap called Major Tony Jarvis, who helps out. He normally works with DDD's Civil Aid Department, led by Major Martin Robb. The Civil Action Teams, known as the CAT teams, are the boys who move in after the army have secured positions on the hill to set up and run the basic support systems and distribution networks. Jarvis is the Civil Liaison Officer (Dhofar), known hereabouts as CLO(D). I think he used to be a District Locust Officer in Africa.

'Interesting background,' I said.

Well, he spends a lot of time here at the stables, unpaid I think, acting as John's eyes and ears. I think John finds it helpful particularly when HM pays an unexpected visit. A signal to Jarvis will ensure everything is as it should be if John can't get here.

Although Shenoon did not speak English, a Pakistani called Rasul Bux did. He had been hovering in the background, but now came forward and saluted smartly. He had learned to speak English in the army, he told me, and had always loved horses. He said he had the rank of Sergeant-Major in Pakistan and at the Royal Stables he was in charge of the small pharmacy and did some basic foot-trimming. He was effectively the Veterinary Assistant and seemed to divide his time between Muscat and Salalah.

I slipped into a stall and picked up a foot of a friendly-looking grey mare to see what sort of a farrier I had in Rasul Bux. The foot was trimmed well but unshod and rock-hard with virtually no frog. In most horses, the frog is a V-shaped rubbery structure on the underside of the foot that acts as a shock absorber and helps pump blood back to the heart. Evolution and breeding, combined with the hot sand and hard going, had produced a tough, resilient hoof in these Omani horses with less need for a frog, or

46

metal shoes. Rasul Bux's job was to keep a reasonable and functional shape to these unyielding, granite-like feet.

His appointment as Veterinary Dresser gave Rasul Bux a higher status than the other *syces*. He led me to a small wooden room which was the pharmacy and also contained his bed and personal possessions. A locked cupboard contained various drugs and packs of Epsom salts. Next door was a small, cramped dormitory, crammed with half a dozen beds. Then there was the feed store, with its bins and small hessian sacks of dark brown, sticky, fly-covered dates.

The prize exhibit was the tack room. Like a magician completing an illusion, Shenoon pulled away the large dustsheet covering the royal tack. It was an incongruous sight in this primitive shack in the sand. There were British, Swiss and US Cavalry saddles and bridles of the finest leather, and all in excellent condition. Someone was a stickler for tack-cleaning. In addition, wrapped in heavy polythene sheets, were traditional, Arabic saddles with blankets intricately embroidered with blue, red and gold threads. The matching bridles had silver buckles and gleaming bits with gold braid decorations. I could see that *Reem el Fellah* would look exquisite when turned out for her sovereign.

I complimented Shenoon, who beamed happily. I turned to Scott.

'Where does HM ride?' I asked.

'Seems to depend on his moods,' he replied. 'Sometimes he'll ride through the coastal villages, meeting the people and listening to complaints or distributing cash; other days he'll just go for a gallop along the beach.'

'Doesn't that present something of a security risk?' I asked, having realised how much the future of this fragile land depended on the survival and success of Sultan Qaboos.

'Wait till you see the performance,' said Scott. 'Wherever he goes, he is surrounded by the Royal Guard and a band of *askars* as well as a load of hangers-on who are all armed. Then there are the vehicles – often a dozen or more; armoured cars, Land Rovers, even an ambulance! The RG run alongside the horses – no wonder they are an elite!'

'Who runs the RG?' I asked.

'A guy called Major Geoff Harcourt is Commanding Officer. I heard he used to protect Jomo Kenyatta in Kenya. He has a very difficult job – he is the only British officer in the Regiment. No one envies him.'

The task of keeping a Middle Eastern ruler safe and well in a country at war was not going to be easy. The Sultan was said to dislike the claustrophobic fuss over his wellbeing and safety and it was encouraging to hear stories that he loved nothing more than sneaking out of his palace to drive around Salalah quietly in an unmarked Datsun. This would in part help to explain why it was said there was not much that went on in Dhofar that he didn't know about.

'I heard one funny tale,' said Scott, 'that one day he wrapped a *shemagh* around his face and walked around the fruit market with his Aide de Camp, Major Sayyid Al-Mutassim, who was similarly disguised. There are fairly strict price controls and regulations about charges for food and the story goes that HM just walked up to a woman selling oranges and asked the price. She told him and he went on to the next stall and asked the price there. When he heard it was cheaper he went back to the first woman, removed his *shemagh*, and said "So! You would overcharge your Sultan, would you?" The poor woman nearly died of fright.'

We were leaning restfully against the wooden bars across the stable of a pert chestnut mare.

'Is he a benign ruler?' I asked.

'Oh, I think so,' said Scott. 'Fighting on the *jebal* is one thing, but he seems to prefer reconciliation and forgiveness. If a terrorist freely surrenders, Qaboos will usually help him to start life afresh. Defeat the enemy by showing how much better life is on the other side. That's why we are here.'

It was just after noon when I got back to *Bir Bint Ahmed*, having dropped Scott at the Mess to prepare for his audience. Saleh was squatting outside the main entrance under the shade of a leafy date palm chatting with a man who was accompanied by three goats, each held on a string tied around its neck. The goats nibbled listlessly at anything green they could reach. Each animal was covered with dozens of small lumps from head to tail. The nodules were all just under the skin surface and about the size of small marbles.

'Uttaria,' said Saleh, 'skin uttaria.'

I looked blankly before I realised that he meant urticaria, a word he must have learned from one of my predecessors. Urticaria literally means 'nettle burn'. Eruptions appear in the skin due to a reaction to something, perhaps a toxic chemical, insect bite, dietary allergy or heat. I asked Saleh whether urticaria was common in Salalah. He said it was – especially in warm weather.

Saleh was relaxed about the condition and muttered something about 'inject Betsolan'. I went with the tide and we gave the goats some intramuscular corticosteroid and, as Saleh knew the owner and where he lived,

I said we would call in the next day to see how they were progressing. The goats looked perfectly happy, and they were really quite plump and so must have good appetites. Despite looking uncomfortable, the lumps seemed to be causing no distress. I gave an optimistic smile at the owner as he shuffled off, leading his goats by their cords.

Back in my office I found a note from Jeremy Raybould, the Harbour Master. It was roughly scrawled and read: 'To the new vet: Welcome. Unexpected dhow arrived from Africa this morning, 1,500 goats. Am awaiting your inspection before off-loading. See you soon. J.R.'

I yelled for Saleh and Hafeedth, who were not thrilled at having to go to the harbour so late in their working day. We clambered into the Land Rover and sped off on the 12-kilometre journey to Raysut. Following Scott's example, I remembered to shout *'tabeeb'* at the *askars* guarding the exit from the perimeter wire and gave them an optimistic wave. It seemed to do the trick – but maybe it was just that Saleh was in the passenger seat.

Dhofar Province Quarantine Station was situated at the top of a hill overlooking the harbour. After leaving the tarmac road, you had to bounce and cough your way along a bumpy track with the tyres throwing up asphyxiating clouds of fine, clinging sand that got into the cab whether the windows were open or shut. From the top of the hill, there was a breathtaking view over the small port on the edge of the shimmering, rich deep blue of the Indian Ocean that stretched south from Oman past the Yemeni island of Socotra and the Seychelles to Madagascar and on to the South Pole. Later in the year, during July and August, the tides and currents would be seriously affected by the monsoon such that no ships could get into the harbour. Before then there would be a big push to get animals (and all the other supplies which had to be routed through its congested waters) in before the monsoon started. Another bottleneck occurred before big Moslem feasts such as *Eid el Fitar*, which marked the end of the fasting month of Ramadan, when huge numbers of animals were required for the celebratory parties.

Walls of rusty, sand-filled *burmails* demarcated the large pens housing groups of up to 2,000 sheep and goats at any one time. A wealthy Dhofari merchant, Said Ahmed Said Al Shanfari, later to become Oman's Minister of Agriculture, was the chief importer. His men were responsible for feeding the animals during their time in quarantine and for ensuring that the *Wali's* import regulations were not broken. Because of the difficulties BATT Vets had experienced in getting any rules agreed at all, it was not surprising that we had to ensure they were enforced. This meant regular visits by the veterinary team. Fortunately, Saleh and Hafeedth had fully grasped the need for such controls and were authorised to isolate and slaughter animals showing signs of infectious diseases (although they

49

preferred the vet to make all potentially unpopular decisions). There would obviously be abuses but the regulations were essential and on the whole the system worked reasonably well; after all, there was little need to smuggle, as Shanfari was perfectly happy for his men to sell sheep to customers at the station gate as long as they were killed on site.

In a cove at the end of a peninsula was the small port. It was run with naval precision by Commodore Jeremy Raybould. In his crisp white shorts and shirt, Jeremy was everything one would expect from an English Harbour Master, complete with naval beard. As well as Harbour Master, Jeremy was also Pilot, Customs Controller and Chief Loader and Unloader – in fact he *was* The Port. He and successive BATT Vets had established a routine for quarantining imported animals. When a dhow approached Raysut crammed, say, with a consignment of Somali sheep, Jeremy would order it to anchor outside the port and send a message to summon the vet. The VO and Saleh would then drive to Raysut and Jeremy would take them out in the Pilot's launch to the dhow. If the VO was satisfied there was no overt disease risk, Jeremy would allow them to be landed on the Quarantine Station's beach from where they could be herded up the hill to their *burmail* compounds. Here, Saleh would spray an indelible mark on each new batch to distinguish them from earlier or later arrivals and the vet could examine the delivery more closely for signs of disease.

Today I could see twenty or thirty modestly sized cargo vessels and dhows waiting patiently to find a berth in the congested port. Alongside the one main jetty three ships were moored, including a Brooke-Marine Fast Patrol Boat of SOAN, the Sultan of Oman's Navy, steel grey with its Bofors gun neatly stowed. Next to it was a dhow and beyond that was a small cargo vessel flying the Panamanian flag. Two or three mobile cranes stood on the quayside and, as I drove down towards the entrance, I could see one unloading what looked like pallets of cement from the bowels of the dhow.

The quay was chock-a-block full of cargo, but as a credit to its Harbour Master, everything had an orderly look to it. Lorries from Taylor-Woodrow, DDD and the army waited uncomplainingly in a long line to collect their loads. Other trucks were being loaded or unloaded, or were arriving or departing. Workmen and sailors busied themselves at their respective duties and there was a definite hum in the little dock. As we drove through the harbour gates, I saw Raybould driving a fork-lift truck that seemed to be piled high with sacks of potatoes. He saw us, pulled over and pointed at the only concrete building.

'Go over to the office,' he said. 'I'll be with you in a mo.'

With that, he backed away and went to collect another batch of King Edwards. We sat and drank tea until Jeremy arrived.

50

'Another bloody consignment of Somali goats,' he said briskly after the briefest of introductions. 'No idea it was coming – I'll speak to Shanfari about that. Scott left yet?'

I said he was leaving the next day.

'Give him my salaams.' Raybould was clearly in a hurry and turned to his cluttered desk and rifled through some files. 'Here's the paperwork for the goats.'

He handed me some flimsy yellow sheets.

'Useless of course,' he added unpromisingly. 'You can go out in my boat now and give them the all clear so we can get them landed and up to the quarantine station.'

I glanced at the paper and the illegible scribble of some Somali government vet and an obscure rubber stamp. The document claimed that the consignment of animals was 'free of any disease'.

I followed the Harbour Master to a motor launch with 'PILOT' marked in large white letters on the sides. 'You seem to be everything around here,' I remarked.

'Too right,' he said. 'Mind you, I have been here for seven years; built it from nothing – and through the coup. It's been fun.'

He said something to the helmsman and turning to me he added, 'See you later – try not to be too long with the launch.' He leaped back into the fork-lift truck and drove off to resume his stevedore duties as we cruised swiftly towards a rather old and worn-looking dhow.

Dhows have plied the commercial sea routes of the Indian Ocean since the Dark Ages. Like Chinese junks, which preceded them, they have survived into the modern day. By 1974, most had engines to supplement their large triangular lateen sails. Dhows were coasters and usually kept land in sight as they voyaged up the Gulf or down across to Zanzibar, or to Bandarbeyla in northern Somalia. There was usually a crew of six or seven men and boys who had little comfort as the vessel was usually open-decked, with a canvas awning at the stern under which the crew would eat, sleep and steer. Also at the stern, but to one side were the heads – a barrel-shaped device attached to the outside of the vessel and usually painted in bright and cheerful colours. Sometimes the face of a crewman could be seen peering over the top as he squatted. Experienced helmsmen like Jeremy's wisely approached from the bows.

There was much shouting and gesticulating as we pulled alongside. The only way on board was to climb a rough rope ladder, which flapped against the side of the dhow. I looked at Saleh and his middle-age spread and long dishdash. He smiled wanly and shook his head, pointing at the youthful Hafeedth. The helmsman held the launch against the boat waiting for me to make a move. So I clambered up, followed by Hafeedth in his

51

tight bright trousers and shirt. Saleh stayed contentedly in the launch, bobbing gently in the swell.

The small weather-beaten and toothless Arab Master smiled as I stumbled aboard spluttering out 'Salaam alay koom'. Then my eyes moved on beyond the ancient mariner to a startling sight. The dhow was crammed with hundreds, perhaps thousands of sheep. Halfway along the deck there was a large gap, which opened into the inner reaches below. In disbelief I pushed my way through the milling, bleating animals towards the hold. The bottom of the ship was 6 or 7 metres below, and as I peered into the gloom I could make out layer upon layer of animals piled upon each other.

The nineteenth-century anti-slavery campaigner, Sir Fairfax Moresby, wrote passionately of man's inhumanity to man in the slave trade of that era when he discovered African men and women stowed in bulk, layer upon layer, in large, unwieldy open boats. Today I saw man's inhumanity to beast. The successor of the slave trade was thriving. The bewildered animals were perched perilously on improvised lower decks just as Moresby had described for the human trade 150 years before. There was a clearance of only a few centimetres between layers and I guessed that after the first layer of sheep was loaded, ribs in the dhow's structure, supplemented by crates, ropes and oil-drums had enabled planks to be placed across enabling a second layer to be added, and the procedure repeated. The only relatively fortunate animals were those on the deck itself. They looked thin but well enough.

This living cargo would have endured several days at sea – the length of journey dependent on wind and weather – with seasickness, inevitable injuries and no food or water. I hardly dared think about the dead and dying bodies in the depths that could not be reached. The smell was awful and I felt sick. Deep below the deck I could hear sheep coughing and sneezing but it did not sound too serious, which was encouraging as my primary duty was to check for signs of infectious or contagious disease that would prevent them landing. I was also supposed to keep an eye out for possible smuggling of arms, but whoever made that suggestion had never visited a dhow full of sheep. It was impossible to see anything other than a sea of wool, hair, tails, heads and shit. They could have hidden a Chieftain tank on board.

I squeezed down to the first platform and the steamy ammoniacal smell of faeces and urine grew increasingly intense and unpleasant. And I was only at level one. Hafeedth shouted at me from the deck. I looked up and saw he was holding a torch, which he had grabbed from a crew member. He handed it down to me. Slowly and very cautiously, I made my way around the second deck. Most of the animals were not too bad apart from

Paddy King-Fretts, Commander
'A' Squadron March 1974.
(*Paddy King-Fretts*)

The entrance to RAF Salalah.
March 1974.

Loading up a Skyvan for a veterinary trip to the *jebal*. The BATT Vet Land Rover and the team.

Salalah from the air in 1974. Taken from a Skyvan as it began its descent into RAF Salalah

The vet's office at *Bait al Falaj*.

The *falaj* (aqueduct) irrigation system at *Bait al Falaj* supplying water from the deep well to fields used mostly for the cultivation of fast-growing alfalfa (lucerne) to feed the cattle.

The Dhofar Development Department's herd of dairy cows at *Bait al Falaj*.

The new bull pens at *Bait al Falaj*.

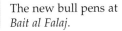

The author with Veterinary Dresser Number 1 Saleh bin Hassan Al Yafai and sick goat.

The author among the sheep and goats in the quarantine station at Raysut.

Veterinary Dresser Hafeedth bin Ahmed Al Theeb draws milk from the udder of a sheep with mastitis.

n Taqah with, from left to right, camel with its owner, Hafeedth, Ahmed Ali Fat ('Taqah Ahmed'),
he author and Saleh.

Breakdown on the beach between Taqah and Salalah as the tide comes in.

Driving south along the Midway Road towards the *jebal* with Salalah beyond.

BATT vehicle on the hill. Ben Higson and Hafeedth in the back.

The author and Hafeedth at the White City water trough as a small herd of thirsty camels arrives with their *jebali* owners.

The tranquil old Royal Stables at Wutayyah near Ruwi outside Muscat. Note the cool *burusti* stabling.

The author demonstrating his riding skills at the Royal Stables.

Assistant Manager of the Royal Stables, Tony Brunton, with a typical Omani-bred Arab.

The grumpy Marabou stork mingling with the pelicans in the Royal Gardens at Seeb.

some coughs and runny noses, aggravated by the ammonia fumes. I tried to get down one more layer, but it was useless so I gave up and heaved myself back into the sunshine like Odysseus emerging from Hades.

'All OK Sahib? Very good sheep, yes?' said the skipper of this floating hell.

I just shook my head. I had no idea what infections I might be letting into Dhofar. Fortunately there was plenty of space at the quarantine station, so in the interests of the animals' welfare I told Hafeedth they could land. We would check them in the morning after they had eaten some food and breathed some fresh air. The captain thrust a grubby piece of paper at me. Hafeedth said it was the landing authority that I had to sign. So I did.

Back in the port, I went up to Jeremy and just opened my arms in a helpless gesture. He smiled sympathetically.

'I wonder how many died on the way,' I mused.

'Dozens, hundreds, who knows?' said Raybould. 'I only hope they remembered to slit their bellies before turfing them over the side or we'll have them washed up on the coast for weeks. Right, let's get them ashore.' He barked an order at someone and I knew the sheep would soon be on dry land.

For the first time I began to appreciate the problems of keeping diseases out of a country, and some of the facts that had been drilled into me at university suddenly took on a new reality. I was responsible for the health of all animals in an area the size of Hungary and for the first time I saw how easily epidemics can arise. Viruses are no respecters of border controls or war zones. Animals that may look healthy on board a dhow can easily be incubating diseases that will be transmitted not only to the others in that festering ship but also to those they mix with on land. A whole country can become infected with a new disease as fast as foot-and-mouth disease spreads in Britain. And I was the only qualified man in Oman to prevent it.

We drove up the hill to the quarantine station to see if there was a secure and remote pen in which to put the new arrivals. There were already a lot of sheep there, certainly more than I had ever seen together in one place. I felt lost as I gazed blankly at thousands upon thousands of animals and realised I should also be checking these animals for any warning signs of disease. To Saleh, however, this was just another routine arrival and he was getting increasingly hungry and grumpy. He grunted that the batch we were looking at had arrived only two days ago, they were all fine and it always took a day or two to get over the stress of the journey.

I pointed to a couple of thin specimens with tails and hind limbs badly stained with liquid faeces. Saleh and Hafeedth, muttering to each other, dutifully dived in and dragged the sheep to a small isolation area where we could check them again after twenty-four hours. I soon learned that selected animals rarely survived long; one of Shanfari's men would immediately try to sell them off cheaply as it was not in the merchant's interests to keep ill animals around. Saleh spoke to the men and reported back that there was plenty of fodder and fresh water and, in case I got any more ideas, promptly reminded me that it was well past lunch and prayer time. Animal health was all very well, I soon learned, but in Dhofar there were certain immutable and non-negotiable priorities.

Chapter 7

A Good Audience

The day of Scott Moffat's departure dawned clear and hot. He still had some packing to finish and some goodbyes to make in the Camp before his royal audience. A lot of interest had been generated in the Mess with bets being taken on what he was likely to be given. It was known that the Sultan loved his animals dearly and appreciated the time and effort that had been put in by successive BATT Vets at the Royal Stables on top of their military duties in Dhofar. Directly after breakfast I drove Scott to *Bir Bint Ahmed* to see the veterinary staff for the last time.

There was quite an assembly waiting for us. In addition to Saleh and Hafeedth, the two *askars*, and the Pakistani lab technician, there were also, to Scott's evident delight, three of the four Veterinary Assistants who were normally based in various outlying villages. They rarely came to *Bir Bint Ahmed*, so it was a touching recognition of Scott's popularity that they had made the effort to see him off. It was also the first time I had met them.

Mohammed Aydrus had come from Awqad Bait Fadil, a small village just inside the perimeter wire on the road to the harbour. Next there was Ahmed, who had travelled in the opposite direction from Dahariz, a village on the Taqah side but again just inside the Wire where some of Sultan Qaboos' mother's family lived. Finally, there was Ahmed Ali Fat, the Taqah Veterinary Assistant, who was generally known as 'Taqah Ahmed' to distinguish him from 'Dahariz' Ahmed. The fourth Assistant, Mohammed Awath al Mahysun, was based at Mirbat, 75 kilometres away and inaccessible by road, but sadly he had not made it.

Taqah Ahmed was in his thirties and said to be an alcoholic – not easy for Moslems in Oman. Scott had warned me not to leave surgical spirit lying around. I never found out where he got his liquor from and Scott said the advice was not to worry too much if he disappeared for a couple of days – the *Wali* of Taqah knew about the problem and would probably lock him up if he was incapacitated. Ahmed was also unusual in that he lacked much of his nose, possibly due to syphilis. This small, curious but agreeable man spoke English remarkably well and told me improbably that he had once visited Grimsby. It seemed that at some stage of his early life he had been a seaman. I liked Ahmed's independent approach to life and throughout my stay in Dhofar we always had a good rapport.

Also employed at *Bir Bint Ahmed* was a cheery tea boy called Ali. He worked for a couple of hours each day before school and was always smiling. Education was expanding fast under Sultan Qaboos and new schools were opening at a rapid rate. After the lapses and ignorances during Sultan Said bin Taimur's rule, there were so many Dhofari children needing educating that schools operated in shifts. Ali's shift that morning was from 11.00am until 2.00pm, which meant that he too could come and see Scott. He beamed with pleasure to be part of the send-off team and today looked particularly smart in his school uniform of clean white dishdash and *tagiyah*. Uniform was *de rigueur* for all schoolchildren in Salalah and it was common to see a crocodile of Arab boys dressed in school kit and clutching a plastic satchel or brief-case, usually out of proportion to the size of the bearer. The girls had their own smart pink uniforms. Only four years before, girls had not been educated at all and had practically no status in Omani society. Now they were entitled to the same education as the boys and were seen equally as the future of Oman. Saleh and Hafeedth had been lucky. Both of modest origins, they had been educated at the one school available in Said bin Taimur's Salalah. Their standard of literacy was uncommon among their age group and accounted for their relatively prestigious posts within DDD.

The veterinary team was standing in a group outside the office as we drove up. I reckoned it might be a bit emotional, so I left Scott to it and wandered across to look at the cows grazing gently in a nearby field of alfalfa. We had about fifty milking cows at *Bir Bint Ahmed*, most of them crossbred between *jebali* cattle and one of Mike Butler's large imported bulls. The local animals were tiny – an adult was about the size of a six- or seven-month Friesian heifer, if that. Yet they were tough and disease-resistant. Mike's plan in crossbreeding was to encourage productivity and milk production while hopefully retaining some resistance to local diseases.

A large covered yard housed the cattle at night. There was also a basic milking parlour, a simple system with a pressure line and separate machines to allow the milk to be drawn easily from the cows as they ate their concentrate rations. However, the Dhofaris had not taken to mechanical milking and ignored the machines. In *jebali* tradition, the milking of cows was the man's responsibility and they saw no reason not to continue to milk their cows by hand as their fathers and grandfathers had done before them. This generally meant a rodeo as two or three men were needed to chase, corner and capture a cow; the excitement would reduce the animal's milk let-down process that is best with gentle and quiet handling. Yet these were tough, wiry *jebali* cattle, and almost as fierce and independent as their owners. Once captured, the beast grabbed greedily at its food and one of the men would hobble its hind legs with a twisted cord and then take hold of its head as another squatted beside her with a large wooden collecting bowl clasped between his knees. Milking involved drawing milk from two quarters at the same time yielding, perhaps, one or two litres of milk a day – a poor comparison to the twenty or more litres from a British dairy cow.

I gazed at this strange herd peacefully eating the legumes that flourished thanks to *Bir Bint Ahmed*'s efficient flood irrigation systems. Unlike many indigenous cattle in the tropics, these cows did not possess a neck hump and some said they may have been the ancestors of our own Channel Island cattle, the Jersey and Guernsey. Looking at the golden coats of some of these well-fed *jebali* cows as they lazily chewed the cud in this early morning sunshine haze, I could almost see the similarity.

Scott was a little sad after his farewells and we drove back to the Camp in silence. I promised to collect him promptly at eleven o'clock and get him to Maclean's office by eleven-thirty.

By the time I got back to *Bir Bint Ahmed*, the boys had dispersed and Saleh and I decided the most important thing was to return to Raysut to see how the new arrivals were faring in the quarantine station. It didn't look promising when we arrived. The partition of *burmails* between those animals already halfway through their twenty-one days' isolation and the previous day's newcomers was now a barrier in name only. Nobody, including me, had thought to fix the gaps or check the integrity of the oil-drum walls before admitting the newcomers. As a result, goats and sheep were freely intermingling and hopping from one section to another through several goat-sized gaps. There were thousands of sheep and goats at the station and I cursed myself for not thinking things through. I had to learn there could be no short cuts in this job; everything had to be checked and double-checked.

At least we knew the newcomers as the older ones had a coloured spray mark identifying the particular batch. I decided it would be pointless to try to sort out the two groups as any hope of isolating sick animals that might be carrying an exotic disease had vaporised. Both lots would have to be treated as having the same health status and must start a full three-week quarantine from the beginning.

Surprisingly, the recent arrivals seemed none the worse for their voyage and had settled remarkably well. Some showed absurd energy and agility, with the more adventurous goats leaping on top of oil-drums from where they could survey the scene around them and hunt for more space and food. I told Hafeedth and the herdsmen to get the gaps repaired. Saleh meanwhile, holding his dishdash out of the way with his left hand, was spraying away at the new Somali sheep and goats, marking each with a red cross and getting increasingly irritated at the incompetence of his helpers.

57

I walked over to the boundary fence and looked down into the Raysut Headquarters and training camp of the Frontier Force below. A bunch of recruits was being put through their paces by a loud, barrel-chested and formidable-looking Pakistani Sergeant-Major. The soldiers were out of step and, as they were not yet in uniform, looked as if they had just arrived. FF was one of Oman's two tough Baluchi regiments. To get into the regiment was an opportunity to escape from the poverty and hopelessness of one of the poorest regions of Pakistan. Selection was rigorous and the standard of recruitment high, but there seemed a long way to go with this lot. It said a lot for the British Commanding Officer and his team to get such a team up to fighting strength within a few months.

Just in front of the quarantine station, on the seaward side, two wooden posts were stuck in the ground about 3 metres apart. Between them was a crossbar fastened with rope to each upright so they looked like miniature rugby posts. On this structure, animals bought at the station were slaughtered, skinned, eviscerated and dressed. I was surprised to see so many goatskins lying around; surely it was only a matter of time before an enterprising Dhofari saw there was money to be made in curing and tanning the leather? At present, the hides seemed only to attract clouds of flies as well as vultures and crows that hovered in finger-licking anticipation waiting for the next victim.

When the marking was completed we set off back towards Salalah. Saleh was in the back of the pick-up with the veterinary bag and clinging on like a limpet as we bounced our way towards the road, and he shouted directions to me through a partition behind the driver. Soon he wanted me to leave the tarmac and we weaved our way through a maze of little roads between walls and small stone houses. We passed shops with tables and chairs outside and chatting occupants. Here was a mosque with a tower that made Pisa look like a plumb-line. There was a coconut plantation and a field of succulent alfalfa. Eventually we arrived at a large, solid wooden door set in a less solid-looking sandstone and mortar wall. Most of the houses in and around Salalah seemed to be in varying stages of ancient decay or modern rebuild. However, bricks were expensive and as most householders did their own building, a house could take many years to complete.

We were there, said Saleh as I pulled up, to check a bullock with lumps. The steer, an interesting cross between a Friesian bull and the local *jebali* breed, had a football-sized abscess on his chest. I wondered how these crossbreds tolerated the climate compared to indigenous animals. They seemed to adapt pretty well. Saleh produced an old paint can and we drained the abscess into it, producing an impressive volume of smelly, greenish liquid pus. I dressed the wound, gave the animal an injection of antibiotics and told Saleh to say to the owner that we would be back tomorrow. It was odd to be treating animals for free, but that was why I was there.

Later, back at the Mess, I knocked at Scott's door. He was nervous and unexpectedly dressed in a charcoal grey suit, RAVC tie, gleaming black shoes, and with a white handkerchief neatly tucked into his top pocket. He looked ready for an audience, if rather warm. Suitcases and boxes lay around his room three-quarters full, with an assortment of souvenirs scattered around the floor.

I opened the door of the scruffy Land Rover and used my hat to dust down the plastic passenger seat before he climbed in. We got a few stares, some cheery waves and a couple of rude shouts as we drove out. Leaving the Camp, I pointed out a neat Falcon jet on the main apron with three RGR soldiers around it. 'That must be HM's aircraft,' I said, 'so at least we know he's here.'

I dropped Scott at the inner courtyard to the Palace just inside the town walls and was curtly ordered by a tense member of the Royal Guard to move on immediately. There were a lot of RG about now that the Sultan was in town and, having spotted two GPMGs pointing directly at me from the roof, I moved. I wished Scott luck as he disappeared into the mysterious world of Arabian monarchy.

Parking the car alongside DDD, I wandered into the *souk*. Two dusty alleys made up the narrow thoroughfares of this tiny market. Each was about 50 metres long by 4 or 5 metres wide. Tiny shops opened to each side and most had a small counter against which an Arab or Indian trader sat watching, haggling or niftily working his abacus with dextrous and nimble fingers. There was no room to expand within the ancient walls of the old town, so the fruit, vegetable and fish markets had moved outside the walls. This small inner *souk* now only sold household goods such as carpets and radios, trays and cloths as well as spices and coffee, dates and sweetmeats. Flour and rice were weighed out from sacks using massive brass scales suspended from the ceilings and tipped into paper cones or plastic bags. There were no heavy items like washing machines, fridges and cookers; these had to be bought from merchants outside the old town – and at huge cost. Nearly everything was imported through Jeremy Raybould's congested port but the variety and enterprise were impressive; shelves groaned with stock of unimaginable variety: there was trouser cloth from Yorkshire and gold-threaded brocades from Pakistan, glasses from Red China, flip-flops from Korea, velvets, satins and silks from India and cool Egyptian cotton.

Arab and African women, black-draped and veiled or wearing colourful fabrics, bustled and jostled with the men – *jebalis*, Dhofaris and Northerners, Indians and Pakistanis, soldiers and a few British expatriates

59

all pushing their way through the narrow passageways. The most romantic stalls were those selling spices and herbs. The colours and smells were exotic and mystical: there were sacks of green cardamom pods, yellow and red saffron, white poppy seeds and black cumin seeds; there were jars of cloves, coriander, cinnamon sticks, curry powders and chillies; endless evocative and new sensations to excite the senses.

Outside the *souk*, a young man was sitting with his back to a wall spinning yarn into thread by rolling it between his two hands with the other end fastened around his big toe. He had a large bag of yellow wool and he smiled self-consciously when he saw how intrigued I was by his task. In other countries he would be a tourist attraction, but here he was getting on with the only life he knew, maybe not realising how the ending of the war and the oil revolution would remove his ancient craft from Oman for ever.

I meandered back to DDD and chatted to Robin Butler. It was almost one o'clock when Scott burst into the office. With the audience over, he had loosened his tie and held his jacket over his shoulder in a small acknowledgement of the midday sun. He was flushed and happy.

'Well? How did it go?' Robin and I both asked at once.

'What a charming man,' replied Scott. He related how an Indian clerk had met him at the entrance to the Palace and taken him up to Maclean's office. Within half an hour, the telephone had rung and Scott had followed Maclean through the old royal apartments until they reached a very deep and rich carpet outside the Sultan's suite. There was a hushed atmosphere and the ADC, Major Al-Mutassim, sat quietly rustling some papers at a desk. Suddenly the door opened, and the ADC leapt to his feet as Sheikh Braik, the *Wali*, emerged, nodded at Maclean and left. Al-Mutassim knocked gently and went in. Scott said he was sure his heart could be heard beating at the RAF Camp. Then Al-Mutassim came out and beckoned to him. His Majesty had been sitting behind a large desk with his back to the window. Through the glass, Scott said he could see the sun glinting on the tranquil sea and a couple of dhows softly passing each other in the distance. The office, he said, was not extravagantly furnished, but there was a fine Persian carpet on the floor and the walls were panelled. The Sultan had smiled, risen from his desk and come round to shake hands. Scott said he was surprised to find the Ruler was quite slight. He was wearing a grey dishdash and purple *musar*, and had a neatly trimmed black beard with black hair greying at the temples. His eyes were very large, black and penetrating but friendly. Scott sat opposite him with the desk in between with a miniature Omani flag on it, blocking his view so he had to peer at the Sultan from first one side and then the other.

The meeting had lasted about ten minutes and Scott had been impressed by how much the Sultan knew of the work of the BATT Vets. He had thanked Scott for his work in Oman and for looking after his animals. He had asked about Scott's family and where his next posting would be. Then the Sultan had stood up, wished him well in his new job in Cyprus and asked if he would accept a small token of his appreciation. Scott was handed a green leather box and after a bow, he found himself outside the polished door. The ADC shook his hand, told a Royal Guard soldier to take him to Maclean's office and turned to usher in three large and important-looking Omanis, all wearing impressive *khunjas*. Maclean had said good-bye and taken him to the main door of the Palace from where he had walked over here, pausing only to take off his jacket and loosen his tie.

'Well. Let's see the watch,' said Robin.

He showed it to us. A dress watch on a leather strap, it had a green face and gold hands and the Sultan's royal crest on the dial. Scott was very pleased: 'Perhaps not for wearing at the stables,' he observed realistically, 'but it'll be fine with Mess kit.'

Scott said his goodbyes to Robin, and I drove him back to RAF Salalah for a fine send-off as he happily displayed his present for all to see. He was repeatedly toasted and it was around four o'clock when we poured him happily onto his flight to Masirah – still in his suit and still clutching his little green box.

It was sad to lose my adviser and friend who had helped so much to introduce me to the vagaries of Arabia and had tried hard to minimise the culture shock. A wave of loneliness washed over me as I watched the Viscount taxi to the runway and take off, realising that I would have to handle all that Dhofar would throw at me – camels, Sultans, *adoo*, BATT and dogs from Harrods. I turned those thoughts over in my mind as I headed for *UAG* for a cup of tea with Ben Higson, the PSYOPS Officer.

'When are you going up the hill?' Ben asked.

'Dunno. When I'm told I suppose,' I replied honestly. 'Why?'

'I'd like to come up with you,' he said, 'I'll bring a photographer and take some shots of the animal treatments.' I said I would speak to Paddy King-Fretts and let him know as soon as anything came up.

Prayers started promptly at 1745 hours every day at BATT HQ for everyone who was not on the hill. No one was late. About twenty of us assembled outside the Ops Room around a large map of the Operational Area, which leaned against the wall of the hut. By now, most of the BATT men in Salalah knew me by sight as I had been at the last two nights' prayers and I got some friendly nods. Fred, the SSM, was drawing lines on the map with coloured crayons, copying details from a pile of Situation Reports in his other hand. Then Paddy King-Fretts came out of his office and began quietly and factually to brief us on what had happened during the previous twenty-four hours across the war zone and the impact on the BATT units.

61

Each evening I learned about military successes or advances, *adoo* killed, captured or surrendered, areas under heaviest attack, arms caches located, and the Squadron's own score of hits. Since Sultan Qaboos came to power the rebels had been progressively pushed westward. The threat to cut off the much-needed water supplies and aid wherever there was enemy action was paying dividends. On the west side, a squadron of Jordanian engineers and British sappers, often under enemy fire, were building a massive physical barrier composed of razor-sharp Dannert concertina wire and anti-personnel mines from Mughsayl on the coast northwards up the *jebal* for some 50 kilometres. This was the Hornbeam Line, which later proved to be successful in blocking movement of humans, camels and donkeys and therefore arms and supplies into Dhofar from PDRY. We learned too of any casualties on our side. After the briefing, which lasted perhaps twenty minutes, Paddy would call over anyone he needed to talk to in closer detail and the rest of us repaired to the bar.

That night there was to be a film show, but I was due at the Butlers' for dinner. I calculated that if I dashed back to the RAF Camp I could shower, change and would just catch the *Tom and Jerry* cartoon before leaving for Salalah. The films were shown against the armoury wall, and chairs, crates and empty ammunition boxes were dragged over for the BATT men to sit on. I sat at the back, sipping a can of Heineken and lazily enjoying the warm, sultry desert evening air. A shooting star fell in the crystal clear sky. It was otherworldly, and as we waited for the projector to cough into life, I wondered how Scott would be getting along in Masirah trying to fix his connecting flight on the VC10.

After the cartoon I slipped away, pushing through a crowd of a hundred or more Asians who worked in the Camp and who gathered outside the BATT fence whenever a film was showing. Entertainment opportunities were limited and the men crushed together, silently shoving and pushing to watch a smart cartoon mouse outwit a dense cartoon cat. I had to politely ask four or five spectators to get off my Land Rover's bonnet and roof, and I drove into town for dinner.

Like most of the other British civilians, the Butlers lived in a small compound of several dozen, single-storey, two- or three-bedroomed prefabricated bungalows on the sea front near *Bir Bint Ahmed*. Most expatriates had an Indian or Pakistani houseboy and the lucky ones might also have a cook, but the Butlers preferred to live alone with their two sons, both under ten, who went to a small English school that had recently opened in Salalah. Both boys had the same flaxen hair of their father and they all seemed so happy and relaxed living as a family near the sea in a lovely warm climate. What could be better?

During the evening Robin told me how she had met Mike when she was in the Foreign Office and he was in the army. Mike had applied to be a

62

contract officer in the time of Sultan Said bin Taimur. After the coup, they stayed in Muscat for a while before coming down to Dhofar when Mike took up a post as Agricultural Development Officer under Robin Young. I also learned something of Mike's plans for agricultural development in Dhofar and how I would be replaced by a civilian vet. In fact, Mike was flying to the UK the following week to interview the potential candidates. A good salary and lots of perks had been offered to make an attractive proposition.

Time flew by and it was something of a shock when I glanced at the clock and realised I would have to make my way back to Camp. The gates closed at midnight and I just made it back in time. As I drove through the town, some of the locals were still drinking tea and coffee and chatting outside the little shops and cafés lit with their harsh neon strips. *Askars* dozed fitfully outside the gates to the town; the Sultan's flag hung limply in the still air above the Palace and another shooting star fell lazily across the busy sky. I decided I could fall in love with Oman.

Chapter 8

An Iron in the Fire

I soon discovered there was a cosmic difference between working in the shadow of an experienced mentor and friend and having to take decisions with no moral or professional support. However, I was exhilarated and excited by the challenges facing me and the next morning set off enthusiastically to *Bir Bint Ahmed* to see what the day might have in store.

A *jebali* man had hitched a lift in from the refugee camp at Raysut. His Sheikh wanted a visit, explained Saleh. Also, he added, there was the quarantine station, yesterday's goats with 'uttaria' and, scrabbling in the deep recesses of his dishdash, he produced a note from Tony Jarvis asking me to call at the Royal Stables before lunch.

I decided to start with the refugee camp and as we would be following tracks into the foothills of the *jebal*, I took my 9mm Browning from the locked drugs cabinet, snapped on my holster and rammed my floppy green hat on my head. Ali the tea boy asked if he could come for the ride and so with Saleh and Hafeedth beside me, and Ali and the *jebali* behind, we set off. It was a fine morning and I enjoyed the short drive along the coast. Saleh and Hafeedth seemed to have accepted that I was now the boss and both began a gentle interrogation in broken English to try to find out more about me. Did I have children? No. Wife? No. Family? Well yes ... but not in quite the same extended sense as a Dhofari family. Why? Oh, a bit difficult to explain. What was I doing before? The problems of Northern Ireland sounded as if they were on a different planet. Did Saleh really have any idea of our own very different sectarian troubles? It was with something approaching relief when we turned right onto a sandy track leading off the harbour road and, following Saleh's directions, I drove the Land Rover bumpily along an undulating and twisting route towards the foothills, swerving to avoid large rocks projecting out of the barren hard earth.

The camp was only a kilometre or so from the tarmac road but it seemed a lot further. Saleh was anxious that I kept off the vehicle tracks as much as possible, as it was known that mines had been laid along some of them in the past. Indeed, 'A' Squadron had lost a 4-tonne truck only a few days before. The track was well worn and marked by the ruts of dozens of other vehicles, but the *adoo* were cunning and had been known to roll a tyre gently over sand they had sprinkled on top of a mined track to make it look safe. I reassured myself that we had a local tribesman travelling with us; he should know better than most if there were mines around his camp and was hardly likely to want one detonated under him. Even so, wherever possible I drove parallel to the trail. It did not make driving easy, or comfortable, especially for the passengers.

There were three settlements, each containing perhaps ten or twelve dwellings mostly built from *burmails*, corrugated iron, salvaged wood and *burusti*. Shanties were constructed by the very poor from whatever they could find. On the hill, the *jebali* people lived in pastoral tents, low mud dwellings and limestone caves – almost as minimalistic as these improvised houses on the plain; the transition must have been hard for pastoralists who, after generations of semi-nomadic life had to adapt to an alien, peri-urban existence. This particular group had made the difficult decision to break away from the *adoo* but had still to be fully assimilated within Salalah which is why they remained in this limbo of a camp outside the Wire.

The Qara people were considered to be among the most primitive societies in the Near East. They may have been descendants of Abyssinian Christian conquerors who invaded South-West Arabia in the years before Islam began to expand rapidly in the seventh century. The tribes were divided into 'sub-tribes', which in turn had been split by various blood feuds over the years. There was no doubt that the present war in Dhofar had created countless further divisions and hostilities.

The Headman of this settlement lived in the only wooden house in the camp. In size, it was little more than a large garden shed. The house was crudely painted a bright blue colour and had a flat roof from where the Omani national flag flew. There was a small yard next to the house, fenced off by *burmails*, and a few camels strained their long, elegant necks to gaze at us. Although tiny, the house was inhabited by several *jebali* women and children who peered cautiously out of the doorway when they heard us approaching. Older children, barefoot or with shoes made from car tyres fastened with string, faces decorated purple with indigo dye, and with flies like halos around their shorn heads or settling on their eyes and noses, scampered around us as we got out of the Land Rover. An army water bowser, or tanker, was parked nearby and women from the camp were queuing to collect their ration of drinking water, which was delivered daily from Salalah. Wisps of smoke drifted skywards from many of the small homes.

The old man, probably the head of what might have been one extended family, was small and wiry with a thin, lined face, prominent nose and experienced eyes. His clansman, who had survived the bumpy journey remarkably well, jumped down from the back of the Land Rover and ran to greet him, touching noses and kissing him in the traditional gesture of affection and respect. The Sheikh greeted me warmly and after we had exchanged a few good-natured remarks, he led me to a nearby ramshackle *burmail* dwelling. He spoke authoritatively and a muffled reply came from within. In moments, a small cow came out of the tiny doorway, followed by a scrawny man, then three goats and finally a haggard-looking woman.

I saw why smoke rose from so many of these houses. It was not only for cooking but also to keep away the flies, which were a real problem when the family's livestock, sheep, goats and cattle, freely entered the house and slept for security with the family. Incense, tapped from the hill's famous and exquisite frankincense trees, was thrown on the fires to sweeten the smell. The Sheikh started talking to Saleh who coped brilliantly with simultaneous *jebali*, Arabic and English translations.

The old woman walked to the back of her house where a small pen had been constructed using wooden boards. *Jebali* men are devoted to their cattle, but goats are often considered the responsibility of the women. From the movement behind the boards I deduced that this was where the sick animals were. Saleh told me that the goats had been unwell for some days with very bad diarrhoea, which had now turned to blood-streaked mucus. They wouldn't eat or drink and the problem was spreading to other animals.

There must have been eight or nine depressed-looking goats in the small dank enclosure. They were pathetic, emaciated creatures, with drooping, sad heads and bloody stains down their hind legs. Yet more distressing to me was to see patterned across both sides of their wretched little bodies many angry and festering black marks of the hot iron.

I knew that it was important to get this in perspective. It was not mindless brutality on helpless animals, as firing, or *wussum*, was an ancient and traditional form of treatment in Dhofar. Modern medicine had an up-hill struggle to demonstrate that it was better than the deeply entrenched tribal practices. There were many stories in Oman, not only of animals but also of children, grossly disfigured by burn scars and brand marks. Yet a nomad with nothing except cattle and family, and no education, had only the cultural remedies offered by herbs, plants and fire. I reminded myself that many so-called conventional drugs were derived from ancient herbal remedies and, as for the hot iron, in 1974 many vets in the UK were still firing horses' legs and convincing themselves and their clients that it would do some good.

Saleh explained that the refugees probably had no idea that such a thing as a vet existed, so the solution had been to apply the *wussum* burn. In Dhofar, the practice was something of an art form, often administered by a specialist medicine man in the tribe. On these particular goats, horizontal brands 10 to 12 centimetres in length had been seared with a red-hot iron across the sides of the abdomen of each affected animal; two 6-centimetre lines had then been burned vertically down either end of the horizontal lines. The goats had also been scorched along their sensitive underbellies and there were more brand marks on their heads and backs. Then the burns had been smeared with camel dung. No wonder the animals looked despondent.

There was a certain irony in using Western treatment in parallel with traditional medicine. If the animals were not treated by me but recovered, the *wussum* would be widely acclaimed and the practice perpetuated. On the other hand, if I treated the goats successfully, the chances were that the *wussum* would get the credit anyway. Of course, if the animals died, it would be my meddling that had interfered with the *wussum*. The Qara's medicine men were still widely respected and feared by the superstitious tribesmen and it would take time before the fires of the witch doctors were finally dowsed in the cool waters of progress. Still, there was hope. After all, the Sheikh had called me in and asked for my help.

I asked Saleh to explain that the fire only hurt the animals and made it harder to get them well. Saleh had experience of numerous similar conversations over the years and had been well drilled by my predecessors. As he rattled off a lesson on firing, emphasising the cruelty of the hot iron, I did what I could to dress the festering wounds and injected the goats with antibiotics and anti-inflammatory drugs to ease their discomfort and stop skin infection compounding their other problems. I gave Saleh some orange sachets containing gut-active antibiotics, vitamins and electrolytes and he demonstrated to the owner how, using an old tin can and a twig, he must mix the powder into a drench and pour it down the throats of the goats daily for several days. I stressed the need to feed appetising fodder such as fresh alfalfa and to provide the goats with lots of clean water and, importantly, to keep the infected ones as isolated as possible from the family's other goats, which were out grazing but would return at night.

Word had soon got round the camp that a *tabeeb* was there and a string of men and boys began to appear to ask me to see this goat or that cow. I steadily worked through the list and was about to walk back to the Sheikh's hut for a cup of tea when Hafeedth suddenly grabbed my arm and asked me to come with him. I had noticed him talking to a group of women outside a *burmail* hut and he looked serious and worried. He shouted something at Saleh who was packing our things back into his Bergen.

'What is it?' I began.

'Woman here,' said Hafeedth. 'Big problem with baby.'

Following Hafeedth, I joined a small cluster of anxious-looking women outside the hut. Hafeedth explained that the woman had been ill with a discharge for several days. He indicated that I could go in so I bent over and entered the hut. It was gloomy and stale inside. A young, very sick-looking, heavily pregnant woman, perhaps seventeen or eighteen years old, was lying on some rugs along one side of the room with her husband beside her. Sweat glistened on her forehead. Gently, looking for the man's assent and getting a gesture I took for agreement, I put my hand on her brow; it was clammy and hot. I took her pulse; it was racing. The woman seemed exhausted and I saw she had a serious infection, possibly metritis. The prognosis was not good unless she was professionally and promptly treated. Already she had been left too long. Her baby might even be dead inside her.

Jebali women were said to insert salt into their vaginas after giving birth, supposedly to keep them tight to please their husbands. However, when scar tissue forms, the womb can no longer relax fully. So if they become pregnant again, there may not be enough space for a fully-formed baby to pass through the birth canal. If this woman had been on the hill, her fate would almost certainly have been sealed, but here in Salalah at least there was a hospital where she would have a chance. I told Hafeedth that we must get her at once to the town.

I was puzzled by the husband's quiet refusal and the obvious apprehension in the girl's eyes when this was translated. I was also surprised that my decision had been rebuffed so quickly.

'Come on Hafeedth, we'll talk to the Sheikh,' I said, smiling reassuringly at the woman and leaving the hut.

The husband trailed behind us and once we were before the Sheikh a long and emotional discussion in Arabic ensued. Hafeedth showed a passion I would not have expected from one of his tender years. Eventually, the old Sheikh held up his hand and spoke a few words quietly and authoritatively. The husband started to protest but a sharp word sent him back to his hut silently.

'OK,' said Saleh to me, 'she come.'

Saleh later explained why they were so reluctant. The hospital was overcrowded and had a reputation for long waits, abrupt, cursory examinations and unsuccessful treatment, although this was unfair and most likely a reflection of the late stages of an illness when patients were seen. Still, I could understand the terrified girl's fear at leaving her family for a town she barely knew, and a hospital so alien to her world on the hill. There was a military Field Surgical Team at RAF Salalah (55-FST) but they were simply not geared up for infectious obstetrics, and I felt that if she didn't go immediately to the Salalah hospital, she would probably die. I told Hafeedth and Ali to clear the back of the Land Rover and do what they could to help load the woman as comfortably as possible.

Meanwhile the Sheikh thanked me for my time and said that although he was sad he could not entertain me properly, he insisted I took a little refreshment while we waited for our patient. A man was given a battered aluminium bowl and he disappeared around the back of the hut, returning after a few moments with it full of steaming frothy milk which had obviously just been taken from the udder. I tried not to look alarmed – *jebali* cattle were hardly likely to have been tested for tuberculosis or brucellosis and raw milk was a classic carrier of these and other infections.

'This,' beamed Saleh encouragingly, 'from camel.'

I think my smile must have frozen momentarily, but what the hell? It was impossible to refuse such a generous gesture from someone who had so little. I decided this was part of life's rich experience. The Sheikh thrust the warm bowl into my hands. It was a large bowl and several dozen flies were competing with me for the first taste. I nonchalantly raised the bowl to my lips and took a preliminary sip, then a swallow. It was bland, warm and salty-sweet, and really rather good.

I muttered '*Shukran*', thank you, and handed the bowl to Saleh. He took a deep draught and passed it on to the Sheikh. A couple of others also took mouthfuls, and soon, just as with the coffee in Sudh, I found the bowl back in my hands again. Another quick swig and on to Saleh who, to my surprise, declined any more. I later read somewhere that camel's milk is an excellent laxative, which may, at least in part, have explained Saleh's uncharacteristic reticence. The others had another drink and the bowl was back with me. This time I had the confidence to decline with lots of praise and thanks and insistence that the rest must be for them. I was beginning to get the delicate balance between hospitality and subsistence nutrition where every mouthful of nutrients was significant. The bowl was laid to one side and was at once invaded by a battalion of swarming black flies. The *jebali*'s immune system must be mighty powerful. I hoped mine would cope.

Ali came running up, excited with all the activity, and told Saleh the woman was in the vehicle. She was swathed in clothes and wore a rigid black mask over her face in accordance with traditional modesty. Her husband, looking apprehensive, climbed in the back beside her and another masked woman came too. I got behind the wheel, waved goodbye to the Sheikh, and we set off for Salalah.

I knew of two expatriates who worked in the hospital. One was the Matron, a large and formidable-looking but totally dedicated English woman. The other was Jeremy Raybould's wife, an attractive and highly professional healthcare worker from New Zealand. Leaving everyone else in the Land Rover, I pushed my way through the crowds at the entrance and went in search of one of them. Sick patients and their relatives were everywhere and the corridors were full. A new hospital was being built and there could be no doubt that it was urgently needed.

69

It wasn't easy to find my way around but I eventually spotted the Matron. She was one of those women who never seem to get flustered and can cope with the most difficult of situations calmly and efficiently. She listened to my story and came with me to the Land Rover. It was exasperating to find the vehicle empty but for Ali. But he pointed at the main entrance and there we saw our party – Saleh with commendable initiative had commandeered a trolley and offloaded our patient onto it. He was in the process of wheeling her through the hospital to look for me. The Matron took command and I shook hands with the sick woman's husband, feeling we had done our best for his wife. Saleh said that she would recover, *Inshalla* – and I also added my small contribution to that hope.

We left the hospital and drove into Salalah to see the lumpy goats. I had been thinking about those lumps and had concluded they were probably due to an allergy to insect bites although I did have a nagging worry that it might be a viral disease, such as goat pox, which is transmitted by biting flies. Pox is widespread where the insects are common, but although it looks unattractive, the animals generally recover. We found the goat-owner in a *Bedouin* tent in part of the town that was being developed. The adult goats were shut in an improvised pen made from wooden sheets. There was a plaintive bleating coming from somewhere and I looked around to see two tiny muzzles peering out from a wooden lid covering a hole dug in the ground. This was where the young kids were kept between feedings – if they had constant access to the mother, there would be no milk for the humans. They didn't look too happy in their earthy dungeon but I could see that at least they were shaded from the sun.

The lumpy goats were neither better nor worse after yesterday's injection. I noticed that the man's neighbour also had goats and went over to look at them. They too were covered in the marble-sized lumps. Yet despite having dozens or, in some cases, hundreds of lumps, the affected animals seemed fit enough in themselves. I got out Ben Higson's Polaroid camera that I had borrowed for the occasion and took some snaps to send to one of my professors at the Royal Veterinary College in London. I then gave the goats a shot of antihistamine and told the owner I hoped the lumps would eventually disappear.

We dropped Ali at his school and went to see a couple of other cases before driving out to the Royal Stables to meet Tony Jarvis. Wearing breeches, boots and a tweed jacket, which looked a bit incongruous under the palm trees, he strode up to greet us, swishing his whip as he walked. I knew that Tony, the former locust-spotter and a key player in the Dhofar CAD teams, harboured an ambition to become Manager of the Salalah Royal Stables. His voluntary work with the horses was certainly raising

70

standards but his approach was not wholly appreciated by old Shenoon and the other *syces* who were accustomed to looking after their charges in the old traditional way.

'Hullo there ... Scott got off OK? Heard he got a watch – lucky sod. Still waiting for mine after four years!'

'How are the horses?' I asked.

'Couple I'm a bit worried about,' he replied. 'I've already discussed them with John Clarke who says to get on with it. He'll be down anyway next week.'

I was getting used to the idea of a week that ran from Saturday to Thursday with Friday the holy day, *Juma*. As today was Thursday, 'next week' could be anytime from Saturday onwards.

There were two horses to see. The first was a brown mare, with both front feet badly affected with sandcrack. Breaks in the wall of the hooves were quite common in arid desert conditions and were compounded by the hard ground and the lack of shoes to maintain the shape of the foot. The mare was slightly lame. Fortunately, the cracks only extended from the toe for about 3 or 4 centimetres, but it was necessary to prevent the crack spreading up to the coronary band at the top of the hoof. If this happened, the whole wall could split.

A good farrier could make a shoe to contain the split, but this was probably beyond the skills of the Stable's veterinary dresser, Rasul Bux. So I got my rasp from the Land Rover and told Saleh to borrow one of the *syce*'s primus stoves. We lit it and I heated the rasp to red heat, watched curiously by Tony Jarvis and the *syces*. I then took the red-hot rasp to the horse and made three horizontal grooves in the hoof wall. This was a quite painless procedure and the mare stood placidly as her keratin singed and clouds of smoke rose about us. I made one burn, about a centimetre wide above the top of the crack, and others at intervals along its length. This was an old British cavalry trick and the theory was that it eased the pressure on the crack, allowing it to heal and, crucially, stopping it reaching the coronet. It usually worked but I was very conscious of the paradox after my earlier tirade against *wussum*.

The second horse was clearly lame. He was a gelding, castrated by one of my predecessors in Muscat, and sent to Dhofar by dhow. The journey had been uneventful, but when unloaded at Raysut the gelding had slipped and had been intermittently lame ever since. With rest, the lameness had improved, but now he was obviously in pain and distress and was reluctant to put any weight on his left hind leg. If he did take a few steps, the leg was extended and abnormally turned out and he dragged his toe in the sand. Something was seriously wrong in his stifle, the joint that corresponds to the human knee, and he did not like me feeling the joint.

71

I reckoned the patella, or kneecap, had become fixed out of alignment. I prodded and probed and tried to manipulate the joint but was pessimistic. Tony was all for firing or blistering the joint, but I persuaded him to rest the horse for a month and see how it went. I was sure that if there was no change, the only humane option would be to shoot it.

Sadly, the poor horse lasted less than a week. It was getting thinner and was in increasing pain. I shot it with my Browning. A *post mortem* examination of the knee showed severely torn ligaments, which justified the action but didn't make it any more pleasant. I have a strong emotional tie to horses and never find it easy to kill them. I gave John Clarke an autopsy report so he could inform the owner. I was later relieved to hear from Mac Maclean that the Sultan was very philosophical about such matters and took the view that he employed experts to advise him.

I dropped the boys at *Bir Bint Ahmed* and by the time I drove back to RAF Salalah Tony Jarvis was already in the bar talking about the horses and the sandcrack treatment.

At prayers that evening, Paddy King-Fretts told me he had fixed for me to go up the hill the following week. 'They want you at Jibjat,' he said, stabbing his finger at a red star on the map. 'There are a lot of goats and camels up there.' He added: 'It's a strong defensive position and has its own airstrip; one of those places where a water hole was drilled early on and hundreds of animals and their minders call in every day for water.' I told Paddy that Ben Higson had asked to come too and he said he would get it fixed.

Three years before, in 1971, there had been an extraordinary vigorous showdown around Jibjat. Several *firqat* families had threatened the government with mutiny by driving hundreds of goats and cattle into the area and demanding that if the Omani government was serious about helping the people, they must provide water for the animals and a market for their meat. It was a tricky time for the military commanders, but Dhofar's shrewd *Wali*, Sheikh Braik, despite considerable opposition, ordered SOAF to fly the goats to Salalah by Skyvan and told the *firqats* to drive the cattle down to Taqah. What became known as Operation Taurus took place amid some of the toughest fighting of the war. General Tony Jeapes called it a unique operation in military history – a Texan-style cattle drive supported by jet fighter cover and artillery fire! Many of the cattle had been owned by *adoo* and were confiscated by the *firqat* during the drive. Jeapes recalls that on the following day the herd, surrounded by armoured cars, moved from Taqah to Salalah to be greeted by rejoicing inhabitants and he considered that this single example of government support did more to impress the people than all the leaflets and broadcasts put together. The *adoo* were not, after all, invincible. I looked forward to seeing Jibjat.

It was the end of a long and emotional day and I was glad to get back. The Foreign Office room I had occupied since my arrival was only ever going to be a temporary home. My plan had been to move directly into Scott's room which was a larger, more comfortable pad, but a quick-witted Rhodesian helicopter pilot had grabbed it and I was left with the pilot's old room. At least it had its own shower, and as it was only a couple of doors down from Ben Higson's room I hammered on his door and told him we were off to Jibjat.

'Two sappers blown up there last month,' was his only impassive comment.

Chapter 9

Up the Hill

I signed out my Armalite and ammunition and, as we were going into an operational area, I also took overnight kit. Saleh carried the veterinary Bergen. It was hard to decide what medicines to take and how much. We were not going to Jibjat to treat anything specific, just to pay a call and show the flag. I tried to work out the type of animals I might see and to estimate what drugs and equipment might be required. Eventually I crammed a selection into the Bergen and hoped for the best.

Paddy King-Fretts had arranged for us to travel up on the daily Skyvan. A Skyvan called most days at each of the main hill locations. The ATLO at Brigade HQ said he would try to get us up and back the same day if possible, but he couldn't guarantee it. I told Saleh he might not get back that night but he shrugged and said it was all up to Allah.

We met Ben and the photographer at 0600 hours at the ATLO's office. The PSYOPS duo both wore civvies, with Ben in his 1970s pink jeans with a 9mm Browning in a belt holster. Still, who was I to comment on psychological operations? The photographer, who looked as if he was still in his teens, was unarmed but laden down with the usual paraphernalia of his profession. Ben said mufti, the old army term for civilian clothes, was important to relax and reassure the *jebali*. I did wonder about the pistol accessory.

It was the aircraft's first trip of the day. The Baluchi Loadmaster was busily securing fuel drums, ammunition resupplies and crates inside the stocky little aircraft and carefully positioned the four of us on small canvas seats. He stressed the importance of balancing the load for take-off. The Skyvan was a strange shoebox of an aircraft. Short Brothers built 150 of them in the 1960s and 1970s and SOAF had at least a dozen. The plane was only about 12 metres long and its maximum take-off weight was said to be around 6 tonnes, so it could carry cargo or a dozen or so passengers, admittedly in pretty cramped conditions. A big advantage in Dhofar was its very short take-off and landing distance, often with a stomach-churningly rapid rate of descent.

Our aircraft that day was in the hands of a pilot called Phil who greeted us jauntily as he walked round the aircraft making his final checks. The noisy propellers started and the rear ramp closed, sealing us into the rattling casket. The Loadmaster completed some final safety checks and in no time we were chugging down the runway.

A few minutes after take-off, Phil turned round and beckoned for me to come forward and sit in the empty co-pilot's seat; SOAF Skyvans usually only carried one pilot on routine short trips around Dhofar. I put on a set of headphones so we could talk and he pointed out landmarks and sites of action during the war. When I saw the rocky, hostile terrain, the valleys or *wadis*, the endless number of caves, and thought about the vegetation cover during the monsoon, it was truly impressive how SAF and BATT, even with their local *firqat* support, had managed to flush out the enemy so effectively in such a relatively short time. The new civil aid developments on the hill on which so much depended looked unimpressive from the air – a few tin huts and sandbag shelters surrounded by a mixed collection of *Bedouin* and army tents.

In about twenty minutes we reached Jibjat, some 50 kilometres north-east of Salalah. Phil told me that an old SAF airstrip known as Lympne, 6 or 7 kilometres east of Jibjat, had been the site of a major operation in 1971. Operation Jaguar had involved two SAS squadrons and hundreds of SAF soldiers and *firqats* in a successful attempt to get a solid base on the *jebal* in what was a major defeat for the *adoo* but which had cost the lives of many men on both sides. He had been one of the pilots flying in SAF reinforcements and it said a lot for the sturdiness of his beloved Skyvan that he had been able to land and take off on such a rough, long disused landing strip.

Phil circled and called up the BATT team on the radio. The current strip looked almost as uneven and bumpy as I imagined Lympne had been. It was also very short. There was a crackle in the headphones and a BATT voice confirmed the runway was clear. We spiralled rapidly down and landed with a few metres to spare as Phil skilfully pulled to a halt after a few impressive bounces. He spun the aircraft round, as if we were on a skid patch, turned off his engines and the door opened.

The BATT team leader introduced himself as Dan. Probably in his late twenties, he was powerfully built, deeply tanned and very fit, wearing only shorts and desert boots. He had arrived in his SAS pink panther [Land Rover] along with a pick-up truck full of *firqats*. The compound was next to the strip and everyone had come out to see the new arrivals. After brief introductions, we all helped unload the Skyvan and Dan handed the Loadmaster a bundle of letters to post. Half a dozen *firqats* piled on board the aircraft with their guns and various accessories; the Loadmaster manually positioned them where he wanted them and the propellers spluttered into life again. Within minutes the aircraft was airborne once more. It circled us once before setting course for Salalah. The whole turnaround had taken about ten minutes.

Although Jibjat lay to the east of the main war zone, it was an uncertain location. While the *adoo* had been considerably suppressed on the eastern *jebal* and their major enclaves were being progressively cleared, incursions did still occur and surprise attacks were not unusual. One reason for Jibjat's strategic significance was that it was a focus for many of the Qara tribes. The pastoralists had fierce tribal loyalties and there were frequent inter-tribal squabbles, some of which could be serious. Nevertheless, the government's Civil Aid Teams were in action here, with Indian and Pakistani workmen employed by the contracted construction company starting to develop the location's facilities and infrastructure.

Dhofar was bisected east-west by a sand track known as the Midway Road that ran due north from Salalah and across the *jebal*, after which it turned north-east through the desert for 900 kilometres to Muscat and northern Oman. About 70 kilometres north of Salalah was a location known as Midway, although it was midway to nowhere. Midway was the remains of an old oil exploration site at Thumrait and the road, built by the Mecom Oil Company in 1953, had significant strategic and psychological importance as the *adoo* had managed to keep much of it closed. The steep, winding section that snaked up through the foothills of the *jebal* had been largely a no-go area for years, and SAF convoys attempting the route were often ambushed. Now, SAF, with the help of Iranian forces, had forced open parts of the road south from Thumrait enabling it gradually to be graded and improved.

Dan seemed slightly irritated that BATT Headquarters had advised that I was likely to leave that evening. He explained that it took at least one day for the word to spread that there was a *tabeeb* on the hill and stressed that visits needed to be at least two or three days in length. With all my kit and belongings accounted for, we all piled into his pink panther for a tour of the site.

We started work at the newly-completed cattle trough about a kilometre or so from the camp. A second Land Rover travelled behind us across the rocky ground. In that vehicle were three *firqats* with another member of the BATT team driving. Dan kept off the tracks pointing out a site where the two engineers had been blown up by an anti-personnel mine a few months before. He said that BATT tried to lead by example and by teaching the *firqats* common-sense precautions. After all, he added, they were going to be around a lot longer than the SAS. I wondered how safe an open Land Rover would be if it hit a mine. I guessed that with luck, and depending where it hit, the passengers had a chance of being thrown free and less risk of being killed than in a closed vehicle.

Dan pointed out the new bull-pen, which was being built out of *burmails*, steel piping and cement. It was a curious design but appeared solid enough to restrain all but the randiest or most ill-tempered of bulls. As part

76

of the DDD programme, Mike Butler intended to provide at least one good bull at each of the main hill positions. His plan was to import them from Kenya as they were likely to be more tolerant of the climate and of Dhofar's endemic diseases than exotic European stock. As the low-producing *jebali* cattle were gradually upgraded the government would buy all the resulting crossbred male progeny (traditionally most of the male calves were slaughtered), transport them to the plains where they would be fattened for slaughter and marketing. Meat prices were astronomically high as demand hugely outstripped supply. Butler's exciting scheme was to be a market-driven and consumer-led enterprise to benefit the whole Province.

The Jibjat water trough was 15 or 20 metres long, made of concrete and contained beautiful, clean, clear water. A pump chugged away spewing out blue diesel fumes as it drew water from the recently-dug well. It all looked so simple but the product was the outcome of a complex and expensive engineering feat, drilling 200 to 300 metres or more through limestone rock to create a well capable of generating thousands of litres of water per hour. The relaxing chug chug of the pump and the splash of the water arriving from the depths seemed somehow symbolic of every-thing we were trying to achieve; the clash of old and new and proof that hard work, ingenuity, cooperation with the locals, and modern methods could achieve a positive outcome that was beneficial to everyone involved.

As we arrived at the trough, twenty or so small dromedaries were drinking thirstily from it. Oman's camels were famous throughout Arabia for their hardiness and speed and, in some parts, Oman is known as *Umm al gimal*, or mother of camels. They can happily survive several days without water but then drink copiously and fast when they get the chance. This oasis was a chance not to be missed. The owners looked at us warily but Saleh wandered over and spoke to them in *jebali*. Ben's photographer nonchalantly took a few pictures of the animals. After a few minutes, Saleh came over and explained there was a lame she-camel and a sick calf and the owner would like me to look at them. Dan and the others lit cigarettes and began to talk among themselves.

I was still beginning to find my way with camels, and I approached the task in Jibjat with some care. I think the *jebali* owner was relieved to see that I was gentle with his animals, but probably did not realise that this was largely due to my own unease. Both he and his animals were surprisingly responsive to my prodding and probing. The camel was pretty lame and I guessed that she must have trodden on a sharp rock as her large flat footpad had been badly bruised. I could see no sign of a penetrating wound nor could I detect any other injury but there was one very sore spot on her foot, which, like a well-trained horse, she obligingly lifted for me to examine. I injected her and gave the owner some bute sachets. Saleh somehow conjured up an empty bottle and explained to the owner how to mix the powder with water. No one teaches British vets about medicating camels but I reckoned a horse dose would be about right.

Following Saleh's instructions, the owner got the camel to go down on her haunches. With just a few taps from his camel stick, she went easily on command with a few mild grunts and complaints. He then tied a rope around both flexed knees, effectively preventing her rising. Lifting her head, Saleh showed how to pour a drench down a gurgling camel's throat. Most of it went down but there were a few more grumbles until the patient was allowed up and, head held haughtily aloof, she stalked off with considerable dignity. We handed over a week's supply of bute and hoped for the best.

The calf was a bit more worrying as it was scratching and rubbing its head. My first thought was *djarab*, or mange, a bad disease of camels that is contagious and debilitating, although it can be treated. Happily it wasn't mange which would have had serious implications for the rest of the herd, and as I had no idea what was the matter I gave the calf a shot of multivitamins, a useful standby, and hoped it would be better tomorrow. The owner seemed satisfied with this pragmatic approach and took his herd back to their grazing.

Some 50 metres from the trough was a small herd of tiny black and brown *jebali* cattle, staring at us with bovine balefulness. Saleh and I went over to meet the herdsmen and soon we were treating a variety of minor ailments including a couple of cases of acute mastitis, a common condition of the udder that is not only uncomfortable and painful for the cow but can seriously reduce milk production and so affect nutrition, both for calves and for humans.

Gradually, more and more people arrived, some alone with a long and complicated story about a sick animal somewhere over the next hill, others with the animal in tow. Obviously, it was easier when the animal was there and I began to appreciate Dan's frustration at the shortness of our stay. Most animals by day were scattered around the hill in the tribal grazing areas and it was clear that I needed to be there for more than one day at a time simply so animal owners knew I was around. Diagnosing and treating at a distance was impractical at the best of times and completely impossible when the clinical picture was being described by superstitious and often suspicious herdsmen speaking in the *jebali* language. Yet, we did our best and dispensed endless treatments for worms, drenches for bloat, antibiotic powders for infections, ointments for streaming eyes and sprays for wounds.

Leaving the trough after a couple of hours, we drove round some of the nearby settlements. The people around Jibjat lived in basic tents and everything they owned centred on their cattle and what was portable. As well as the animals, I also treated several humans with complaints ranging from malaria to an old man who, I concluded from his illuminating gesticulations, was having difficulty satisfying his wife. I gave him some multivitamins. He seemed delighted. I hoped she was.

It was obvious that there was a lot of malaria about and I tried through Saleh to explain the need for preventing as well as treating it. The military were supposed to take daily Paludrine, a foul-tasting anti-malaria drug, but the disease on the *jebal* was endemic, and there was a real challenge from the ever present mosquitoes that transmitted the disease. The new water point would compound the problem by providing ideal new breeding grounds. Disease prevention, whether a vaccine against tetanus or a tablet against malaria, is always a hard concept to get across, particularly to people not familiar with modern medicine. Also, in their minds it was invariably up to Allah to decide when and where a disease struck, so the urgency of prophylaxis was rarely appreciated.

With my stomach growling, Saleh and I headed back to the BATT *basha* for some compo rations and a brew. The guys were good company and having visitors was a great excuse for Dhofar stories. It was cooler on the hill than in Salalah and the breeze was refreshing. Dan updated Ben Higson on the effects of the propaganda machine. Ben had spent the morning touring the nearby settlements and replacing posters and photographs on the notice boards. He had also brought new portrait-sized photographs of Sultan Qaboos to post up in the little CAT shop, as well as in the medical room and schoolroom. An Egyptian schoolmaster had recently been recruited and was reported to be having some success teaching the local tribal children. He was delighted with his new picture of the Ruler. Our photographer persuaded Saleh to pose with some children and to pretend to inject their animals. This would be our own propaganda.

It was late afternoon when Dan said he could hear an aircraft. I had just finished suturing a goat's torn perineum and gave it a quick jab of antibiotic and smiled positively at the owner before packing up and hopping into the pink panther. A Skyvan was circling above the camp as another BATT man came out of the *basha* and said the pilot had been on the radio asking for the all clear. We gathered up the rest of the party, drove along the airstrip and parked to one side. Dan whipped out a blue smoke flare and fired it to show the pilot both the wind direction and that he was cleared to land. Our day's work had ended abruptly, but I knew we would have to return regularly. With quick handshakes all round we clambered on board the briefly stationary Skyvan, ready to return to RAF Salalah.

I sat on the canvas strip seat at the back of the Skyvan and peered down as we circled. I thought the visit had been a success in that we had treated a good number of sick animals and people and at least I now had a greater understanding about Hearts and Minds and how it operated in practice. Ben's photographs with Arabic captions would soon appear showing Saleh treating cattle, camels and goats on the *jebal*, and these would be distributed throughout Dhofar including those places where the *adoo* may still have some influence.

As we tumbled out of the aircraft at RAF Salalah, Saleh surprised Ben and me by inviting us to have supper with him. This was quite an honour and impossible to turn down. So, later that evening Ben and I set off from the Mess and trawled the tracks of downtown Salalah looking for Abdullah's Café, which was where Saleh had suggested we meet. Eventually we found it – a small, square shop, with a few stainless steel tables and plastic chairs, a glaring strip light and a Formica-covered counter presided over by a rotund owner, presumably Mr. Abdullah. The tables were all occupied and there was a buzz of chatter above the background of a statically noisy radio blaring out Lebanese or Egyptian music. Saleh leapt up as we arrived and was visibly elated that we had turned up. He must have already briefed the men sitting at the tables about our trip to Jibjat as we were viewed over the coffee cups by expressionless eyes that followed us as we got out of the Land Rover and walked to our seats in front of the shop. Saleh looked after us well and fed us a very good curry with the best *khobz* I had ever tasted, washed down with cups of Nescafé. With true Arab hospitality there was no question of us paying. It was rare for a couple of Brit officers to able to enjoy the benign Salalah nightlife with Dhofaris instead of propping up the bar of the RAF Mess. We felt privileged.

It was during this meal that Ben came up with the innovative idea of putting Saleh on the radio, and within days he had made his first broadcast on Radio Salalah, which was beamed to all parts of the *jebal*. It was valuable PR, Ben reported later, and Saleh had spoken clearly and knowledgeably about the work of the Veterinary Department of DDD and how they could help all the people of Dhofar. He had stressed the need for early diagnosis, the futility of *wussum*, or firing, the inadvisability of feeding rice to ruminants as it caused bloat, the need for shelter, water and why we had quarantine. It was the first of a series of broadcasts and boosted awareness as well as Saleh's reputation throughout the Province.

Chapter 10

The Royal Connection

There was something strange about this morning. I had woken as usual at seven, blearily fumbled for the radio and listened to the undulating waves of *Lillibulero*, the irritating seventeenth-century Irish jig arranged by Purcell and the signature tune for the BBC World Service News.

I survived the headlines before dropping off to sleep again. When I woke, the News had ended. So had Radio Newsreel and I had even missed the wistful announcement that the BBC's Eastern Relay Station was now closing and a Very Good Morning to You All. RAF Salalah's own station, Radio 219, then took over and, as I resurfaced, was playing rock music, introduced by a chirpy airman, hidden somewhere in the depths of the Camp who fancied himself as Oman's answer to 1970s DJ David Jacobs.

I looked at my watch. By now it was 0745. Mohammed, the Pakistani Mess man had not shuffled in as usual with my early morning cup of syrup which, despite its taste, brought me to my senses fairly sharply. Outside, the Camp was unusually quiet. What was wrong? Then I got it. It was Friday, *Juma*, the holy day and the Mess man's day off. It was also Dhofar's day off. Robin Butler had pithily summed it up by saying Omani animals never got sick on Fridays. If there was a real emergency, she said, the *askars* at *Bir Bint Ahmed* tended to point people in the direction of her house and she then played Hunt the Vet.

I yawned and got up, pleased at the prospect of not having to wear OGs. I shaved and showered, pulled on a pair of jeans and a shirt, and strolled across the silent Camp to the Officers' Mess. On a normal working day there would be great activity by now, but on *Juma* hardly a soul moved in the warm, still desert air. There was a handful of officers in the Mess reading the previous Sunday's British newspapers, which had just arrived. One of them asked if I wanted to join them for a swim and barbeque at a beach near Raysut. It sounded good but I had to explain with faint self-consciousness that I had been invited to call on the Sultan's Private Secretary.

I wondered if the *adoo* respected *Juma*. Probably, I thought, as the 25-pounders of Cracker Battery were also uncharacteristically silent. Things were equally quiet when I drove over to *Umm al Gwarrif* to check for post. It was weird. Like a twenty-four-hour armistice at the end of each week. Apart from a few wireless noises that came out of the Ops room, BATT HQ seemed as dead as the RAF base. Paddy King-Fretts was not resting, however, but was in his office poring over a map. He seemed pleased to have some company and I filled him in on my activities during the week. He took me to the map, briefed me on some of the trickier locations and showed me where the main watering holes were that he wanted me to visit. He also told me he would be up on the hill himself in a few days' time for an operation that could be important.

I decided to have a gentle drive around the town to get my bearings without the pressures of having to visit cases. Near *UAG* was Robat Palace, its white walls gleaming in the morning sun. A country residence where Sultan Qaboos could relax away from his official duties in the Old Palace. Above the building the royal standard rippled in the breeze. The walls prevented intrusive eyes seeing much but through the heavily-guarded gates one could glimpse luxuriant, well-tended and well-watered gardens.

As I passed the gate, I noticed a flurry of activity and a bunch of red berets moving rapidly around just inside the entrance. Before I had driven 100 metres, I heard wailing sirens behind me. A builder's lorry in front of me suddenly swerved to the side of the road, stopped and the driver at once jumped out. A couple of cars coming towards me skidded onto the sandy verge and their occupants also got out, one of them gesticulating frantically at me. I suddenly realised what must be happening. I'd been warned that when the Sultan drove past, all vehicles were to pull right off the road and all male occupants make themselves apparent by getting out of their vehicles.

Rapidly I pulled in behind the truck and leapt out just in time. The sirens drew closer and more persistent. A black and white Volvo police car with lights ablaze raced past with siren wailing, shattering what had been a quiet, peaceful morning. A maroon Datsun estate car came next, crammed with Royal Guard soldiers with two of them sitting either side of a GPMG in the luggage compartment at the back with the rear door open. Behind this came a shiny silver Mercedes sports car with no number plates. I straightened myself up into something resembling attention as it was pretty clear who must be in that car. As it swept past, I saw the Sultan himself was driving. Wearing a blue dishdash and white *tagiyah*, he was instantly recognisable from the countless posters and pictures of him throughout Dhofar. Next to him, in uniform, was, I presumed, an ADC, and there were two young black men squeezed into the rear seat. Three more Mercedes followed, then two RG army personnel carriers and, bringing up the rear, the famous red ambulance. It was said to carry blood matching the Sultan's and to go wherever he went.

It was quite a procession. Gradually, everyone got back into their vehicles and, negotiating through the little traffic jam the unexpected motorcade had caused, continued on their way.

By midday the sun was at its most scorching. Despite this, I decided I would drive back to the Mess, shower and put on a fresh shirt and tie ready for my call on James Maclean.

Like most houses in the officials' compound by the sea, Maclean's neat prefabricated villa had a small garden in front of it. Maclean seemed to grow only grass but some of his neighbours had been more adventurous, proudly boasting displays of huge tomatoes, vegetables and exotic flowers. There were two wooden steps up to a small veranda where there was a double door – the first being a fly screen. To the side of the steps was a magnificent, if slightly unruly bougainvillea with a shock of rosy and purple bracts. This scrambling, fast-growing plant, named after the eighteenth-century French navigator and explorer Louis-Antoine de Bougainville, grew widely in Salalah and provided a colourful contrast to the otherwise drab expat houses.

On the veranda squatted two old *askars*, each clutching an old Martini-Henry rifle. They stared at me and as I started for the steps they shambled to their feet. I gestured with a smile at the door. 'Mr Maclean?' I asked.

'*Na'am, Sa'ab.*' The answer was affirmative.

With a toothless smile of encouragement, one added '*T'fuddl*'. This expression seemed to have a number of meanings or uses depending on circumstances. It could mean 'Help yourself' at a meal, 'You go first' at a doorway, 'Welcome' or 'Please sit down' on arrival, or, as here, 'Carry on in, mate.'

I pulled open the mesh screen and knocked on the glass-fronted door, which was already ajar.

'Come in,' came the voice from within.

The house was small but well designed – a couple of bedrooms, bathroom, sitting/dining room and kitchen. It was sparsely but adequately furnished with utility-type furniture, but it was obvious that Maclean did not spend much time there. He was seated at an unmemorable table, which was covered in papers that spilled out of a large black leather Gucci brief-case.

'Good to see you,' he said, rising from the table. 'Be with you in just a moment,' he added, gathering his papers into assorted files that all seemed to be marked 'Secret' and 'For His Majesty – Pending'. He placed the red folders into the brief-case and snapped it shut, rotating the combination locks as he did so.

'Now come and sit down,' he said, gesturing to a couple of armchairs. 'It's always the same when His Majesty just arrives – one frantic rush.' He turned to open the kitchen door, 'I'll just get the family.'

A frantic scurrying accompanied by excited yapping and barking followed as three puppies were woken from their slumbers. In ran a brindle Boxer, a Dalmatian and a yellow Labrador, all males, all about four or five months old and all boisterous. They looked as though they each had long and distinguished pedigrees. The happy trio scampered up to me and a great show of boot-sniffing went on. As this was happening Maclean had fetched two large gin and tonics.

'This one,' he said, pointing to the Boxer, 'is mine. A present from the Sultan. He told me to get two for a couple of servants and one for myself. I'm trying to think of a good name for him.'

'Are they all from Harrods, Mr Maclean?' I asked.

'Firstly, my friends call me Mac. And yes, we get them all from a marvellous woman, Miss Rita Strator, who runs the Pet Department at Harrods. She knows just what we need. I always had Boxers when I was young.'

I told him of my love of German shorthaired pointers, and how George Yeandle in Long Kesh had introduced me to them. I gave the pups a quick once-over but they looked in peak condition and had clearly travelled well. I checked their pedigree certificates and treatment records and was pleased to see Harrods had done a thorough job and, importantly, had ensured the dogs had been given a shot against rabies as well as all the routine vaccinations.

'I've told the boys to come and collect their pups this morning as I knew you were coming. They can take them to Robat and show His Majesty and report that the vet has checked them.'

'What about the two black Labs at Robat?' I asked.

Maclean shook his head:

'Totally out of control,' he said. 'When they were younger, His Majesty liked to drive around with them in the back of his car; now they'd jump out of the window and be away across the desert in two winks. Trouble is they never get enough exercise.'

'Who looks after them?'

'Abdul Malik. One of HM's Household servants. I'll fix for you to go over in a day or two to see them.'

I said I had seen the cavalcade that morning with the Sultan driving himself.

'Oh yes, he likes to drive around to see what's going on, so don't be surprised if you bump into him again. Like a lot of Dhofaris, His Majesty sometimes takes his mother and sister for a drive on Fridays.

As a matter of fact, they often take a turn around this compound. It's the only chance the women get of going anywhere and seeing what's going on. There's a lot happening here and things happen at an incredible speed.'

I asked him about the changes since Sultan Qaboos took power.

'It is unbelievable,' said Maclean. 'I've been in Oman for eleven years and cannot believe what I am seeing. It used to be so old-fashioned. Do you know,' he went on, 'only a few years ago it was a legal requirement for people walking the streets in Muscat at night to carry a hurricane lamp as identification. I've still got mine,' he added with a note of pride.

'It must have been a very repressive society,' I ventured.
He looked straight at me:

'Not as bad as people make out. The old Sultan was one of the kindest and most courteous of men. He steered Oman through some terrible times and was a great friend of Britain. But, yes, he was old-fashioned and a strict Moslem and he did not want his country to develop into a seedy society as he believed was happening in some of the other Arab countries.'

I realised Maclean had retained a deep affection for his previous employer. He went on:

'I knew nothing about the coup. I was in London when it happened and had no idea it was planned. I resigned at once but the new Sultan asked me to work for his uncle, Sayyid Tariq bin Taimur, who was appointed Prime Minister after the coup. I was with him for six months before the new Sultan invited me to work for him.'

I admired his allegiance and Sultan Qaboos' trust in re-employing a man who had worked for his deposed father. It had been an interesting ploy to test Maclean out on his uncle first in order to assess his loyalty. Obviously he had met the test and continued looking after the Sultan's personal affairs.

There was a knock at the door and a well-built, middle-aged man with close-cropped grey hair walked straight in. Mac introduced to me Gren Gayler, the Salalah Palace Engineer whose challenge was to ensure the royal properties were maintained properly and to oversee the new and planned projects for the royal household.

'I spend my life unblocking drains, mending air conditioners and arranging emergency power sources to keep the Boss happy,' said Gren by way of introduction. He joined us with a gin and I complimented him on

Robat Palace, which looked so attractive both from the roadside and from the air.

'Yeah, it may look good,' said Gren, 'but when HM is in town the whole place gets over-loaded and fuses spark like Catherine wheels on Bonfire Night. Then they all want to use the phone and there just aren't enough lines. Or HM takes one look at the colour scheme and asks for new curtains or bathroom fittings to be fitted immediately. Last week we had to fly carpets in from London at three days' notice.'

Yet it was not all maintenance and fire brigade work, and Gren had a lot of exciting new projects under way including Royal Guest Houses, a Family Home for Princess Mizoon, 'The Queen Mother', a Regimental Head-quarters for RG and a major renovation of the old Salalah Palace. His biggest construction headache, he said, was the building of a series of houses for His Majesty's servants. These were being built close to Robat Palace and were an ambitious combination of traditional Arabic style with all Western amenities, and had been personally designed by HM. Gren and his wife were living in the first completed house, so that he could be on site and try to identify problems and iron them out before the rest were handed over.

'Yesterday evening, Mac,' said Gren, warming to his theme, 'just after HM got here, I was unwinding with a beer or two when Joy comes dashing into the bedroom and tells me she thinks I had better come quickly as the house was being surrounded by soldiers. I hurried downstairs to find HM, a gaggle of servants and half the Royal Guard outside the front door. Joy was in curlers and had her washing-up gloves on! The Jack Russell was going mad so Joy grabs him and dashes up to the bathroom to get her hair sorted and I went to the door. "May I have a look at the house please?" HM asks politely. He hadn't seen the finished version. So they all swept in and had a quick tour of the ground floor, pointing out various features. HM thanked me and asked when the other houses would be finished. I said it was our top priority. Then he left. Moments later Joy comes downstairs, hair looking great, and all ready to be presented. She was a bit disappointed to miss him!'

We chuckled and Mac poured the next round of drinks. I could see it was going to be a heavy day.

A car drew up outside and there came another knock at the door and in walked two of the black servants. They were about nineteen or twenty years old, slim, elegant and immaculately dressed, each in a pure cotton dishdash, one pink, one blue, with gold tassels at the neck and a white *tagiyah*. Each carried a large *khunja* made of fine silver, which was strapped to their stomachs by a finely-woven silver mesh belt into which was also tucked a black Browning pistol. Leaving their gold-strapped sandals at the door, they came into Maclean's house brimming with self-confidence and discreetly scented with something exotic. Their names were Nafis and Loqman. Both spoke English and were extremely polite, apologising to Maclean for the *Juma* intrusion. I stood up and shook hands but their attention was totally focused on the puppies. Both boys got to their knees and started playing with their new acquisitions. Nafis was to have the Labrador and Loqman the Dalmatian.

'You'll have to give them names,' said Maclean.

'This is Bron,' said Nafis proudly and promptly.

'And I shall call mine Mac after you, Mr Maclean,' said Loqman to great amusement.

'Now this,' said Maclean, pointing at me, 'is the Doctor. Any problems with the dogs and you go straight to him. Do you know what to feed them?'

'Abdul Malik will show us,' said Nafis.

'Yes, all right,' said Mac, speaking to them rather like a nanny, 'but don't forget they are your dogs and you must look after them properly.'

'Of course,' they replied in unison.

'You'd better take them to show His Majesty,' said Maclean. They took the animals lovingly in their arms, thanked us and glided out to their gleaming silver Mercedes parked next to my scruffy Land Rover.

'I'll have to show you where the boys live now,' said Maclean to me after they had gone. 'Those two have never had puppies before and you'll need to keep a close eye on them; they'll never be bothered to train them properly so you must check them every few days.'

I nodded, feeling apprehensive. I had a gut feeling that the *jebalis* might be easier to handle than the courtiers.

Maclean turned to Gren and said, 'I told Brian Hewson I might drop over for a drink this morning – can you come?'

'Love to,' said Gren, 'I'll just phone Joy.' He moved to the phone and I made to leave but was waved down by Maclean.

'Why don't you come too?' he asked. 'Brian's the Master of the *Al Said*, the Royal Yacht, and it just docked yesterday at Raysut. He and I go back a long way. He was a Royal Navy Commander when I was a Chief Petty Officer. You'll like him. With luck he'll give us lunch. You've nothing else on, have you?'

I said I was free barring any emergencies. Gren rejoined us, and Mac picked up the Boxer, who now looked rather lonely without his two companions and was whining softly as he looked about the room for them.

We were about to leave when a further visitor arrived with a tentative knock. Friday seemed to be the day for house calls in Salalah. This time it was a small, round-faced doctor called Dr Raffay, who lived next door and who had, he said, just popped in to say hello.

One of two Royal physicians, Raffay was originally from what is now Pakistan but his family had been tragically torn apart at the time of Partition in 1947 and as a result he had been brought up in India and had later joined the Indian Army Medical Corps. He had been recruited to work for Sultan Said bin Taimur in the late 1950s and now looked after Bibi and all the female side of the Sultan's family. He told me there was also a serving Indian Army doctor called Major Rashid who was attached to RG and was HM's personal physician.

'There is a very strange attitude to medicine in this country,' said Dr Raffay, sipping a lemon squash as we settled down for our third gin. 'We constantly have to deal with folk lore and traditional medicine. There is so much quackery. And even some of Bibi's family believe in the old cures, it is so entrenched in their way of life.'

I recounted my experiences with the pregnant woman earlier in the week.

'She is very lucky you were there,' said Raffay. 'Otherwise some filthy witch doctor would have invaded her body and probably killed her. I am surprised you got her to hospital so easily – they seem to have such a fear of our hospital.'

'Is that because they leave it so late that the patients are often at death's door before they get to see a doctor?' I asked.

'Oh, just so,' said Raffay. 'They think of it as a place of death, not somewhere to get well.'

'And have you come across many major diseases in your time here?' I enquired.

'We have so much,' said Raffay. 'Malaria, syphilis, trachoma, TB. And diarrhoea and dysentery are very common. It is such an uphill struggle,' he sighed.

Maclean got to his feet. 'Sorry, Dr Raffay, you must excuse us but we have a lunch engagement.'

'Of course, of course,' said Raffay, extending his hand to me. 'You must come and have dinner with me and we will have a long talk.'

Maclean and Gren Gayler went off in the Datsun with Mac at the wheel and I followed in the Land Rover, relieved that breathalysers had not reached Oman.

We sped through the Wire and soon reached Raysut. Our progress into the harbour was expedited by the Datsun's Palace number plates and the gates flew open with the *askars* leaping to attention. The port seemed very quiet and still after the bustle of the working week and we parked by the grey bows of a handsome ship of about 1,000 tonnes moored at the end of the jetty. The Sultan's flag flew from the stern as we made our way to the gangway. Three men and a dog. There was no ceremony. In fact, apart from a couple of sailors on guard duty who dispassionately watched us arrive, there was no one else to be seen as we climbed up the gangplank.

We were met on deck by the *Al Said*'s captain, Commander Brian Hewson, an imposing man who looked like the popular British character actor James Robertson Justice. He wore a neat beard, perfectly creased white shorts, white deck shoes and socks and a shirt bearing his rank and the insignia of the Sultan of Oman's Navy. He introduced me to his Chief Engineer, a Scot, and as Mac and Greg went below with Hewson, the Chief gave me a tour of the ship, which had originally been commissioned by Sultan Said bin Taimur. He explained that both he and Brian were retired Royal Navy officers. There was a mixed Omani/Baluchi crew and the ship was always in attendance whenever the Sultan might need to use it. His visits were unpredictable but when 'the Boss' was in Salalah they were constantly on stand-by and on Fridays there was always the chance he might on impulse decide to take a trip along the coast. I was surprised to see a cluster of .50 and .30 Browning machine guns on the *Al Said*'s deck and the Chief explained that for most of the time the *Al Said* doubled as a patrol boat helping to guard the Dhofar coast under the command of Dhofar Brigade.

We went below to the engine room which gleamed obsessively with polished steel and brass, and then through to the elegant but not particularly luxurious sleeping accommodation and finally the cramped Wardroom. We squeezed ourselves around a small mahogany table where I was immediately given a Horse's Neck, a cocktail made from brandy, ginger ale, Angostura bitters and a snaking neck of lemon peel. It sat easily on top of Maclean's three hefty gins. Lunch was a superb curry produced by a skilful Baluchi cook in the tiny Wardroom galley and the hospitality continued well into the afternoon, interrupted only by more Horse's Necks and periodic loo walks along the jetty for the Boxer pup.

'Are you coming to the Taylor Woodrow barbeque tonight?' Maclean asked Hewson as we were leaving.

'Yes, we've been invited,' he replied.

'Well, see you there,' said Maclean. Turning to me he added, 'You can come too as my guest.'

The social life of the expat was tough. I replied that I would love to come and arranged to meet Mac at six o'clock. By now, I was beginning to feel the toll of the day and a nap was definitely called for. That would give me a couple of hours on my bed at the Mess in preparation for the next round.

Taylor Woodrow was probably the largest British company operating in Salalah. Sir Frank Taylor, its founder and managing director, took his firm resolutely into Oman soon after the coup, and had capitalised successfully on the urgent need for new buildings and redevelopment. Outside Salalah, where they were much in evidence, the company had contracts for drilling wells on the *jebal* and were working with BATT and SAF on building the new road between Salalah and Taqah. Taylor Woodrow had developed a reputation for producing the goods against incredible odds. Their standard of workmanship was reported to be superior to many of their competitors and they employed a lot of British foremen, managers and technicians. Salaries were high and tax-free and many of the staff volunteered to stay on for several years, becoming established members of the Salalah expat community.

As things had gradually become safer, wives had begun to join their husbands and about fifty families now lived in the Taylor Woodrow compound, which was a small fenced-off village of prefabricated houses on the sea front, next to the quarters where the civil servants such as Maclean and the Butlers were housed. The company had its own social centre, the Taywood Club, and membership was jealously guarded by those outsiders who were lucky enough to get it. Mac and Gren were honorary members as the Sultan's construction projects formed a major part of the company's business in Dhofar.

Mike Foster-Turner, known to his friends as Mufti, was TW's manager in Salalah. He was in his late thirties and a Rhodesian by birth. And he was tough. He chain-smoked and the size of his stomach bore witness to life spent to the full. He made much of Maclean's arrival at the barbeque that evening. I was immediately welcomed and in no time a can of cold Heineken had been thrust into my hand. It was a jolly evening with the coloured lights, the smell of roasting meats in front of the Goanese and Indian chefs in their white aprons and hats, the 1970s music and the endless flow of drink, which seemed by now to be a normal part of *Juma* life.

The cream of British society in Dhofar circulated as guests leisurely mixed with each other and the TW staff. I saw Robin Young, the Butlers, the Rayboulds and the Gaylers. The Brigade Commander, Jack Fletcher and his wife, the CO from RAF Salalah and his Adjutant, our hosts from the *Al Said*, and to my surprise I found Paddy King-Fretts and John Innes from BATT, both looking remarkably relaxed in casual kit. I was introduced to Norman Jackson, known as Norman the Bank, who was a Dhofar grandee and manager of the Salalah branch of the British Bank of the Middle East, or BBME.

Tables were loaded with delicious offerings, which had been laid out around the brightly lit swimming pool. People ate, drank, swam and generally had fun. It was barely credible to think that we were in a war zone. It was a weird mingling of British military and civilian society in an alien land. There were no Omanis among the guests and I felt I had translocated a hundred years to life in India under the British Raj where expatriates created a cocoon of social security around them as protection against the local people whom they often misunderstood and rarely mixed with. Yet whatever the PFLOAG propaganda said, the British in Oman were not colonisers. Britain had signed a treaty with the Sultan of Muscat as far back as 1798 offering protection in exchange for trade concessions. As far as Taylor Woodrow was concerned, their work was a natural extension of that treaty. I took the opportunity to mingle and meet as many people as possible with the confidence that comes with alcohol that had been free-flowing all day. This was some party – a tropical beach, a great crowd of people, fantastic food, attentive staff, a warm sea breeze and stars shining brilliantly in a still dark sky above. 'I could really grow to like this,' I thought to myself.

The following morning, nursing a massive hangover, I went to find the royal servants' houses. They were located in a small, unprepossessing alleyway behind Salalah hospital. Fortunately Saleh knew the place. The houses were unexpectedly ordinary and unpretentious, unlike some of the large merchants' homes that were beginning to appear around the town. The Sultan had decided to build the new up-market homes for his friends next to the palace at Robat. When they moved, this odd narrow road of old, traditional, mud and brick walled Salalah houses, which I guessed had been the town's slave quarter and home to families of favoured black Omanis for generations, would probably vanish for ever.

Saleh did not like the flamboyant, extravagant lifestyle of some of the servants. Nor did he particularly like dogs – even puppies from Harrods. He was unusually quiet when we called on Loqman and Nafis, with none of his usual banter or cosy suggestions that we might linger for tea or coffee. The servants were close to the Sultan and were to be treated with caution and reserve.

We called first on Loqman. His house, like the others, was made of stone coated with limestone plaster. It had a large, solid wooden door, which opened into a courtyard and there were attractive carved windows, shuttered to keep out the sand and sun. In Loqman's case, the yard contained a covered well, animal pens and a cooking area; chickens scratched about looking for insects and titbits. Around the periphery were a number of doors, which opened into the living and sleeping accommodation. Clothes and colourful wraps hung to dry outside. At one corner of the yard was a *maglis* where the men would gather to drink and chat around a small fire. There was a handful of black women sitting in the yard preparing food or involved with various minor household chores. Their faces were

91

uncovered and they made no attempt to conceal them as Loqman, who seemed to be a son of the house, let us in.

The Dalmatian puppy, Mac, was sitting quietly in the yard. He did not give the impression of being particularly happy, but did not look ill, just a bit unsettled having lost his friends and finding himself in a situation far removed from Knightsbridge or even Maclean's comfortable sitting room. Loqman was affectionate towards the dog and picked him up gently and brought him over for me to check. Conscious of Saleh's discomfort, I talked to Loqman in English, interspersed with my broken Arabic. I checked if the pup was eating, drinking enough, where he slept, what was coming out of the other end and the sort of routine he had. Loqman was clearly fond of the puppy and I hoped this would last and would be shared by his extended family who would probably see a lot of the little dog.

Loqman then took me to some of the other servants' houses. In one, there were two grossly overweight yellow Labradors which, he said, had been in Salalah for a long time. It looked as if they spent most of their lives scavenging in the alleyways and sleeping in dust beds in the courtyards of their respective homes. The owner was not around and I sensed that Loqman felt awkward and embarrassed at their appearance.

In another house, there were two brown-spot Dalmatians; both looked too thin and were affected with mange, causing them to scratch and bite their skins. I told Saleh to arrange for them to be brought to *Bir Bint Ahmed* where we would bathe them and keep them for a while until they got better. In the meantime I gave the itchy pair each an injection to ease the discomfort.

Nafis was not at home and his family told me that he had his new yellow Lab, Bron, with him in his limo. So with my visit over sooner than expected and no other calls planned for the day, I was able to return to *Bir Bint Ahmed*. I would have to check on Bron some other time, but for now I could use the unexpected free time to catch up on paperwork and other mundane chores.

The next morning, Maclean had arranged for me to check over the Sultan's dogs. We rolled up at the gates of Robat Palace at the appointed hour, and were met by a perfectly turned-out Royal Guard sergeant. He spoke briefly into his radio and a junior officer swiftly appeared, exchanged a few words with Saleh, looked at me and pointed at a small gate some 50 metres further along the perimeter wall. Not the main entrance for us!

After ten minutes or so, the gate opened from the inside and a rather rotund middle-aged servant came out. This, Saleh told me, was Abdul Malik. He was impeccably dressed in a spotless white dishdash, complete with large silver *khunja*.

Abdul Malik opened the gate and we went into the Palace grounds. He bolted it firmly behind us and we found ourselves in a private, walled

92

landscaped garden at one side of the Palace itself. I was relieved to learn that the Sultan was not at home but noted that there were still a lot of soldiers about the place. I reassured myself that their primary remit was to keep people out of the Palace and that they were probably less concerned once you were on the inside trying to look as if you belonged there.

The gardens were very attractively laid out with brick paths meandering through the grassy lawns. Seats were strategically placed and I could hear a pitter-patter that I supposed must be fountains playing nearby. The ubiquitous bougainvillea abounded and, along with other exotic-looking climbing plants, provided bursts of colour against the white walls. Bare-footed brown gardeners squatted everywhere like shrubs, weeding flower-beds, pointing hoses or simply, it seemed, meditating. The Palace was smaller than I had imagined, but opening on to the gardens were large windows of smoked glass that kept out the bright sun and inquisitive eyes.

Abdul Malik led the way along a winding path of crazy paving. I followed and Saleh brought up the rear clutching the veterinary bag. I could see a swimming pool and tennis courts ahead but we turned right along the side of the main building. There was an outburst of frantic barking ahead, and as we rounded a bush I saw the chain-link fence sur-rounding the compound containing Oman's only two black Labradors. The dogs were large and very excited. They were bedded on clean, fine sand and had some 30 square metres to tear around. I took my hat off to Taylor Woodrow who had built an impressive polygonal concrete kennel. Concrete tables had been ingeniously put in the runs so the dogs could jump off the ground and onto the roof of the kennels.

Just outside the compound was a stack of cans of *PAL* dog food and some tins of condensed milk. With Saleh translating, Abdul Malik explained that every morning he gave each dog a can of milk with two tins of meat each in the evening. To demonstrate the dogs' versatility, he picked up a can of dog food, unlocked the door and threw the can in for one of them to catch. The larger of the two Labs dived at the can and started gnawing it possessively. The party trick, I saw, was to let him bite through the tin and eat the meat. Abdul Malik beamed. I sighed. The quantity of food given to these obese, hyperactive dogs was bad enough but then to encourage them to chew through metal and risk not only breaking their teeth but also lacerating tongue and mouth as they struggled to get the food out was hopeless.

Abdul Malik was disappointed at my lack of enthusiasm for his little show. I asked why they had a can of tinned milk each day. There was no real answer. I suspected they had been given it as part of their diet when they were growing pups and no one had suggested it should be stopped. Although they were a bit fat, they were very active dogs and I reckoned they were fit enough. I went into the compound with Abdul Malik, who at my insistence dolefully retrieved the macerated tin from the indignant animal.

Saleh followed me in rather more cautiously as the dogs rushed at us bouncing up and down with the energy of coiled springs. Young Labs need a couple of good runs every day and, without exercise, they soon get bored and overweight. The arrival of three of us must have been hugely exciting. I tried to get hold of the smaller of the two to look him over. He was friendly but in no mood for being peered at and prodded.

Suddenly, Abdul Malik gave a yell and leapt towards the gate. To my horror I saw it was open – Saleh had warily entered, leaving it ajar. As I had been looking at the smaller dog, the larger of the pair had nosed open the gate and charged out. I made a quick but unsuccessful attempt to grab hold of his chum, who swerved past Abdul Malik and dashed through the gate before he could close it.

'Oh bloody hell!' I cried, adding quite unnecessarily, 'Quick – after them.'

Watched silently by countless, blank-faced Indian gardeners and puzzled RG soldiers, the two black Labradors raced delightedly across the Palace lawns, followed by a greatly distressed Veterinary Officer in his OGs clutching his hat in his hand, and a puffing Abdul Malik in his billowing dishdash with his large *khunja*-embossed stomach quivering before him. A worried veterinary assistant, still holding the medical bag and with his spare hand hoisting up his dishdash to increase his speed, brought up the rear. We ran around the swimming pool, over the tennis courts and along the perimeter pathway. I was seeing far more of the Palace grounds than I might have expected.

It all happened so quickly but it was with a feeling of impending doom that I realised the dogs were making for the guardroom and main gate. The soldiers were gazing in amazement, not sure what to do. 'Shut the gates!' I yelled hopefully, but it was in vain. One or two of the bemused guards tried to wave their hands at the dogs to divert them but the canny canines knew exactly where they wanted to go and that was out of the Palace grounds and into freedom.

'Oh great,' I groaned as I raced through the gate after them, adding some more choice Anglo-Saxon words. Saleh jettisoned the bag at the gate and added a few words of his own in Arabic. We hit the main road and the dogs turned left to run towards the town. A hundred metres or so along the road Taylor Woodrow were building the new RGR barracks and it was in this massive building site that we lost them completely.

I asked Abdul Malik to go and explain the situation to the RG duty officer and try to secure his help. I would go to *Umm al Gwarrif* and put out a message that the Sultan's personal and favourite dogs had escaped and were on the run. Saleh, who had ignored the golden rule about shutting gates behind him, was not in my best books at that precise moment and I told him to go and requisition some Taylor Woodrow workmen and scour the site.

I drove rapidly to the Camp. If the soldiers on gate duty were a bit surprised to see a hot and flustered BATT man roar up, they did not give me any hassle. I jumped up the steps to the office of the Adjutant of the Muscat Regiment, a middle-aged contract officer who was sitting behind his desk puffing on a cigarette. He looked mildly surprised as I threw open his door and breathlessly blurted out my problem. He got up and came round the desk, putting his arm around my shoulders.

'Come and sit down, my dear boy,' he said, steering me towards a chair. I could see he was smiling sympathetically. 'There's really absolutely nothing you can do about it. Don't worry – it has happened before – usually when the Sultan goes to visit them! Last time, they turned up at the RAF Camp and, after giving them a meal and endless TLC at the Mess, they took them home. They'll wear themselves out after half an hour or so.'

He told his clerk to issue a warning that the Royal Labradors were on the loose again, and then gave me a much-needed cigarette and a cup of strong coffee.

A few minutes later, feeling calmer, I drove back to the Palace and saw two tired but happy dogs rolling playfully on the ground cheerfully resisting the endeavours of Abdul Malik and Saleh to get collars and leads on them. Their efforts even made the Royal Guard laugh. Eventually, we got them back to their kennels and Abdul Malik firmly padlocked the gate. I told him his master's dogs were very fit and that he was pretty athletic too. He loved that and we parted the best of friends.

Inevitably the story spread fast, and from Officers' Messes to the coffee houses of Salalah the tales of the Great Escape caused merriment for several nights, and cost me a lot of drinks.

Chapter 11

The Winged Dagger

It took me some time to work out what it was that made up an SAS soldier and I am not sure I ever got there. Since my posting to Oman and the knowledge that I would be working with probably the most professional soldiers in the world, I realised that I needed to try to sort out in my own mind the truth from the fiction that surrounded the Regiment. Stories about the SAS abounded, reflecting its anonymity, secrecy and often secret missions that British governments would sometimes deny. Some of the media-driven accounts were plausible, others less so and often, of course, it was fantasy. Even so, the public interest driven by the mystery and derring-do was understandable. I was curious to know what sort of person joined the SAS and what did the Regiment look for in applicants?

My first impression was of the total normality and good company of those around me in 'A' Squadron, together with a calm orderliness with which they all set about their work. There was no arrogance, flamboyance or bravado; more a disarming humility and a quiet maturity about the job in hand. One or two members of the Squadron seemed taciturn and many were passionate about keeping fit, but there had to be more to it than that. So one evening after prayers, Paddy and I sat chatting with Bronco and John Innes in the small dining room where I sometimes ate with the others. I asked them outright, 'What is it that makes an SAS soldier?'

There was a pause. Eyebrows were raised. They looked at one another.

'Reliability and self-reliance, I suppose,' was Paddy's reply. 'The big difference is that we don't operate like other regiments; we don't have people chasing around after each other, NCOs shouting, lots of noise, parades and so on.' He thought for a moment, then went on: 'We need people who can act for themselves, think for themselves, sort themselves out and you *know* you can trust them, no matter what.'

'That's it ... the last bit,' chipped in Bronco. 'Each guy's got to trust those around him; we have to have complete faith in each other.'

'Maturity is important,' added John. 'A bunch of mixed-up teenagers like you get in most units is not for us. We couldn't function with their wild music, endless chatter and lack of discretion. Living with them would be hell.' The three of them laughed and shook their heads at the thought of it. John continued: 'Our guys must have settled down and got the riotous youth out of their systems; you have to know that in a crisis, everyone is going to keep their cool, stay focused and stick to the plan.'

'What's the average age in the Squadron?' I asked Paddy. 'Twenty-nine,' he replied. Almost ten years older than the average young infantryman I had worked with in Ulster, and four years older than me.

'There is nothing wrong with the youngsters in the military today,' added Paddy quickly. 'They're mostly good lads and they are the army's future. But they couldn't cope with the jungle or *jebal*. They simply would not have the stamina or determination.' He glanced at the other two. 'The vital thing is to see a job through. You need resilience, determination and sometimes ruthlessness. It can be a bloody difficult job but you have just got to go for it.'

'Killer instinct?' I asked.

'Yes,' he replied, simply. He paused. 'There is no point in having a unit like this if there is going to be any dithering or hanging back.' Paddy's pale blue eyes seemed to have become steely as he held my gaze steadily. 'If a man has the killer instinct, then Hereford will teach him the rest.'

'And then screw the nut,' said John with a laugh, easing the tension. He grinned at my puzzled look. 'One of our expressions,' he explained. 'In plain English – just shut up and crack on.'

I thought a lot about this over the weeks. It came down to self-reliance and dependability. It had to be the inner man that the selection team at Hereford was looking for. Skills could be taught and developed – but not personality. And who at home would really understand the strain these men were under? Their only real relief in the course of a five-month tour were the occasional, but compulsory, R and R breaks at *Umm al Gwarrif*, when they could recharge their batteries, sleep, drink, eat fresh food and get into their own casual clothes.

The pressures were immense. Home for five months was often little more than a rocky dugout, or shack if they were lucky, a *basha* with no electricity (other than from a portable generator), no running water or ablutions, no facilities for washing clothes and only basic cooking and food storage capabilities. Fresh rations came up maybe once a week and lasted little more than twenty-four hours. If there was no well, water also had to be flown in or delivered in jerry cans. The men lived and worked from the shelters they had built, week in week out, month after month, and in weather that varied from the stiflingly hot to the choking, menacing sand storms to the pervasive, misty drizzle of the *khareef*.

Then there was the constant cluster of *jebalis* – dozens, sometimes hundreds of unpredictable tribesmen who we were supposed to be wooing and protecting. They lived in increasing numbers around the BATT teams, which were often no more than four or six strong. The *jebalis* saw BATT as a sort of welfare state and as the providers of every creature comfort. During my brief visits to the teams I was pestered relentlessly for ammunition or more or better weapons; for medicines for the sick; for materials to improve their shelters; for feed or veterinary attention for their animals, and so it went on.

Within all this was the relationship between the men themselves. Paddy told me that teams were selected as near as possible for compatibility. Many were good friends and on the whole everyone got on remarkably well. Yet, inevitably from time to time there were differences – a petty niggle, bad news from home, a stomach upset – things that normally they would take in their stride. On the hill there was no escape and contact with the enemy could be frequent, ruthless and vicious. Occasionally, Paddy would mount an extensive operation but it was often left to the team itself to coordinate mortars, artillery, infantry support and air strikes, and always with the unreliable and temperamental *firqat*. Still, it was their country; they provided the intelligence and BATT was only there in support.

It was great to be able to share, however modestly, in the Squadron's achievements, such as when Paddy himself led a successful operation on the *jebal* and captured several wanted *adoo* leaders. A cheer went up at evening prayers when Bronco reported this to the few of us left at base. Such victories sometimes caused their own problems. The morning after the Op, I was flown urgently up the hill to treat a herd of cattle with bullet wounds. SAF was convinced that the shooting must have been a determined and deliberate retaliation by the *adoo* for Paddy's success the previous day. The animals were said to have been shot as part of an inter-tribal settlement against those *jebali* families who had helped BATT.

On one occasion I arrived in Jibjat just as an Op was being mounted. It was mid-afternoon and I went up in the same aircraft as two other members of BATT with their full fighting kit. The cattle I had been asked to come and see were not due at the watering point until morning, but I wanted to get up the day before to check on the new trough as there had been several complaints that the water was contaminated and a row was said to be developing between some of the rival tribal chiefs.

As usual we were met by Dan, the team leader, who at once explained that the plan had changed as they were going out that night on a forty-eight-hour operation into one of the deep *wadis* running south from the high *jebal*. The two men who were with me would remain at Jibjat as caretakers while the operation was in progress. Dan said he had decided not to postpone my visit as he wanted to demonstrate to the *jebalis* that help for their animals was available under all circumstances; I was to continue with my mission and catch a return heli or Skyvan as soon as I had done my business.

I had got to know the Jibjat team quite well and was pleased to be back. One of the caretakers made tea and, having dropped my kit on the usual bed space, I went over to the main *basha* where the whole team was assembling. There were smiles of welcome and a bit of shuffling until a space was found for me to sit down. Apart from the BATT team, three *firqat* were also in the *basha*, squatting on their haunches. I thought I recognised a couple of them as leaders of local tribes; they seemed to have forgotten any differences over the water trough as bigger issues were clearly up for debate. There was a tense, charged atmosphere in the room; everyone was focused on a particular task. One or two people smoked and everyone was studying their notebooks and maps. I watched, fascinated to see the team in action.

Dan gave out his final orders for the night's operation. It did not involve me so I sat and studied the six SAS men as they sat around a central map on the ground next to a carefully prepared model of the terrain made from stones and sand. As Dan took them through his plan point by point, Trevor, the Arabist, explained it to the *firqat* leaders who muttered quietly together before nodding their approval or asking a question.

The soldiers sat quietly absorbing every detail. If necessary, Dan would go over a point again and again. Nothing seemed to be missed. The men were totally focused on the job ahead of them, oblivious to anything else, including me. This single-minded concentration and focus was another special attribute of the SAS.

The rapport between troops and *firqat*, Brits and Arabs, was striking. A sort of mutual respect – not so very different, I felt, from what I was trying to achieve in my own field. In Hereford, Peter de la Billière had told me that the four pillars of Operation Storm all depended on trust. They may be at opposite ends of the spectrum, but both counter-insurgency operations and animal health would only work in this campaign if the *jebali* people and the military had faith in each other. Hearts and Minds.

When the meeting was over, several of the team went down to a shallow, rock-strewn *wadi* to test their weapons. Alistair, a burly, jovial Scot pointed at my Browning 9mm and grinned: 'When did you last fire tha' thing?'

'About two weeks ago,' I replied a bit sheepishly. It really did look rather inadequate compared to the other hardware on display. 'Had to shoot a couple of donkeys.'

'You wha'?' He rounded on me looking genuinely shocked and thought for a moment. 'I couldna' do tha' man,' he muttered. 'Couldna' go shooting wee animals like tha'. No way.'

The evening meal was earlier than usual as the team wanted to get themselves organised well before dark. My name had been added to the guard roster for the night but that was normal. There was the usual chat around the table but I could feel the tension rising as the hour for departure approached. One by one the men slipped away to attend to their own responsibilities. A *firqat* appeared at the door. *'Salaam alay koom.'* Trevor turned round and listened to the tribesman, nodding. After a couple of minutes he turned back to Dan and me. 'Remarkable,' he said. 'Never known this before. In fact I don't think I've ever heard of it happening. They've asked us to join their evening prayers.'

This was a great compliment to the team and an indication of how close their relationship was with the *firqat*. Dan got up immediately and we all silently followed him to stand behind the line of *firqats* facing towards Mecca as the sun set over the glorious Qara hills. Somewhere the hills boasted a footprint and the tomb of the prophet Nabi Ayoub (Job), and others say here it was here that the Virgin Mary's father died. Somehow all this seemed no surprise. We remained a short, respectful distance behind the Arabs as the Imam led the prayers and blessed all those about to do battle. It was very moving and spoke volumes about the bonding, maturity and judgement of the men of 'A' Squadron SAS.

A short while later, as the stars began to appear like bright jewels in the darkening Arabian sky, I watched our heavily-armed team join up with what must have been a hundred or more tribesmen. After the ritual hand-shakes and pleasantries, they sat together finishing the last of their cigarettes before suddenly, at some unseen command, there was a rustling of equipment, the clink of a weapon or two against a rock, the shuffling of many feet, and they were off and away into the night.

Two days afterwards I heard that the Op had been aborted, but the *firqat* had captured a herd of *jebali* cattle from the enemy. Paddy was philosophical and explained that when animals were involved the operation of the moment invariably collapsed as the *firqat* became far too concerned about dividing up their spoils of war; a reminder of just how important cattle were to these people in the battle for their hearts and minds.

It was now the height of the Ops season and the Sultan's forces were making a determined effort to break down the remaining enemy resistance east of the Midway Road. Operations were being launched regularly from bases on the *jebal*, many with a number of different *firqat* forces involved and sometimes with a battalion or more of SAF troops deployed. As a result, air travel was at a premium which hampered my work and I had to cadge lifts however and whenever I could. The war was the priority, so the timing of my return flights became highly unpredictable and I had to go up the hill prepared to stay several days if necessary.

100

One strong BATT location to the east of the operational area was Tawi Atair, the Well of the Birds. There were a lot of *adoo* around the location and Tawi had been a centre for considerable enemy action over the past three years. It was an amazing place. The well itself was 150 metres wide and must have been 200 or 300 metres deep, with much of the wall frighteningly sheer. There, in the silence, you could hear the birds sing as they nested, rested and refreshed themselves in the ancient cavern. Sand grouse and doves fluttered around the well revealing how Tawi Atair must have got its name. A steep, dangerous-looking, boulder-strewn path wound crudely down towards the black water far below.

The sappers had recently installed a pump with pipes leading to cattle troughs and water points. As a result, hundreds of animals were able to drink there each day. I loved visiting Tawi; it had a peacefulness that belied the surrounding *adoo* activity. I wanted to station a veterinary assistant there which might provide encouragement to the *jebalis* to come in for water and CAT support.

Tawi had to be approached by air as parts of the Mirbat road remained exposed to surprise enemy attacks. As there was only a very small landing strip the Skyvans spiralled downwards with nauseating tightness, roaring to a halt with the by now familiar furious reverse thrust and braking. Only a few months previously an SOAF de Havilland Caribou had crashed at Tawi and landings were always a heart-stopping, nerve-wracking experience. As I walked unsteadily away from the aircraft, which was already revving up for a swift departure, I was told that Paddy was on the hill commanding an operation. I hadn't realised the boss himself would be here. Jack, one of the two BATT men still at base, told me there had been some hard fighting at the bottom of two enormous *wadis*. Paddy, it seemed, was currently at a vantage point between the two and artillery and jets had been used that morning to draw the operation to a close. No wonder the pilot had corkscrewed down even more sharply than usual.

The men were expected back shortly. I felt particularly helpless. The SAS would return to their Spartan quarters, filthy and exhausted, with nothing but a bowl or cattle trough to wash in, an empty camp to open up and a horde of *jebalis* clamouring for attention. I did what I could to help the guys get a meal on the go and hot water ready for the instant brew that would be welcomed the moment the others got back into the Camp. The team and their *firqat* finally arrived mid-afternoon and it was obvious they had been engaged in a hard slog. Unshaven and hollow-eyed, their faces drawn and gaunt, the men raised their hands wearily in greeting as they approached us. Paddy was not among them; he had been flown back to *UAG* by helicopter for the debrief.

I knew Lee, a gunner, fairly well and went over to help him with his kit. I tried to take his Bergen as he slipped it from his shoulder, but it was so

101

heavy it was nearly torn from my grip. He eased his shoulders and then removed his belt which must have weighed 20 kilograms with the remains of his tightly-packed ammunition and water bottle. 'How did it go?' I asked, offering him a cigarette.

'Three, four maybe,' he answered matter-of-factly.

'Killed?'

'Yep. And we captured three.'

For a moment I was taken aback. We were not talking here of slaughtering goats. It brought into sharp focus the contrast between my relatively civilised life in Salalah, the tranquillity of Tawi Atair's fluttering doves and gently chugging water pumps, and the savagery of the war, just a few kilometres away. I looked at Lee's back; the shirt still dark and sodden where the Bergen had pressed in stark contrast to the white rings of sweat which had been dried by the hot sun.

'There you are, Boss,' said Lee pointing, a wide grin breaking on his stubbled, tanned face. 'See the *firqat* with the three we captured? You wouldn't believe it would you? Two hours ago they were knocking the shit out of each other, now it's all kiss and make up.'

It was true. The captives were squatting in a ring of *firqat*, sipping tea and chatting away to their captors – at least two were; the third sat a little distance away.

'Bloody hell,' I exclaimed. 'One's a woman.'

'Yeah,' said Lee. 'She gave as good as she got until the game was up. Still it's really unusual to capture a bint; as far as I know they like to surrender to the locals in their own time and place. Never heard of one being captured before.'

I gazed at her. Her face was uncovered and she was very attractive, maybe in her twenties; it was hard to tell. She had a nose ring set with a red carnelian stone – the gem that the Prophet Mohammed was said to wear in his ring. She smiled demurely at us then turned away with a shy laugh. It was hard to see the killer in that soldier.

Suddenly something struck me. 'Lee,' I said, a note of alarm creeping into my voice. 'They've still got their weapons.'

'Yeah, that's normal,' he replied. 'Their personal weapons are their pride and joy. We let them keep their guns, they get to keep their dignity. Here it's really important not to lose face.' He smiled. 'We've taken the ammo though!'

He slung his Bergen on his back again as if it was a school satchel and together, we walked towards the *basha*.

'What about the dead?' I asked.

102

'They get shipped down to Salalah for identification unless one of the *firqat* recognises them. They often do – somebody's cousin's wife's brother. That helps as they can be buried at once out on the hill, which the Moslems prefer. So do we, actually.'

Keith, the Tawi team leader, was nearby, cleaning his Armalite. I watched the ritualistic way in which he carefully examined each part before re-assembling the weapon. He caught my gaze as he looked up. 'Got to be done before dark whatever happens,' he said. Standing up, Keith raised his voice slightly.

'Right, you guys,' he said, calling the team together. 'Let's run through it step by step.' The team each grabbed a drink and gathered round. Wash, rest and food had to wait. It had been a hard contact – I later learned two BATT men had been hit with shrapnel, fortunately neither seriously. As Keith started to review the Op with his men, I eased away.

These were extraordinary men, I thought. Regular guys. Often family men with a wife and children at home. Yet there was something about them that I just could not quantify. They were soldiers first and foremost; tough, professional ones at that, but there still remained a difference – an independence of spirit which, combined with their dedication and pro-fessionalism, put them in a warrior class of their own. Many had been to Dhofar several times, the older ones to Aden and Borneo before that. It was, as 'A' Squadron's Captain Simon Garthwaite had once told me, in their blood, and none of them had a clue why they kept coming back for more. What I was beginning to see was that their achievements were not brought about by luck or some macho Superman formula as the media myths might imply, but by constant effort and honing of skills.

Chapter 12

The Muscateer

The Court returned to Muscat after a brief but intense stay in Salalah and an air of relative tranquillity once again descended on the town. John Clarke had remained for a few days after HM left and I had dinner with him and his new Swiss wife, Clody, at the Raybould's'. Clody was tiny and delightful and I thought she was remarkably composed having made such a radical transition from urban Basle to the deserts of Arabia. She and John shared a love of horses but she was barely half his age.

In some ways John was an odd man; tall, thin, slightly stooping, with glasses and a dark moustache on a rather mournful face. His conversation sometimes seemed a little eccentric until you got used to his droll sense of humour. Yet, as befitted a former officer in the Trucial Oman Scouts, he was utterly loyal to Sultan Qaboos and Oman.

John had served as a contract officer for SAF in the *Jebal Akhdar* campaign in the 1950s. The *Jebal Akhdar* was the focus of a rebellion in 1954 backed by Egypt and Saudi Arabia against Sultan Said bin Taimur. The leaders of the revolt were based on a high fertile plateau 2,000–3,000 metres above sea level and towering above the arid deserts below. It was an ideal site for a conflict, as there were said to be only twelve approaches to the plateau, making it virtually impregnable. The guerrillas were well stocked with arms and, despite air attacks from the Sultan's Air Force, they managed to stay entrenched for several years.

In November 1958, the British government, eager to ensure stability in this volatile region, secretly deployed the SAS and this turned out to be a pivotal moment in the Regiment's history. One of the SAS troops was led by Captain Peter de la Billière who, in his own autobiography *Looking for Trouble*, describes with unabashed enthusiasm his exploits in the campaign, for which he won the Military Cross, as indeed did another SAS commander and later Major-General, Tony Jeapes. Two troops of Trucial Oman Scouts had also taken part; one led by the man who was now Director of the Royal Stables, Major John Clarke. John had been in charge of a group of irregulars – fifty *Beni Ruawha* tribesmen who accompanied the SAS squadrons to the top of the seemingly inaccessible hill, which was heavily defended by the Saudi-backed militia. The tribesmen's local

104

knowledge had been superbly complemented by the military precision of the SAS. Colonel David Smiley, who commanded the Sultan's Forces at the time, wrote of John surveying his men with his habitual air of profound gloom, but that behind his melancholy manner were efficiency and courage as well as a wry sense of humour. When asked if his boys knew what they were supposed to do, John replied: 'Yes, they know what they're supposed to do; God only knows if they'll feel like doing it.' In the event John and his men got to the top of the plateau and persuaded the tribesmen to surrender. With leadership skills like this and his dedication to the country, John was a good choice to head up the Royal Stables.

One day, after a particularly busy morning, I called for a coffee with Gren Gayler. He often worked from home and was usually pleased to have visitors. Today my arrival was greeted with unconcealed relief.

'Thank God you're here,' he burst out as I walked into his office. 'Mac is desperately trying to reach you. Have you been to DDD yet today?' I said I had just got back from Raysut.

'Well you'll have a message there, and another at BATT HQ and at the RAF Mess.'

I was puzzled.

'What on earth is up?' I asked.

'As far as I can gather from Mac,' he said, 'some Under-Secretary in one of the Ministries in Muscat went walkabout with HM in the Palace gardens at Seeb – Seeb's a village about 50 kilometres from Muscat, near where they've built the new airport.'

I nodded. He went on, 'It seems that in conversation, HM mentioned that it would be good to have a few animals in the garden – peacocks, deer and the like.'

He paused and lit a cigarette. 'Have one,' he said pushing the packet across the desk to me. 'You'll need it.' I lit my cigarette, wondering what was coming next. Gren continued:

'This Under-Secretary took HM at his word and hopped on a plane to Bombay. He managed to find some animal export firm, bought dozens of zoo animals and birds, and got them shipped to Muscat. No one knows what he told HM, if anything, but he didn't tell anyone else, neither did any of HM's staff.

'Yesterday,' he paused for effect, 'an Air India 707 arrived and Seeb airport was suddenly filled with crates of weird and wonderful creatures destined for the Palace. Officials didn't dare to question the shipment for obvious reasons. Needless to say, there were no cages for

105

them, no anything. Everyone's in a flat spin up there and Mac wants you there now.'

Gren seemed rather satisfied with my reaction. The prospect of Seeb airport full of zoo animals with nowhere to put them was bad enough. The fact that they had come from India was a further complication. I had a feeling that I was about to sink completely out of my depth into the quicksands of Arabia. My only experience of unusual animals had been a couple of visits to London Zoo, and a few lectures at veterinary school. Exotic animals were not given priority in the undergraduate syllabus in the 1970s. However, I told myself, a professional man should always try to convey confidence, so I smiled wanly and said I would be pleased to do what I could. Gren told me he had already booked me on the next day's Viscount.

I drove thoughtfully to *Umm al Gwarrif* and explained the position to Paddy King-Fretts. He agreed that I must go at once. 'Hearts and Minds also extends to His Majesty,' he said with a smile, turning back to his charts.

Next stop was DDD, where I poured out the story to Robin Butler. She smiled encouraging.

'You'll like Muscat,' she ventured.

I lamented how little information there was to go on and she suggested I should try to ring Maclean. Telephone communication between Muscat and Salalah was, however, very difficult in 1974 and it took half an hour to get a connection. Through the crackles and echoes of the ancient telephone system Mac explained that he had not seen the arrivals himself, but understood they had now been transferred to the Sultan's Palace at Seeb. Around the Palace was a small complex of new buildings and of course the gardens. Gren's boss, the Palace Chief Engineer, Alex Williams, had managed to accommodate the collection temporarily but badly needed advice. Maclean shouted down the line that he was pleased I could get up the next day and he would arrange for me to be met at the airport by John Clarke's Assistant, Tony Brunton.

I spent a long afternoon and evening poring over the few veterinary textbooks we had accumulated at *Bir Bint Ahmed* trying to revise as much knowledge as possible about zoo animals. The next morning, grasping my drug bag and the *Merck Veterinary Manual*, a handy-sized clinical bible with a small section on exotics, I caught the early morning flight to Muscat. It was an excursion into the unknown. Other than the contract officers, many of the British military posted to Dhofar never left Salalah and it was exhilarating to be flying north to see the capital. I realised with a mix of excitement and trepidation that I was facing a quite different sort of challenge. Saleh saw me off with a cheery wave, quite happy to be left in veterinary charge of Dhofar.

The elderly former *Aer Lingus* Viscount covered the 900 kilometres in just over two hours. The aircraft rattled noisily and was uncomfortably full of Baluchi and Omani soldiers going on leave. The British pilot chirpily welcomed us on board as if we were flying to Dublin for the weekend, but instead of a pretty *Aer Lingus* stewardess there was a large, sweaty Baluchi Flight-Sergeant who offered a plastic cup half full of warm orange juice.

We followed the coast east past Mirbat and Sudh, nestling cosily in their shiny blue inlets. Once out of possible enemy range, the aircraft turned across the rocky and bleak Khuriya Muriya islands, with their impoverished and isolated fishing communities, some 40 kilometres from the coast. The seven islands had been ceded to Britain in 1854, but in 1967 were returned to Oman. The Viscount then followed the tracks north across the Great Sandy Desert, known as the *Rub al Khaya*, or Empty Quarter, said to be one of the hottest and most inhospitable places on earth. Endless dark brown or beige rough plains with little human or animal life spread flatly and uninspiringly to the horizon.

As we approached Seeb airport, the aircraft was lifted jerkily by a series of air pockets over the high, bare jagged rocks of Mount Shams, the Sun Mountain, clawing its 3,000 metres to the sky amid the green spots and villages of the stunning Akhdar Mountains. We landed on a long runway laid in an unexciting, brown terrain and the aircraft chugged its way past a gleaming new passenger terminal to an unimpressive old concrete structure, which turned out to be the SOAF building. A couple of Strikemaster aircraft were parked on the apron with a squadron of helicopters and two other SOAF Viscounts. I could see another Viscount in a nearby hangar. We disembarked into the dry, oppressive early afternoon heat of the North. The pilot had warned us it would be 43 degrees Centigrade. It felt like it as I joined the straggling line of passengers as we made our way to the stuffy arrivals area in the dingy building.

Assorted kissing and embracing went on as friends and relatives met the passengers and there was the usual turmoil until all the baggage had been offloaded and safely reclaimed. I looked about for Tony Brunton but there was no sign of him and I had no contact telephone numbers.

I made my way over to the British SOAF Movements Officer.

'Brunton?' he said. 'Yes. That'll be Major Brunton; works at *Bait al Falaj*, SAF HQ. Something to do with quartering, I think.' I explained that my Brunton was someone of about my own age who worked for the Royal Stables.

'Oh, that must be the son,' said the officer. 'I think I met him once at a party. Nice Irish wife.' He made a few quick calls and passed the phone to me. It was Mrs Brunton Senior. She was totally reassuring. Yes, Tony had been to lunch with them and was now on his way to the airport to meet me.

I was relieved to hear a friendly voice although the mention of lunch made me realise that one glass of tepid juice had not done much to boost flagging glucose levels. I sat in the office until Tony turned up. He was a slim chap with fair hair and the slightly swaggering, bandy-legged walk of a horse-man. He was full of apologies for getting the arrival time wrong.

'So sorry about the mix-up,' he said. 'Things are always a bit unpre-dictable here. Follow me, the car's outside.'

We piled into his grey Datsun saloon with Palace number plates. One of the perks of these plates was that Tony could park in the airport's No Waiting areas. This meant the car had been left right outside the terminal doors and under cover, which meant a lot in the stifling heat. Thankfully the Datsun was air-conditioned. We drove towards Muscat for about forty-five minutes making for a town called Muttrah, just outside the capital, where Tony and his wife, Beatty, had a flat. We talked on the way but kept off the subject of zoos as Tony knew little about the problem and was really only interested in the horses. Horses were his life. He had served with the Household Cavalry for three years after working for a racing stable in Newmarket. His parents had been in Oman for years and his father had a staff job as a contract officer with SAF. When the chance came for Tony to work for the Royal Stables, he had jumped at it.

'Be mad not to at this tax-free salary,' he added with a smile.

As we drove along the good single carriageway tarmac road, one could see how oil revenue had enabled a lot of development to take place in the North. The stark landscape in the powerful afternoon sun was harsh on the eyes after the gentle greenery of Salalah. As we passed Wutayyah, a village on the outskirts of the Muttrah/Muscat complex, Tony pointed out the Royal Stables in a shady wooded area of acacia trees near to the road. The horse lines were made of *burusti*, and as we sped past I could glimpse sandy paddocks with some small pretty Arabian horses standing peace-fully or flicking their tails and shaking their heads to remove flies. Tony told me about the new state-of-the-art stables now going up in the Palace complex at Seeb. The massive project was well under way, but a bit of a gamble as no one had tried to build modern stables in a desert before. He, John Clarke and the architects had spent hours with builders, engineers and Palace officials planning and brainstorming and he reckoned the com-pleted project would be fantastic.

Muttrah, which name means anchorage, had been Oman's major trading centre for years. Sultan Said bin Taimur's friend, the American oil con-sultant and archaeologist, Dr Wendell Phillips, described it as the place where the ships of the desert met the ships of the sea. Muscat was next to it on a small peninsula surrounded by mountains, which prevented expan-sion of the capital. Over the centuries, development had occurred at the only place it could. The entrance to Muttrah from the west was marked by rough, black, volcanic rocks from which rose the remains of an old Portuguese fort. The road narrowed as we approached the town, and became busy with lorries and trucks as a sign of the extensive construction work under way.

The Bruntons' flat was in a small, conventional apartment block. Tony parked the car on a rough patch of ground in front of some dreary-looking shops below the apartments. The hot air hit me like a hammer as I got out of the cooled atmosphere of the Datsun and it was a relief to get into the flat where air-conditioners roared reassuringly as they pumped the hot air to the outside through box-like protuberances in the walls.

Tony's wife Beatty was petite, very attractive and Irish. She was extremely welcoming to this invader in the middle of her siesta time. I was fed and watered and after a shower I felt ready to face whatever challenges Muscat was about to throw at me.

The plan was to call and see Mac Maclean and then John Clarke. Both had flats in Muscat. We set off down the main street of Muttrah which was waking up after the afternoon rest. The road was congested with cars, trucks, bikes, donkeys, trailers and men. There was nothing like this in Salalah, which in contrast seemed a dozy provincial town. Tony pointed out the Muttrah *souk*, a vast covered bazaar beginning to fill with late-afternoon shoppers.

The drive from Muttrah into Muscat was along a stretch of relatively new road, called the Corniche, or coast road, which had been built along the waterfront, taking some of the congestion away from Muttrah's bustling centre. The Corniche was a short sweep of dual carriageway facing the large harbour, Port Qaboos, where twenty or so cargo ships were anchored waiting to unload. Dhows were moored nearer the shore and a host of smaller vessels plied their way between them.

The waterfront had been designed with care, with date palms and concrete benches for people to sit and watch the activity in the port. Local boys splashed and played happily in the shallow, clear water at the shore-line. On the other side of the road were ancient, traditional three-storey merchants' houses, many with ancient rickety wooden balconies jutting out like protruding jaws. Old men sleeping and housewives gossiping could be seen on balconies, draped with multicoloured washing drying in the warm afternoon air. The wide boulevard even boasted an Indian café, the Cornish Restaurant, probably not known for its clotted cream and pasties.

The Corniche ended in a small roundabout. From here, the route into Muscat was along a narrow tarmac road, which threaded its way dramatically around the side of the igneous rocks, across the Muttrah pass and over a small hill that led to the capital. It demanded careful driving as the width was only just enough to allow two trucks to pass. On the seaward side there was a low wall, but rocks jutting in towards the traffic presented a further hazard. The road had been built in 1929 by the Muscat Levy Corps and was the only way into the capital. It had provided an excellent defence in earlier turbulent times, but was woefully inadequate for today's traffic.

The road was busy and one could imagine the chaos and frustration that would arise if there was a crash or someone broke down on this 3-kilometre artery. As the road veered inland, we climbed up a steep rock-strewn hill past an ancient power station that sat in the valley to the right noisily generating electricity for the twin cities of Muscat and Muttrah. Then we reached the summit and a stunning view; unbelievably sparkling blue sea, sheer, stark cliffs with a jumble of cramped sand-coloured and whitewashed houses interspersed with modern concrete buildings. Then we were descending rapidly towards the city walls. The city was as spectacular as the sudden view was surprising. It was compact, perhaps only 2 kilometres wide by 1 kilometre deep.

Muscat lay in a horseshoe-shaped inlet surrounded by volcanic rock faces with two imposing and intimidating sixteenth-century Portuguese fortresses on either side. Smaller towers, also built by the Portuguese as lookout posts, were perched at intervals along the ridge.

Right in the centre of the cove and smothered in a shroud of steel and wooden scaffolding lay a massive concrete monolith that was to be the Sultan's new Palace. This dominated the town like a giant's castle, reflecting the sun off the blues, gold and whites of its part-completed mosaic and marble facing.

Muscat became the capital of Oman in 1784, taking over from the inland fortress town of Rustaq. It had been a major trading post for centuries and of strategic importance to the European trading nations of Portugal, Britain, France and Holland. The Portuguese arrived in 1507 and started a brutal period of colonial rule until they were finally expelled in 1650. After an invasion by Persia in the eighteenth century, Oman negotiated a treaty with the British East India Company in 1800. This benefited both sides. It helped the sea-faring Omanis at a time when they had interests in Baluchistan, East Africa and Zanzibar. And it gave the British a foothold on the Arabian Peninsula and helped to keep the French away from India. However, the first four British Residents died in post and perhaps understandably Muscat was considered an unpopular posting for the Company's employees. The encircling cliffs trapped the air and heat such that a nineteenth-century summer must soon have become a disease-ridden oven where smallpox and malaria vied with the climate to kill vulnerable Europeans.

110

The two large, commanding fortresses were called Fort Mirani and Fort Jalali. Each was built on a cliff top guarding either side of the entrance to the bay. Muscat had been known to navigators as the Hidden City, as it was said to be possible for ships to sail straight past without noticing it. Even when spotted, the encircling spiky and craggy cliff faces and the two massive forts bristling with cannons would seem to have deterred all but the most determined raiders, and it was not hard to see how the Portuguese held on to their possession for almost 150 years until finally dislodged by the Omanis in 1650.

Nowadays, said Tony, Fort Mirani was the base for the Royal Guard Regiment in Muscat, whereas Fort Jalali was the city jail. The prison had a gory reputation in Sultan Said bin Taimur's time when inmates were said to have been kept there shackled in grim squalor. It was rumoured that a former governor of Wormwood Scrubs had now been employed to run it more in the style of a British prison.

I was discovering that Tony Brunton was a mine of information. He told me of one Briton who had killed or injured four Omanis while driving when drunk and had recently been a guest in Fort Jalali until a *Sharia* court could hear the case. Under Koranic law, the relatives of those killed were eligible to claim blood money. This man had refused or been unable to raise the money demanded and so had to remain in prison. After six months or so, the Sultan had released him. Many expats now employed local chauffeurs to avoid the dangers of accidents, but experienced Omani drivers were few and far between and in any case, Tony added, you often felt safer driving yourself.

There was an ancient wall around the old city, and even the desiccated remains of a moat. Muscat's main entrance, with its robust, reinforced timber doors, was known as the *Bab al-Kabir*, or Big Gate. Opposite the gate, an Omani policeman stood on a pedestal under a sunshade energetically directing cars, lorries, bicycles and donkeys with as much enthusiasm as his colleagues in Salalah. We went around the policeman and through the narrow gateway where, on either side of the portal walls, a row of ancient wooden benches were crowded with old men, sitting and chatting to each other or silently watching the moving traffic and reflecting.

Until 1970, the gates had been closed at sunset when a cannon boomed across the city and most of the town's lights had been turned out; pedestrians could then only enter the city through a small door and only if they carried a lantern. This old decree was said to date back to nineteenth-century Egyptian laws and had been rigidly enforced by Sultan Said bin Taimur.

The roads inside the walls were narrow and driving was not easy as people meandered across the road with little traffic sense. Just inside the

111

gate on the left was the police station and next to it a small, fairly modern block of flats where Mac Maclean lived. We looked unsuccessfully for somewhere to park in the shade and eventually squeezed among a jumble of cars crammed into an alleyway to the side of the flats. Tony hoped his Palace plates would prevent any problems. We climbed up to Maclean's flat on the first floor and were let into a small, dark sitting room where I was given an ecstatic welcome by the Boxer puppy that I had met in Salalah and which had now been named Rashid.

Maclean, who had risen from an afternoon siesta, was wearing a colourful *longhi*, a sort of sarong. He made tea, lit a cigarette and he told me about the zoo. I was relieved to hear I had a bit of breathing space as so far only birds had arrived, and Alex Williams, the Palace Engineer, had done a good job putting up temporary cages and getting them housed in the gardens at Seeb. Through the complex and mysterious network that Indian merchants in Muscat had operated for centuries, Maclean had tracked down the supplier in Bombay and a telex had been despatched to the Palace's agents there telling them to get hold of a full list of species that had been ordered and to put a block for the time being on any further shipments. Unfortunately, several animals were already on the way and could not be stopped.

Agreeing that Maclean would pick me up from the Stables at Wutayyah the next morning to take me to Seeb, Tony and I left his apartment and headed off to see John and Clody Clarke, who lived in a newish apartment building near the Sidab road.

John clearly relished his post as Director of the Royal Stables and I could see from the banter that he and Tony had an excellent relationship. John was responsible for the horses both at Wutayyah and in Salalah and also for the recruitment and employment of the *syces* and other staff. In addition, he always had to be at the ready in case HM wanted to ride or visit the stables or to show visitors around, which he often did. John was also overseeing the stables' redevelopment project, which included new houses for the stable manager and his assistant.

The next morning Tony and I left the flat at 0600 hours for first stables. John was already there and twenty or thirty *syces*, some in *longhis*, some in trousers, were beginning the morning's routine. It was tranquil under the trees in the pale, pinkish early morning light. The air was quite still with a hint of cool, moist dew. I watched the men quietly go about their work to the occasional shouted order. The horses were bedded on sand in their *burusti* boxes and snorted happily as they woke from their slumberings and began to look forward to their first feed of the day. *Burusti*, the interwoven palm fronds that provided the fabric of houses and walls as well as stables, made excellent, well-ventilated and cool boxes for horses. Water

112

buckets were on the floor of each box and haynets were fastened to the walls.

As the stables came to life, the first string went out to exercise in the scrubland around Wutayyah. The horses were similar to the mixed Arab-bred horses in Salalah. They were small, nothing much over 15 hands, of various colours and some were very graceful. John ran the operation from a trestle table in an open-sided *burusti* unit under a large tree. From here, with his records in a large cardboard box, John issued directions and planned the day. At 0730 the second lot went out. Several British enthusiasts were among the riders, including Tony's sister, and the wife and daughter of the British General Officer Commanding Oman, General Tim Creasey.

Once fed, the horses were tied up outside their stalls so the sand bedding could be mucked out. John asked me to check several horses, rasp some teeth and look at a couple of lame animals. The teeth were far better than those in Salalah where Shenoon fed all those dates. There was one thin horse, which worried me even though it was eating well and the droppings looked normal enough. It just seemed too listless and lethargic. I asked John to let me know how it got on.

By now the air was getting warm and I appreciated the significance of the early start. At nine o'clock, it was time for the breakfast break and the *syces* disappeared to their tents and huts at the back of the stables to cook their morning meal. Soon the smells of spices and curries were wafting through the lines. We drove the short distance to the Army Headquarters at *Bait al Falaj*, in Ruwi, where Tony's parents lived. When we arrived at their whitewashed villa on top of a hill inside the Camp, a hearty and greatly appreciated English breakfast was waiting for us.

There was a large fort in the *Bait al Falaj* complex. This had once been a palace but it was now the centre of Oman's military complex. Next to the fort had been the country's only airport until the new one at Seeb had opened in 1972. It must have been awesome for passengers and a challenging task for pilots to weave their way through the surrounding mountains and to land successfully on the small runway. *Bait al Falaj* was said to have been one of the trickiest landings in the world.

SAF HQ was very different from RAF Salalah. For one thing there were no 25-pounders booming away all day, or helicopters buzzing overhead, or Strikemasters strafing targets on the nearby *jebal*. But there had been no war in the north of Oman since the *Jebal Akhdar* campaign. Nevertheless, *Bait al Falaj* was Oman's Whitehall – the Sultan's forces' central HQ. General Creasey and his staff officers lived and worked here. The Brunton family seemed to know everyone and everything about the military life in the country.

After breakfast, Tony took me back to Wutayyah where the daily routine was continuing with grooming, tack-cleaning, feed preparation and all the other duties essential to the smooth running of any stable. In due course Maclean arrived, this time with his driver, a young Omani/Zanzibari called Yacoub. It was pretty obvious Maclean had little interest in horses and, after fairly cursory exchanges with John, he whisked me off to Seeb in the back of his air-conditioned Datsun.

As we drove, he told me he had spoken to the Sultan about the zoo animals. HM had listened patiently and said he could appreciate that there was a risk of importing diseases. As a result Maclean had been told there would be no further animals ordered until the BATT Vet had reported, but the Sultan had made it quite clear that he did want a zoo in his garden at Seeb, and he wanted it soon. No point in blaming the Under-Secretary, said Maclean, the orders were from the top.

The salt flats and blue sea of the *Ghubbat al Hayl* coast were on our right with the mountains away to our left. Just past Seeb airport there was a roundabout. One route lay ahead, tarmacked for just a few metres before it became a graded track. This road, originally built by the oil company PDO, was the route to the oilfields and the interior towns of Nizwa, Izki and Ibri. Then it became a long desert road offering a dusty three-day drive to Dhofar. However, we turned right to follow the Batinah coast where a series of coastal fishing villages sit next to the sea right up to the borders with the United Arab Emirates. One such village was Seeb, which was reached along a sandy, graded track from the tarmac road. Its prosperity had been boosted by the closeness of Seeb Palace, the Sultan's country retreat. A kilometre or two from the Palace, on a sandy plain, with the Indian Ocean rolling relentlessly against its shores, was the site HM had chosen for his new Royal Stables Complex.

Contractors' vehicles passed back and forth turning the graded road into a series of ridges. Driving down it was like motoring across a very large sandy sheet of corrugated iron. Then, in a shady, walled and guarded oasis, we came to the place where Sultan Said bin Taimur had built the Royal Gardens.

We got out of the car beside large wrought-iron gates, guarded by a couple of *askars* and two razor-creased, unsmiling RG soldiers. Through the entrance I could see a blanket of different greens and a bouquet of colours forming a vista of stunning tropical tranquillity. A path led enticingly into the centre of the garden, which covered perhaps 15 or 20 acres in total. On top of the high stone wall, coloured electric lights had been fixed, offering a night-time contrast to the multi-hued effects of the plants and shrubs.

Maclean, in his grey trousers, striped Jermyn Street shirt and tie, clutching a folder of papers, looked very much the Private Secretary, and we were ushered into the gardens by the old men. One of the RG soldiers threw up a good salute.

'*Salaam alay koom*,' said Maclean walking ahead, with Yacoub and me following behind.

There was a wickerwork pergola smothered in climbing plants, which formed a verdant tunnel for about 100 metres. The gentle, pulsating throb of the water pumps was hypnotic and the atmosphere was pierced only by the unmistakable shriek of a peacock and the soothing cries of doves and other tropical birds. The garden had been carefully laid out, with spacious deep green lawns from where sprinklers played continuously over ornamental shrubs and flowers. Delicate jets of water criss-crossed each other, showering diamonds on the succulent foliage. It was a glimpse of paradise in the midst of an arid sand and cement dustbowl. The scents of jasmine and honeysuckle and other fragrances filled the midday air and I imagined how intoxicating it would be in the still of the early evening with the sounds of exotic birds singing their evening choruses. Maclean said the Sultan came here a lot.

At the end of the enclosed path was a large round dais, with steps made of marble. A fountain played gently in the centre. Maclean explained that when HM was expected, the dais was laid out with carpets and cushions and a stereo system was made ready so he could play classical European and Arabic music. Staff would arrive with drinks, incense and rosewater and he might stay here for hours with his friends and courtiers.

As I continued my garden tour with Mac, I saw how carefully designed aviaries and animal enclosures could fit in well. There were several shallow ponds, with clear, circulating water. Tucked away towards the rear wall of the garden, there was a partly-built concrete compound. Men were hard at work rendering the walls of what was evidently planned to be a large animal cage. A stocky Englishman in shirtsleeves was talking to an Indian foreman and jabbing at a sheet of technical drawings. He saw us and came over and Mac introduced me to Alex Williams, the Palace Chief Engineer. We shook hands.

'Well,' he said, 'what do you think of the bear pit?' This was the first I had heard about bears being on the agenda and I said so.

'Yes,' said Williams, 'HM has two Himalayan black bears and a pair of sloth bears on the way. Don't ask me what they're like, I have no idea. But, until you got here I thought I had better get on and get something built just in case they arrived by the next flight.'

He led me around the garden and pointed out five or six buildings of various shapes and sizes that were either finished or close to completion. He had cleverly positioned them so as to cause as little aesthetic contrast to

115

the main gardens as possible and had knocked down part of the wall at the rear to allow the contractors discrete and rapid access.

'We've got a lot of birds here already,' said Alex, leading me to a completed aviary full of cockatiels, lovebirds, cockatoos, parrots, mynah birds, doves and two stunning blue and gold macaws. The round building had been designed thoughtfully and skilfully by Alex, despite his self-confessed ignorance of animals and birds. The species were separated by partitions and he had put branches inside so they could perch happily and there was plenty of food and water.

'Yes, I know the cages are not big enough,' he said, reading my expression. 'We can thin the birds out as soon as the next unit is finished. Should be tomorrow. I'm afraid quite a lot of birds died,' he added, 'they were packed too tight and sat in the heat on the apron at Seeb Airport until someone finally decided to put them into the air-conditioned Customs Warehouse.'

Despite any shortcomings in the designs, what Alex had achieved was remarkable and I congratulated him sincerely on his efforts. It was a relief to discover there was also a couple of Indian zookeepers. Alex introduced them and I shook hands. They spoke little English but they had arrived from Bombay with the first consignment and it seemed they were planning to stay.

We turned to the designs for the cages. According to Maclean's intelligence reports from Bombay, we were likely to receive in addition to the bears, a pair of hyenas, assorted macaques, desert foxes, a Marabou stork, painted storks, assorted other exotic birds and a pair of mongooses. I took a deep breath:

'Look,' I said, 'if we are certain that more animals and birds are coming, including some seriously grown-up wild animals, we need to have properly designed housing. We also need to work through disease control risks, safety and management details as well as feeding. If we get it wrong with Himalayan black bears then people's lives are going to be at stake. We'll have to devise capture guidelines, both inside the cage itself but also provide SOPs on what to do should the animals escape.'

I then had an inspired thought. We could call in Oliver Graham-Jones. OGJ, as he was known to generations of students, was a lecturer in medicine at the Royal Veterinary College, but earlier in his life had been Senior Veterinary Officer at London Zoo. One of his University responsibilities was to give the handful of lectures on exotic animals to undergraduates. I liked Ollie a lot and had been fortunate to be on his list when he had been

The entrance to *Umm al Gwarrif* Camp where the BATT HQ was located.

Outside the BATT Camp at *Umm al Gwarrif*.

BATT Ops Room at *Umm al Gwarrif*. (*Paddy King-Fretts*)

Typical back street in downtown Salalah in 1974. Already a rebuilding programme was underway that would change forever the almost mediaeval village appearance of the town.

My predecessor as BATT Vet, Major Scott Moffat RAVC.

A visit to Sudh with Scott and the team. Scott is on the left next to the *Wali* and other elders of the town.

The *Wali's* fort at Sudh with the Omani flag flying.

Scott on his last morning in Dhofar saying goodbye to Saleh (centre) and Hafeedth at *Bait al Falaj*.

A Wessex RAF helicopter tasked for a vet mission and piloted by Flight Lieutenant Alek Tarwid, who commanded the detachment to SOAF.

Dispensing electrolyte sachets for rehydration to *jebali* boys on the hill.

The BATT *basha* at Jibjat.

White City BATT camp. (*Paddy King-Fretts*)

Our new *jebali* Veterinary Dresser for two days, Ahmed bin Salim Al Jaboob, at White City.

Firqat gather near water on the *jebal*.

A donkey in Salalah that had just been bitten by an unknown poisonous snake. You can see the swelling at its brisket.

Peace Corps Volunteer, Chris Klotz, still holding a box of antivenom points to the fetus that was aborted following the snake bite.

A *jebali* woman sits minding her goats waiting for veterinary attention.

A goat herder overseeing the watering of his thirsty herd of healthy and valuable goats.

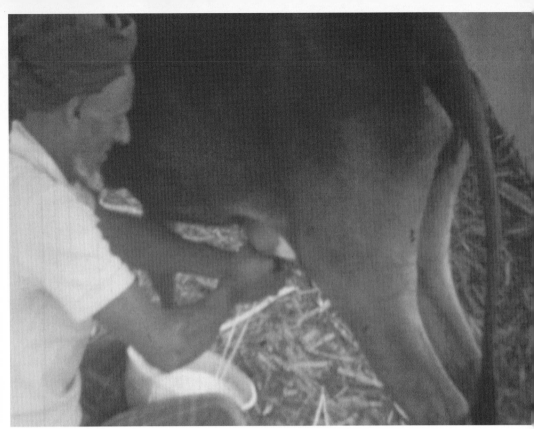

Milking one of HM The Sultan's Mother's *jebali* cows. Most of the milking was done by the men; the cow's hind legs are tied and two quarters are milked together into a bowl clutched between the herdsman's knees.

Saleh picks out the choicest sardines in the Salalah fish market. Those not bought for human consumption will go to feed the animals, including cattle and camels.

Nussum. The use of hot irons for firing the skin of sick animals and people. This was still widely practised in 1974 in the absence of conventional medicine. Here there is a simple horizontal line with two vertical burns along one flank, possibly applied for a digestive disorder; sometimes animals could be severely traumatised. Note how the *jebali* owner is restraining the goat using his toes while Hafeedth injects it.

Ali, a schoolboy who seemed to spend much of his spare time with the Vet Team at *Bait al Falaj*. Here he holds a rather battered and possibly non-functional Martini-Henry rifle in the back of the BATT Vet Land Rover.

A weaver working in Salalah *suq*.

James MacLean, universally known as Mac, Private Secretary to HM The Sultan. Pictured outside his house in Salalah.

A dying horse is put out of its misery with a single shot from a 9mm Browning pistol.

The author, assisted by the Royal Stables' Veterinary Dresser and Farrier, Rasul Bux, completes an autopsy on the dead horse which revealed severe liver damage, sadly not treatable.

Connor McGilligan, the first civilian veterinary officer in Dhofar, performs a rectal examination for pregnancy on a camel in Salalah flanked by Hafeedth and Saleh.

Major John Clarke, Manager of the Royal Stables. John had served in the Trucial Oman Scouts and was a veteran of the 1958–59 *Jebal Akhdar*, or Green Mountain, campaign in Northern Oman, in which the SAS had played a highly significant role in overcoming an earlier internal revolt against Sultan Said bin Taimur. He is pictured with his assistant, Tony Brunton, in his 'office' at the old Royal Stables in Wutayyah.

A Boran bull in the Kenya Highlands and destined for many years' service in Dhofar.

Loading the bulls onto MV *Southern Trader* at Mombasa, Kenya's main sea port.

A young Sahiwal bull *en route* by sea to Salalah and a new life.

MV *Southern Trader* with bull crates loaded and ready to sail for Salalah.

called in to treat a circus tiger with dystocia. He had driven four wide-eyed students at great speed to Birmingham in his Bentley, with a police escort for the final few miles. The man had style and I reckoned he would be the perfect man to advise us. Mac agreed and after a quick look at the rest of the garden and a check that there was enough fresh fruit and nuts to feed the birds we drove back to Muscat.

I first had to clear my proposal with RAVC headquarters at Droitwich, but I did not expect any real problem as Ollie had served as a lieutenant in the RAVC many years before. The five hours time difference between Muscat and Droitwich meant that MOD was just getting into gear when we got through. Mac's dealings with Muscat's primitive telephone system were clearly well honed and soon I was speaking to a staff major in the AVRS Director's office. He calmly listened to my bizarre story, and when I had finished explaining what it was that I needed, he said that he would clear my request and get back to me.

Mac rustled up a sandwich with Rashid yapping excitedly around his tiny flat until he was sent out with Yacoub for a walk. Within half an hour the phone rang and MOD came back to say they were perfectly happy to involve Lieutenant Graham-Jones and they would follow up with further briefing. Would I please send a signal confirming my actions?

I scribbled a list of urgent questions, and thanks to Maclean's influence with the telephone operators I was soon speaking to Ollie at his office in the Royal Veterinary College's Beaumont Animals' Hospital in Camden Town. The line was pretty poor and he thought I was speaking from Moscow rather than Muscat. However, he was extremely helpful with immediate tips for feeding and management of the birds and gave me a lot of useful practical suggestions to prepare for the next batch of arrivals. Best of all, he agreed to fly out himself to advise in person. Mac then spoke to him and assured him the Palace Agents in London, Charles Kendall and Partners of Kensington, would do all that was required as regards air tickets (first class of course) and the issue of a No Objection Certificate. An NOC was mandatory for anyone wishing to come to Oman and was usually only obtainable at short notice with high official sanction.

Mac said I must plan to come back to Muscat when Ollie's dates were confirmed. In the meantime, as long as the holding order on further shipments held tight and the Indian workers continued to look after the existing and anticipated charges adequately, there seemed little more to be done. I asked Mac to try to get the Palace agent in Bombay to get hold of Health Certificates for each of the specimens. At the very least we needed a veterinary statement confirming that the animals were not suffering from any disease or illness when they were shipped and hopefully that they had originated from a part of India relatively free of serious infections.

That night, I went with Mac to the PDO Club. As he had worked for PDO before moving to the Palace and as oil was the kindling on which Oman's financial future depended, Mac was treated well. We talked through the outcome of the day's decisions and concluded we had done all we could for now. I caught the Viscount back to Salalah next morning and Mac said he would signal Robin Butler to get someone to meet me.

Saleh was there as I arrived. He had a big beam on his face. 'Plenty big elephants?' he asked.

'Saleh,' I replied, putting my arm around his shoulders, 'I wouldn't be the least surprised.'

Chapter 13

A Close Run Thing

As the days passed, I found my army duties on the hill were increasingly mixed with civilian work around Salalah. Pet dogs were regular patients too, as British expatriates had a tendency to adopt mangy and unpredictable pi-dogs. It was a rewarding and challenging time professionally, although it took a while to get my head around the sometimes uncomfortable paradoxes presented by, on the one hand, courtiers, parties and tennis matches and, on the other, guns, poverty and goat pox.

Some two months after my first visit, I made a return trip to Sudh. This time I flew with Saleh in an SOAF helicopter with British pilots and without a BATT escort and less fuss generally. This reinforced a quietly whispered consensus that the war was turning our way. The *Wali* greeted me like an old friend and was pleased to tell me that there had been no more deaths and he had issued a firm edict about importing animals from Africa. It sounded improbable but the line between medicine, politics and public relations was so vague that I could only smile and express my delight. We had given the *Wali* a day's notice of our visit this time so I found there were plenty of patients to see and, of course, plenty of coffee to drink.

Government employees are followed everywhere by demands for paperwork and the BATT Vet in Oman was no exception. There were monthly reports for MOD, indent forms to complete for supplies and drugs, memos to respond to, orders to read and letters to write. Sometimes the bumph was challenging, like when Mike Butler passed me a communication addressed to 'THE CHIEF VETERINARY OFFICER' and asked me to deal with it. Who, me? It was from an American company, which had been contracted to import a hundred Holsteins from Arizona into Salalah for a new government dairy farm, currently being built on the outskirts of the town. Would I advise them on prevalent diseases and my current import requirements? I signalled MOD for advice. They suggested contacting the United Nations Food and Agriculture Organization's Near East Animal Production and Health Development Center in Beirut, where there was a British Animal Health Adviser called Dr Richard Wooldridge, DFC and bar.

After long and helpful exchanges of telexes with Dr Wooldridge, and thanks to his guidance, I was able to devise suitable formal import restrictions and forms that I hoped would pass muster. It was one thing to import from Somalia dhows full of sheep destined for slaughter, or even mongooses and hyenas from Bombay for a private zoo at the whim of the Ruler, but it was quite another matter to deal with the formalities of the US Department of Agriculture and get a structure in place for the arrival of high-cost dairy cattle that would be living with and breeding from indigenous livestock.

Thanks to Wooldridge, I was able to make proposals for vaccinating the cattle against some of the diseases I thought might pose a problem, such as anthrax, brucellosis and some of the clostridial diseases such as tetanus. Nobody knew what livestock diseases were endemic in Dhofar, and I could only trawl through my predecessors' reports and make best-guess suggestions in the hope the consignment would survive. I pored over the formidable list of possible diseases and a growing list of vaccinations, but my Peace Corps chum, Chris Klotz, seemed much less worried.

'Relax pal,' he said, 'these Arizona cattle are tough. They'll be just fine,' adding with a smile, '*Inshalla.*'

One day Chris was sitting in my office having tea when Saleh burst in looking alarmed.

'One man outside,' he said. 'Donkey eaten by snake!'

Chris and I looked at each other. Saleh, mistaking our lack of response as a sign that we hadn't understood him, started to repeat his sentence. It was too much and we collapsed in uncontrolled giggles. It was the combination of Saleh's dramatic entrance, the sober pan-faced delivery and the image conjured up. It took a while to recover our composure then, wiping tears from my eyes, I got up and went out with the bemused Saleh.

I felt a bit ashamed when I saw the face of the owner of the donkey. He was clearly worried and told us his donkey had been bitten by a poisonous snake. It was his only means of transport and employment and if it died he would probably not be able to afford another. Chris came up and talked to him in Arabic. The man wanted me to go to his home at once to see the donkey, which he thought had been attacked in the night. An additional cause of worry was that she was pregnant.

There were several species of snake in Dhofar, some of which were totally harmless to humans and animals. Others were not, including the horned sand viper, a small fat unpleasant creature, about a metre long with an odd sideways action that helped it to move across hot ground with minimal discomfort. I had seen a couple of side-winding vipers since I arrived in Oman, usually slithering rapidly away as fast as possible. Chris, working most of the day in the fields, had seen many more species. I had been prudent enough to visit Salalah hospital to scrounge a couple of vials of antiserum against 'Middle Eastern snakes', which I stored in the *Bir Bint Ahmed* fridge just in case.

The man climbed into the back of the Land Rover and we drove to his dilapidated *burusti* house in the centre of Salalah. Inside the yard were a few children and the rather mournful-looking donkey, standing in a corner with her head hanging down and her front legs hobbled together with string. The owner comforted the animal and pointed to her brisket, where there was a swelling the size of a grapefruit. The seriousness of the bite would depend not only on the species of snake, but also the amount of venom that had been injected and where the bite was.

I had a close look at the swelling and could just make out two pinpricks where the fangs had entered the skin. There was a faint trickle of blood oozing from the wound. The inflammation and oedema were the body's best attempt to cope with the bite. The donkey looked in shock so I gave it my stock of antiserum, half by slow intravenous injection and the rest sub-cutaneously around the site of the entry wound. For good measure, I also gave a shot of anti-tetanus and a slug of antibiotics. Chris called me over to where he was standing behind the donkey. He sadly pointed to the ground and bent down to pick up a perfectly-formed donkey fetus, about 20 centimetres long. The shock had provoked an abortion.

A similar case occurred a few days later in the Stables. Tony Jarvis had called me in with a note that a snake had bitten one of the horses. This time the swelling was on the thigh. Discussion between Saleh and the *syces* led to heated debate as to whether it was caused by a snake, a scorpion or a spider. Shenoon pointed to tracks that seemed to clinch the debate, as there was general nodding of heads and agreement apparently that the sting was that of a scorpion. I had never seen a scorpion but I knew there were several species in Dhofar as well as poisonous spiders, including the black widow spider and the long-legged and fast-running camel spider.

It was impossible to tell what had actually happened. Perhaps the mare had been lying down and simply rolled over onto an indignant arachnid. Fortunately, she seemed unconcerned and was contentedly munching her way through a large pile of alfalfa. She wasn't lame and showed no systemic signs. As with the donkey, I gave her injections of tetanus anti-toxin and antibiotics. I told Shenoon to keep a close eye on her for the next day or two, but I needn't have worried. The swelling vanished in a couple of days and I was proclaimed a wise and gifted *tabeeb*.

About this time I decided to make a visit to my Taqah assistant, Ahmed Ali Fat. Scott Moffat had not managed to get to Taqah during his stay and there was very little I could find in the files about the place. All I knew was that 'Taqah Ahmed' made periodic visits to Salalah, usually when he needed to top up his supplies of veterinary drugs. Saleh was delighted at the prospect of a trip to Taqah as his wife's family came from there.

The road from Salalah to Taqah had been mined by the *adoo* for several years and, although contractors had made a start on a new tarmac road, travelling to Taqah still meant either a laborious trip by dhow or heli-copter, or the route we would take, along the beach. I talked it through with Paddy King-Fretts. He liked the idea. BATT had based a team in Taqah until a year or so previously, and now there was a detachment of the Muscat Regiment billeted in a fort on a hill just outside the town. Although there were periodic sorties and attacks, the town was considered relatively secure. Nevertheless, Paddy said a BATT escort with a radio would go with us.

Mike Butler asked me to check on two new bull-pens that were being built in the town, and his Agriculture Officer, Abdu' Sittar Basra, a hugely enthusiastic and competent Pakistani with a sultanic beard and a constant smile, was to come too. Abdu' Sittar talked very fast and incoherently but was very astute and widely respected. He was an energetic man who always seemed to be dashing off to do something. He insisted we set off at precisely 0800 hours so we would make it there and back in the morning and beat the tides.

And so the following day we set off in convoy. In front went Abdu' Sittar driving a smart new Agriculture Department Land Rover with a couple of his staff; I followed at the wheel of the old Vet Land Rover, and the BATT escort Land Rover, with two heavily-armed troopers called Ray and Steve, brought up the rear.

Abdu' Sittar had made the journey many times and I found this re-assuring. When we reached the Salalah Wire, the *askars* waved us off the barricaded road and onto a rough track to the beach, lined by windswept palms. It was low tide. Several vehicles made the trip each day and once we hit the shore I found that despite the early hour there were already half a dozen tracks imprinted in the damp sand.

Abdu' Sittar knew what he was doing. As he drove onto the sand he shifted into four-wheel drive and sped away along the hard sand of the shoreline between the turquoise sea and the sandy dunes. I took a deep breath and followed. The hardest sand was about midway between the high water mark and the water's edge. The recent high tide and the cool-ness of the early morning sun provided a surface that was firm enough to allow steady acceleration. I stuck to Abdu' Sittar's tracks but had several unnerving moments when we hit softer sand and the Land Rover's wheels sank and spun alarmingly for a few seconds until they again got a grip and we resumed the chase. The PSYOPS photographer who was travelling with me told me how a BATT vehicle got bogged down just as the tide came in. It had been at the Salalah end so the soldiers had been able to walk to the road, leaving their pink panther to the mercy of the sea. Although a recovery vehicle got it out next morning, the incident emphasised the importance of getting the timing right for the journey – and the need to take a radio.

We passed a loaded Datsun taxi going hell for leather in the opposite direction. It said a lot for Japanese engineering and the driving skills of the owner to even consider such a journey in a saloon car.

After about thirty minutes, we reached the outskirts of Taqah and left the beach for a trail leading into the town. Once on hard-standing, we pulled up and had a quick conference. Abdu' Sittar had a variety of jobs to attend to and we agreed to rendezvous in two hours' time, which would, he reckoned, give us just enough time to get back to Salalah before the tide came in. He hopped back in his car and shot off in a cloud of dust. Ray and Steve said they wanted to go up to the MR fort and drove off. Saleh said we must call on the *Naib*, or Assistant, *Wali*, who had just been appointed.

Taqah had been self-supporting for centuries. The ancient frankincense centre of Sumhuran was located just to the east of the town and Taqah itself thrived on fishing and agriculture. There seemed to be ample fresh water as there was plenty of greenery – alfalfa, maize, vegetables and coconuts. Two small dhows were at anchor in the tiny harbour. I could imagine how Taqah had developed over the centuries as a small, significant and relatively independent trading centre, boosted by the frankincense trade.

Frankincense. That mystical aromatic resin. The shrub-like tree grows well in Dhofar and its milky sap oozes out of cuts in the bark. The tree is called *Boswellia carterii*, after Surgeon-Major Henry John Carter FRS of the East India Company who identified Dhofar as the world's frankincense centre in the mid-nineteenth century. After the sap is harvested it is dried in the sun and then broken into pieces or ground up. Frankincense has been used widely in religious ceremonies since ancient times and was such an important commodity that the Queen of Sheba's famous visit to King Solomon was thought to have been to negotiate trade routes for her frankincense caravans. Dhofari folklore had it that the frankincense-bearing Wise Man started his journey to Bethlehem from this part of Arabia.

Taqah's *Naib Wali* lived in a newish white house, built in the style of a small fortress. We were shown upstairs to his small receiving room, furnished in a mixture of cultures, and in stark contrast to the very traditional style of his neighbour in Sudh. Two modern three-piece suites stood against the walls replacing the more usual floor cushions. Flimsy coffee tables were strategically placed in front of the seats. The only decoration on the whitewashed walls was the obligatory photograph of the Sultan, slightly askew. A small balcony opened off the room.

We took off our shoes and ammunition belts and I wandered over to the balcony. Beyond the green fields of alfalfa was the gleaming Indian Ocean. A gentle early morning breeze wafted over me. I turned as the *Naib Wali* entered. The others stood up. He was a young man in his early thirties, with a neat black beard.

We sat down and began the meeting with the usual ceremony. Orange juice arrived, followed by bitter tea and Nescafé in tumblers. The *Naib Wali* talked to us softly in Arabic, happily translated by Saleh. It was clear they knew each other. The *Naib Wali* said he was delighted to welcome members of the BATT team who had helped so much to liberate his town. It seemed Ahmed Ali Fat was doing a good job and was popular.

I asked if there were any problems I could help with and the *Naib Wali* said his biggest headache was rubbish disposal. The town had no means of clearing its accumulated garbage and as a result there had been a massive invasion of flies and rats. I promised to relay the message to DDD. The *Naib Wali* thanked me, said he hoped we would make ourselves at home in the town, visit the veterinary pharmacy and join him for lunch. He nodded understandingly when I said that, sadly, we had to return directly to avoid being caught by the tide. Then he sent a messenger to Ahmed to tell him we were here. He rose and smiled and said we would always be welcome in his town.

We left the Land Rover outside the *Naib Wali*'s house and walked to Ahmed's place. Taqah was a small town and it didn't take long. Ahmed was waiting for us. It was good to see him again and, as he spoke excellent English, it was possible to get a very clear idea of how things were going. He unlocked the large wooden doors of his pharmacy and we went in. It was immaculately kept. Drugs were stacked in an orderly fashion on the shelves and Ahmed proudly showed me his record book, where he had filled in the entries in English as well as Arabic. The book suggested that he saw three or four cases a day. We talked through the recent cases but there was nothing too surprising: stomach disorders, the odd lumpy goat, mastitis and lameness prevailed.

Ahmed sat us down and brought some cold Cola from the nearby shop. Saleh asked me if he could go and see his wife's family and I agreed, but told him we could not wait for him if he was not back in an hour. Ahmed then walked me round the small town. He took great pride in pointing out the red light district. Actually, it was less of a district, more one house; even so it was the only one I had heard of in Dhofar. Two Zanzibari ladies leaned out of the window and made what I guessed were interesting proposals with peals of raucous laughter.

The town's beaches were carpeted with acres of sardines drying in the warm air with the sun's rays dancing off the silvery skins of thousands of fish. But the pungent smell permeated every part of the town. We walked through small alleyways with piles of rubbish littering every street, just as the *Naib Wali* had warned. I asked Ahmed why the town had got into this state. He replied that the old *Wali* had been a Said bin Taimur man and no one in the government had really bothered about Taqah for years. With the war, there had been no incentive to make an effort about anything other than survival, water and food. Now the Sultan had appointed a young, educated man as *Naib Wali*, things were expected to change soon. He added with a knowing look that if His Majesty decided to visit Taqah he was sure there would not be a tin can to be seen.

The town market was in full swing. We joined about a hundred people milling around the dozen or so traders, selling meat, fish, fruit and vegetables. The butcher caught my eye. He squatted on the ground with the remains of a goat around him and would cut bits off as his customers required. He then prepared the flesh by placing one end in his mouth and used his knife to work the meat into stringy strips and remove tendon and gristle. The man grinned at me and offered me a slice. I grinned back and told him I was sure the meat must have a very special flavour. Ahmed said the price of meat was very high but everyone loved the taste so every morsel was sellable.

With time at a premium, we headed to the outskirts of the town to see the bull-pens. These were good solid structures, just like the ones at *Bir Bint Ahmed*. I thought they would serve their purpose well and hoped the bulls would too.

Ray and Steve were already waiting in their pink panther with the engine running when we arrived at the rendezvous point. Saleh was there too and a few minutes later Abdu' Sittar screeched to a halt beside us. He gabbled away about not missing the tide, then, crashing his gears in his eagerness to be away, shot off towards the beach. We piled into our vehicles and set off in pursuit. It was now about eleven o'clock and I could see we were cutting it a bit fine. Already our inbound tracks had been covered by the incoming tide. We sped furiously towards Salalah and got about halfway when our luck ran out.

Saleh, who was travelling in the back of the Vet Land Rover, thumped on the roof and yelled at me to stop. I found some relatively hard-standing sand and drew up, flashing my lights frantically at Abdu' Sittar who was racing on ahead. I looked back and saw the BATT Land Rover stationary about 100 metres behind us; Ray and Steve had got out and had the bonnet open. I eased into reverse and slowly backed up with the PSYOPS photographer trying to predict where the safest sand might be and calling out directions.

The BATT vehicle had a perished radiator hose and a steaming radiator. We had reserve water in my vehicle and somehow Ray got the cap off the radiator without seriously scalding himself. When he poured in the water we all watched silently as it sprayed out through the holes in the rotten tube. There was a good bit of cursing, particularly when we realised that neither vehicle was carrying a spare hose. I dived into my vet kit and produced a roll of Elastoplast, which we wound round the leaky pipe. Depressingly, this only held the water for a few moments before it was saturated and the water poured out again as readily as before. In fact by fiddling with the perished rubber we managed to enlarge the holes and aggravate the leaks.

The sea was fast approaching and we had no more fresh water. I realised there was no alternative other than try to tow the BATT vehicle back to Salalah. We looked at each other and the truth dawned on us. Neither vehicle had a towrope.

Ray raised his eyes to heaven and sighed deeply. 'I'll radio HQ,' he said. 'If necessary we'll have to push the sodding thing above the water mark and recover it later.' He swore colourfully.

He grabbed the radio and he and Steve stomped off to the top of a sand-bank to call *Umm al Gwarrif*. Despite stories of ambushes between Taqah and Salalah, there was no sign of life beyond the beach and although Saleh was beginning to look anxious, I only felt in danger from the encroaching ocean, which was already beginning to lap around the wheels of my vehicle. My thought process was interrupted by some heated exchanges between the two BATT guys. It was clear that the radio was not working either. Why do they say troubles always come in threes?

'Fucking thing worked perfectly this morning,' said Ray. 'Tested it myself. Now it's gone one hundred per bleeding cent U/S.' There had been a power leak and the battery was totally flat. The radio operated on a different voltage to the Land Rover's so we could not connect it to that power source.

During all this activity, Saleh had laid out a small mat and was praying. As if in answer to his prayers, we heard the drone of a Skyvan. Five pairs of eyes swivelled skyward. We spotted the aircraft ambling like an over-weight bumble-bee towards Salalah from the east. We all waved frantically at the pilot, trusting that he would realise the problem seeing the bonnet up on the pink panther. It worked. He reduced height, circled us once, waggled his wings at us and drifted on towards Salalah.

'Well, at least the Boss will know all about it,' muttered Ray morosely. 'I know someone who's going to get a hell of a bollocking for this. Two weeks' frigging pay.'

The noise of the aircraft had masked that of a fast-approaching car. It was the returning Datsun taxi we had passed that morning. He stopped and Saleh greeted him enthusiastically. The driver got out of the car, looked at the stricken vehicle and shook his head sadly as Saleh explained our string of mishaps. They walked together back to the Datsun, there was some animated discussion, the driver opened the boot and I could see Saleh's face break into a very wide smile. The smile stayed in place as he hurried back to us carrying a towrope. The Taqah taxi driver had magnanimously lent us his lifeline. He climbed back into the Datsun, waved and roared off, eager not to push his luck with the tide.

There is another common expression in Arabic, *Al hamdu l'Illah*, which means 'Thanks be to God'. It was often used when one of my patients recovered or when things generally went well. Subconsciously the five of us muttered it as Ray and Steve rapidly fastened the stout rope first to the towing ring on the front cross member of his vehicle and then to the trailer hitch point on mine. Ray sat behind the wheel of his vehicle and Steve and the others got into the back of the Vet Land Rover to weigh it down. We set off slowly and warily and, at crawling speed with the sea beneath our wheels, we finally reached the Salalah turn.

As we pulled onto the track leading to the checkpoint we saw a huge army recovery vehicle and SAF Land Rover parked at the side. We got out and spoke to the drivers. Yes, the Skyvan pilot had radioed that there was a broken-down army vehicle on the beach; yes, they were just debating whether to risk a rescue; and yes, he was pleased it wasn't now necessary.

I decided that the Vet team would make a quick exit and we left Ray and Steve to sort out the repairs. Later, at prayers, Paddy King-Fretts was not amused. He said nothing, just looked straight at me. We both knew the message was clear. Although only attached to the Squadron, we all should have double-checked and ensured we were properly prepared for the journey. I hadn't, trusting completely to the professionalism of the BATT guys. Was that good teamwork? Was it hell. Ninety-nine times out of a hundred, it works. It is that hundredth time that sinks you. I guess we all learn from experience.

Chapter 14

His Majesty's Zoo

Things were fairly quiet at the Royal Stables in Salalah. I called in most days when I was not on the hill. Tony Jarvis was increasing his authority and there were changes and improvements in the day-to-day stable duties. John Clarke and Tony Brunton were hectically busy in the north as the new stables neared completion, and must have been relieved that an enthusiast like Jarvis was able to keep an eye on affairs in Dhofar. Among the innovations and improvements, he had managed to get wood shavings for bedding. I was delighted with this as it removed much of the risk of sand colic. He got the bedding from a building contractor but they could not guarantee that the shavings were free of nails and other bits of metal, which could cause serious problems. As a result, hours were spent by the *syces* sifting through sackloads of chips before the bedding could be laid in the boxes.

Gren Gayler had been asked to put up a new fodder store and to roof the wooden boxes with a double layer of corrugated iron sheeting to increase insulation. The standard of tack-cleaning had always been good when John or Tony Brunton were around, but tended to slacken off when they were in Muscat. Not any more. Leather gleamed, brasswork shone and stainless steel sparkled like newly-minted coins. The horses looked impressive too, as Jarvis had not only introduced a daily inspection but also an incentive scheme with a packet of cigarettes going every morning to the *syce* with the best turned-out horse. The Indian grooms had adapted well to the new regime but I could see that old Shenoon, who had bounced baby Qaboos on his knee, resented being bossed about by this *Inglesi*. I knew that Tony hoped to quit his job as Dhofar's Civil Liaison Officer for a full-time position with the Palace as Salalah Stable Manager, and I suspected Shenoon's era was drawing to a close.

One evening, after prayers, Paddy King-Fretts came up to me and handed me a signal. It was from John Clarke and read: 'THIN HORSE MUCH WORSE STOP GRATEFUL YOUR ATTENDANCE STOP CLARKE.'

'Looks like it's back to Muscat for you,' said Paddy. 'Bloody good life you vets have in the military. Here am I stuck here fighting a war and one of my officers is up and down to Muscat partying and having fun with all the nobs.'

I pulled a sympathetic face and told him it was all in the line of duty helping Queen and country. He laughed. 'Sultan and country at any rate.' Then, anticipating my next question, 'OK, I'll get you on tomorrow's flight.'

The timing was good as Ollie Graham-Jones was scheduled to arrive any day to sort out the zoo. I went round to the Butlers' house and called Maclean at home.

'I was just about to contact you,' his distorted voice crackled down the line. 'Your zoo man is arriving the day after tomorrow.'

I yelled back that I was coming up the next day to deal with a horse for John Clarke. Would he be kind enough to ask Tony Brunton if I could stay for a day or two? He said he would do what he could and thankfully I replaced the receiver.

'The jet set vet,' commented Mike Butler to his wife. 'When we get our civilian vet he will not be working for the Palace; strictly DDD only. Tell John Clarke from me that he'd better get his own vet from 1st May.'

'Have you got someone for here?' I asked interestedly.

He nodded. 'Irishman called Connor McGilligan. I got a telex confirming his acceptance this morning. He's been working in Ethiopia. He used to be in the RAVC too,' he added.

It was quite a shock to realise that in another few weeks I would begin handing over. I had been in Dhofar for only a few months but I had become infected by the buzz of Oman and immersed in the work, and I would be sad to move on so soon. I thanked Mike for letting me use his phone and I went wistfully back to the Mess.

Next morning I was on the plane to Muscat. To my surprise Mac Maclean himself met me at the airport.

'I was up at Seeb Palace seeing HM,' Maclean explained as he walked with me to a bright orange Datsun coupé parked outside the SOAF HQ. He gestured at the car. 'I've arranged for you to borrow this for a few days. It's a bit small but it should do to get you and Mr Graham-Jones around the place.'

I inspected my new wheels and fiddled with the air-conditioning, cassette player and electric windows – quite a contrast from the dilapidated old Land Rover I had been used to in Salalah.

'You drive,' said Mac, climbing into the passenger seat.

I had noticed that the car did not boast Palace number plates and I asked Maclean if it was a Palace car.

'Certainly,' he replied. 'But as you are not on the staff, you have to drive on civil plates. Come on, let's go.'

I slipped into gear and sped off towards Muscat. The road was fast. We passed a couple of accidents on the way. There may have been a camel to coupé revolution over the past three years, but driving skills were still evolving.

I asked what news of the zoo.

'Well, the second batch of animals has arrived,' he said. 'Though what His Majesty wants with hyenas and everything else defeats me.'

'Has Alex Williams managed to accommodate them all?'

'Somehow, yes. But I can't think what your friend will make of it.'

Maclean said it had not been easy getting Ollie Graham-Jones to Muscat. The first problem had been for Ollie to extract himself for several days from his University duties. Then, two days before the flight, he discovered that his passport had expired. Kendalls, through managing director John Kendall's highly capable and efficient PA, Eileen Harris, had worked every angle to get the passport renewed in twenty-four hours – and succeeded.

Ollie was scheduled to arrive the following day and Maclean had got him a room in Oman's only modern hotel, the *Al Falaj*. This was hard as the hotel was always fully booked – often for months in advance. Reservations were unreliable and many weary travellers had staggered in after a long flight from Europe to be told that the Ministry of Foreign Affairs or some other government department had requisitioned twenty rooms for a visiting delegation. If the hapless traveller was lucky, he might get a sofa in the overcrowded lounge.

We reached the big gate into Muscat, and I indicated left. A smart Omani policeman stood on his plinth with his back to me. Treating his podium like a mini-roundabout, I drove round the policeman towards the gate, negotiating bicycles, pedestrians and a donkey cart. This decision turned out not to be a good one, as suddenly a shrill whistle sounded.

'Stop,' said Maclean sharply. I stopped. The policeman had brought all traffic to a halt and I saw from my mirror he was leaving his dais and making for us.

'What have I done?' I asked Maclean.

'You drove past him before he waved you on,' he said wearily. 'They can get very officious and I think you have found a difficult one.'

I wound down the window and smiled hopefully, but instead of the usual polite exchanges I had grown used to in Salalah, I received a stream of invective in Arabic.

'Licence' was the one word I understood. I looked at Maclean.

'Have you got a licence?' he asked.

'Only an SAF one,' I replied.

'Give it to him,' he said quietly. 'We'll sort it out later.'

I opened my wallet and removed a rather tatty piece of folded red cardboard, which contained my army details, a photograph and, as was required on all Oman military licences, my thumbprint. The policeman pointed through the gate towards the police station and I gathered he wanted me to park and report there. He tucked my licence into his pocket and marched back to his pedestal. By now there was considerable congestion and a lot of shouting, hooting of horns and ringing of bicycle bells.

I parked outside the police station but Maclean led me to his flat, 50 metres away, saying he preferred to deal with things from there. He told me to fix a drink and picked up the telephone asking for the Deputy Commissioner, Colonel Brian Cooper. He explained the situation and, after a few minutes' discussion, relayed the information that I could now collect my licence.

I murmured my thanks and apologies, grateful for the efficiency and action of the old boy network. In 1974, the Royal Oman Police was still largely officered by British ex-Colonial Service policemen, many having retired after careers in Hong Kong or Singapore. The Director-General of Police, Felix de Silva, was Ceylonese and was a powerful man in this embryonic country, running the police force efficiently and effectively on a paramilitary basis.

As Tony Brunton was away, Maclean had arranged for me to stay with Chuck Pringle, the British Managing Director of the construction company Yahya Costain. Chuck had a modern villa in a tiny cove called Kalbuh, just outside the Muscat walls on the road to Muttrah. We drove there after I had rather sheepishly recovered my licence from the Indian desk sergeant at the police station.

Chuck was in his thirties and had run Costain's operation in Oman after spending several years in Dubai. He had designed and built a striking house beside his office in this tiny, hidden and charming inlet, which was reached by driving along a narrow, bumpy passage between ancient Omani houses. Children played on the beach as the sea lapped languidly on the sandy shore. Beyond the bay, a flotilla of ships waited patiently at anchor to get into Muttrah's port, which was hidden from view behind a large wall of rock to the west. We parked the Datsun next to Chuck's Mercedes and, as his houseboy opened the door, a handsome Samoyed and an exuberant Wire-haired Fox Terrier, which I later learned were called Romeo and Pilotte, leapt out joyfully to meet the visitors.

The house was imaginatively designed and air-conditioned. A fountain played in a small pool in the entrance and a spiral staircase of pink marble wound upwards over the pool to the first floor. The ground floor was open-plan and looked airy and comfortable. Outside the Palace, I had seen nothing like this in Oman.

131

Maclean said with barely concealed pride that he was having a similar house built next door. 'I never asked for it,' he said. 'I've lived in that one-bedroom flat for years, and then suddenly HM asked me why I didn't have a house. Within six months I'll have one like this.'

I drove to Wutayyah for evening stables. John Clarke was relieved to see me and led me to the thin horse that I had seen barely two weeks previously. It was no longer just thin, but pitifully emaciated. Only three years old, it was now a bag of bones. I looked in its eye and the mucous membranes and white sclera were tinged with yellow. The mouth was also jaundiced.

'Looks as if the liver's packed up,' I said to John. 'Is he eating?'

'Just picks at his alfalfa,' he replied. 'He's had no real interest in anything, let alone food, for the last week or so.'

I told John there wasn't much hope. I asked: 'Is there a chance we can get a blood sample analysed in the hospital?'

John thought it was possible so I took samples and we drove to the American Mission Hospital in Ruwi where I explained the problem to a friendly consultant. He said I could have the results the next day but he wouldn't want to interpret them. As we left, John turned to me.

'I'll bring my revolver tomorrow,' he said gloomily.

I nodded. 'Anything else you want me to do whilst I am up here?' I asked.

'Could you castrate half a dozen stallions?' he said. I agreed, and we decided to make a start early the next day.

Chuck Pringle was reputed to have the best cook in Muscat. He was Goanese and I soon learned that he lived up to his reputation as we all sat down to what Chuck called 'a little snack' but which was prepared with the skill and care of a Savoy chef.

Later, as I gazed over the last lingering light dimming gently over the bay and the shimmering Gulf of Oman, I decided the stay in Kalbuh would not be something to explain in too much detail to Paddy King-Fretts, currently on the hill in a rat-infested *basha*. I also thought I wouldn't mention my large, comfortable, cool bedroom, with its sunken bath and marble floor.

Next morning, I called in at the hospital on the way to the stables. The blood tests were conclusive. The horse had liver failure. He appeared a bit brighter but I knew this was only due to the fluids I had injected the previous evening. John had already had a pit dug in the scrub beyond the stable area, so we quietly led the horse there and I swiftly despatched it. We buried the horse and I put its death down to toxic hepatitis, possibly due to ingestion of some noxious plant or other poison. I took samples and a few weeks later the lab reported 'cryptogenic cirrhosis'; in other words the liver had packed up for unknown reasons.

After a wash, a drink of Coke and a cigarette, I turned my attention to the castrations. I had been warned that there was often reluctance in the Middle East to castrate male animals, even though entire horses are less easily handled, especially in stables where there are rival stallions as well as mares on heat. It was encouraging that John had persuaded the Sultan to reduce the number of stallions and keep only those likely to be good for breeding. He told me that my predecessors had gelded a number of horses, always with the animal standing. It was evident that this is what he expected from me. I was still barely a year out of veterinary school and had never done a standing castration; the few horses I had gelded had been immobilised and conveniently lying on their side. Many vets prefer standing castrations, as it is fast and simple; local anaesthetic is injected into the testes through the scrotum, the skin is cleaned, painted with an antiseptic, a twitch is applied and an incision made with a scalpel. The testicles are removed one by one, instruments applied firmly to stem bleeding and that more or less is that. The trouble was that these were not yearlings but five- or six-year-old stallions.

The *syce* led up the first patient. A strutting grey stallion with a fulsome mane, massive balls, and looking remarkably full of himself. Feeling just a little apprehensive I sorted out my kit. I was now committed, and in any case I was determined to teach myself the standing procedure. I gave the stallion a sedative, had a twitch applied, and got a bucket of water ready to wash the surgical site with antiseptic scrub.

I will never know if it was John Clarke's, or indeed the *syce*'s odd sense of humour to select that particular horse to start with, but in the next few seconds, as I leaned round to gently grasp the testicles to clean them, the horse took me closer to death than I had ever been in the war zones of Ulster or Dhofar. With a squeal and a furious squirm, and totally ignoring the heavy dose of sedative I had administered, he shook aside the groom holding the twitch, put his head down, hunched up his back muscles and kicked back both hind legs with such ferocity that I felt the wind ruffling my hair as the hooves passed within a millimetre of my forehead. I was bowled over onto my back with my legs in the air, bucket and sponge flying and my carefully laid-out instruments clattering to the ground. The *syce* meanwhile was struggling to prevent the beast galloping away into the distance, bucking and rearing in fury at my audacity.

I decided that was enough of surgery for one day. I told John I would not be performing standing castrations after all and would signal MOD for a knock-down anaesthetic that would immobilise the animals and preserve my dignity if not my life.

When I had stopped shaking, John asked me to examine a mare for pregnancy. It was one of the Sultan's favourites, he added. Apparently when John and Tony had both been away, she had been accidentally covered, more than likely, I thought, by that precocious bloody stallion with the big bollocks.

'It's the horse he rides most,' said John. 'If she is pregnant I'll have to tell him he can't ride her for months. Not a happy prospect.'

She was an eye-catching little mare, about 15 hands high and an attractive dark chestnut colour. I gently slipped my arm into her rectum and soon felt a well-developed head floating like a lump of wood in the fetal fluids in the uterus below.

'About eight months, I would say,' I told John.

He looked glum, but later told me that when he told the Sultan the news he had solemnly asked how it had happened. John had to explain that he was terribly sorry but she must have been caught by a stallion when he had been away in Salalah. The Sultan's face had creased, the eyes twinkled and he had laughingly said, 'Then you will have to find me another horse to ride, Major Clarke,' and walked off chuckling.

As Mike Butler asked, I told John that DDD had appointed a replacement Veterinary Officer who would be starting in a couple of months and that Mike did not envisage him working also for the Palace. John had enjoyed his relationship with the six BATT Vets. He reflected for a moment and then said there was only one thing for it; I must apply to be the Palace Vet.

I left the stables close to lunchtime. Maclean had told me to meet him in his office in the old palace, an ancient whitewashed building in the centre of Muscat. The administration of the *Diwan*, or court, was run from here while the new *Al-Alam* Palace was being built on the waterfront. Although the Sultan rarely went into the *Diwan*, preferring to operate from his Palace at Seeb, most of his staff worked from Muscat, close to the embassies, Ministries and offices. This split court meant officials like Maclean spent a considerable amount of time on the road between Muscat and Seeb.

The Royal Guard were posted around the Residence and Maclean came to the gate to get me. Inside, his office was large, whitewashed and comfortably cool. The old Omani buildings with their high ceilings, open windows and metre-thick walls seemed to keep out much of the intense heat. Maclean had a large desk at one end of the room under a picture of Sultan Qaboos. Nearby, his Indian clerk, whom he introduced as Hamid, typed busily onto parchment thick notepaper with a large red crest at the top. Two old ceiling fans rotated slowly and erratically, wafting the air and softly rustling the papers. One wall was stacked high with boxes labelled 'Asprey', and in a corridor were dozens of Harrods crates. To the side of Maclean's desk was a telex machine, which coughed into life every few minutes and spewed out its staccato messages. With the poor telephone system, and a decade before fax machines became popular, the telex was the main means of communication with the outside world.

I sat down opposite Maclean and he apologetically returned to a signature book of letters he and Hamid were preparing for the Sultan to sign. A Pakistani servant in immaculate whites brought in coffee. Office hours were 0730 to 1300 and on the dot of one o'clock, Hamid got up to go, putting his last letter in a folder for Maclean to check before politely saying goodbye and leaving the two of us alone. As the building emptied, the Residence became quiet and calm, with the only noise being the soft turning of the fans and the scratch of Maclean's Mont Blanc fountain pen.

Through the open window I could hear the *Moazzhin* begin to chant the *Azhan*, the mystical call to prayer that has rung out from the mosques five times a day for more than a thousand years: '*Allah Akhbar ... Ash hado Allah elaha ellalah ... Ash hado an na Mohammadur rasulalah ... Allah Akhbar ...*' – 'God alone is great; there are no gods but God; Mohammed is his prophet; come to prayer.' The call was echoed around the town through loudspeakers on top of the mosques; the sounds reverberating in the hot still air.

'That's enough for today,' said Mac, getting up and putting the folders into his Gucci case and screwing the top on his fat pen. 'Let's have some lunch before we meet Mr Graham-Jones.'

We walked back to his flat through the intense heat of the early afternoon sun. As we ate a quick sandwich, I filled him in on my activities at Wutayyah that morning and we planned the itinerary for Ollie before leaving for the airport.

Ollie came in on the shuttle from Bahrain, in a slow propeller-driven Fokker Friendship. Mac and I watched from the airport lounge as the passengers disembarked. Ollie was one of the last to get off. Despite the heat he was dressed in a dark worsted three-piece suit.

Immigration Control was slow at Seeb, as everyone's entry had to be checked by the relatively inexperienced police officers who manned the desks under the watchful but discrete control of a British senior officer. With a war in the country, the snail-like procedure was understandable but still frustrating. I appreciated the simplicity of RAF Salalah and the absence of formal immigration controls for arriving British military personnel. Maclean and I waited outside the Customs Hall and eventually we spotted Ollie queuing behind two or three others waiting for his baggage to be checked.

'Oh Lord, do you see what he's got?' said Maclean, suddenly pushing his way through the crowd and reaching in his pocket for his Palace pass. Ollie had innocently bought a couple of bottles of spirits at Heathrow and was about to clank up to an earnest-looking Omani Customs Officer. The import of alcohol was strictly prohibited and, if spotted, Ollie's liquor would be confiscated, and there would be further delays and embarrassment. For the second time in two days, Maclean had to act to salvage a British vet from embarrassment with the Omani Police. I saw him speak to the customs officer, doubtless telling him that the gentleman was His Majesty's guest. I saw the man look speculatively at Maclean and his pass, and then at Ollie, as he worked through the alternatives. Then he expressionlessly chalked a mark on his suitcase and suddenly they were both beside me, Ollie still clutching his duty-free bag.

It had been a long day for poor Ollie. The flights had taken over ten hours with tedious changes. He was hot and flustered and hadn't expected to be suddenly whisked through Customs by a strange, white-haired Scotsman with a red face. However, I made the formal introductions and in no time we had loaded the bags (and gin) into my orange Datsun, squeezed ourselves in and, grateful for the car's air-conditioning, I drove the party to Ruwi and the *Al Falaj* Hotel.

Ollie and Mac hit it off at once. Ollie could be hugely entertaining and he soon launched into a story of an old man in the first-class compartment who wanted to pray as they were flying somewhere over Turkey. The problem was where to find Mecca. The stewardess had to ask the Captain for the right direction, and the man then prostrated himself across the aisle. The other passengers had to wait for the second course of their lunch until he had finished.

We dropped Ollie at the hotel once Mac had double-checked that there was still a room for him. Ollie was more than ready for a shower and change so I drove Maclean back to his flat and, after calling in at evening stables at Wutayyah, rejoined my refreshed visitor to take him to Kalbuh for an evening with Chuck Pringle and his Goanese master chef. Ollie marvelled at the sumptuous meal laid on for us all. Chuck was a great host, as always, and it was nights like these that reinforced my now confirmed feeling that I could get used to this life.

I was not very effervescent next morning at 0730 when I collected Ollie from the *Al Falaj*. Ruthlessly, but with enterprise, freely using the name of 'the Palace' and 'Mr. Maclean', Ollie had managed to block persistent attempts by the hard-pressed receptionist to persuade him to share his room with a couple of stranded German businessmen.

We spent several hours looking round the Royal Gardens, checking the inmates and studying the plans and technical drawings that Alex Williams had produced since my last visit. We now had a full list of the animals so could judge accurately what was needed. Looking around the garden, Ollie felt that if one could start from scratch, it would be marvellous to design and build a state-of-the-art zoo with proper planning, layout and design, but this would destroy forever this peaceful haven.

However, our priority today was the mammals – sloth bears, Himalayan black bears, a striped hyena, a desert fox and some small frightened macaque monkeys, which had all arrived since my last visit. Following the embargo no more deliveries were expected. All of the animals had travelled in crates and about half of the macaques had died on the way; the rest had been kept in their crates for a couple of days until the enclosures had been finished. Alex had done remarkably well. True, the cages were not ideal – how could they be? Yet, given the circumstances, each was functional. Ollie immediately advised how to provide environmental enrichment for the animals – branches, toys, water pools, and even tyres hanging from the ceilings. Food could be put in hiding-places to stimulate the animals to look for it, preventing boredom and to minimise the risk of stereotypic behaviour developing.

Ollie was particularly anxious about the bears. Sloth bears are by nature solitary creatures. Here we had an adolescent male and female, and Alex had understandably placed them together in a semi-circular, well-shaded display area with a cleverly-designed water feature in front. It was reasonably sized, with different levels for the animals to climb and a hiding/sleeping area where they could relax. Happily, the young bears got on well together. Ollie reckoned they were probably litter-mates, and with the absence of competitors and plenty of food, he felt they were unlikely to show aggression towards each other. It was rewarding to see them playing and I hoped the sibling love would last.

Sloth bears are so named as their long claws resemble those of that upside-down mammal, the South American sloth. In their natural forest and grassland habitats in India, sloth bears like to eat nothing more than termites, and they use their claws to probe the nests. They have a gap in their front teeth so they can suck up the insects. Termites were in short supply in the Palace Garden, but Ollie told us the bears would be perfectly happy with fruit and maize. He said that the sloth bear's gall bladder is coveted in traditional oriental medicine and in some countries they are killed just for this trophy. Watching our couple frolicking in the dappled sun, we lamented man's strange desire for such worthless placebos.

The Himalayan black bears were of similar size to the sloth bears, but had black shaggy coats and distinctive white 'V's on their chests. The male was larger than the female, about 150 kilograms in weight, I guessed. Their thick curved claws, designed for climbing trees, looked daunting and Ollie encouragingly told me the breed was known for its aggression. Like the sloth bears, Himalayan black bears were also prized for their gall bladders and other bits of their anatomy, and were still used as dancing bears in parts of Asia. Alex had housed the Himalayan black bears in a smaller but sturdy enclosure. He listened carefully to Ollie's advice about the need to have a foolproof capture area and how to modify his design for the safety of the keepers, whose task it was to feed, clean and look after these wild animals.

Next we studied the carrion eaters. There was an ugly black Marabou stork that stood about 1.5 metres tall, with a pink flabby neck, long beak and grumpy attitude. The keepers had wisely clipped his wings before releasing him, so he stomped disagreeably about the pool, chasing the ducks and anything else that got in his way. He was fed chunks of meat, as was the spotted hyena, who was the sole and sad occupant of a small cage nearby. He padded up and down restlessly, not understanding his confinement. The Bengal fox was an even sadder sight as she was a slight, attractive animal with a pale coat and big ears, but bolted in terror to the back of her cage whenever anyone approached. Both of these animals should have had mates but these had died during shipment.

For the remaining birds and primates, Alex had put up a five-sided enclosure with triangular cages and a central handing area. With branches and foliage, a single unit was just about OK for a handful of lovebirds, or two macaws, say, but not enough for a troop of frightened macaques. With Ollie's advice, we did what we could to provide enough shelter and hiding-places but we badly needed a different sort of building and set to work on a design.

I spent the afternoon in Chuck Pringle's office typing out Ollie's report for him. The recommendations in his clear, neat longhand included the need for new buildings as well as sensible advice on feeding and management. He also advised that a zoo curator and a Palace Veterinary Officer should be appointed as soon as possible. I delivered the report to Mac and we talked the concepts through over dinner. He said he would see it reached the Sultan. Mac said he also wanted to introduce Ollie to the President of the Royal Court, Lieutenant Colonel Said Salem Al Wuhaibi, as he felt he would give added weight to the recommendations.

Next day, after a long unhurried breakfast, and at last having some time to ourselves, I took Ollie for a tour of the sights. I also wanted to see them myself. We started in the Muttrah *souk*. It was an elaborate maze of shops and stalls, far bigger and more intricate than Salalah's market. The hustle and bustle was exciting; Arabic music blared out from radio shops, smells of exotic spices filled the air; money-changers sat at their desks; typists using vintage typewriters wrote letters for people; there were barbers, shoe shops, gold shops, gun shops; there were pawnbrokers and tailors; coffee shops and food shops; one could buy *khunjas*, Maria Theresa dollars, onyx lamps, rare and exquisite scents, bikes and car parts, books and lavatory brushes. Everything seemed to be available in this buzzing hive of activity. We were enthralled. Ollie bought a gold charm for his wife and a couple of souvenirs for his two boys while I just revelled in the atmosphere.

138

From the *souk* we drove to Muscat. Maclean had told me to take Ollie to the British Embassy to sign the Visitors' Book. The British had the oldest and largest mission in Oman and the Ambassador's Jaguar carried the prestigious number-plate CD-1. The Embassy was a modest but impressive colonial building, in a prime position on the waterfront beside the new Palace, and under the shadow of Fort Jalali. Someone once wrote that it had 'one of the noblest verandas in the world' in a city that Lord Curzon described as 'the most picturesque in the East'.

Nearby was the American Embassy and for years it had been a matter of national pride that the Union flag flew higher than the Stars and Stripes. Then, one day (so the story goes), high winds caused the US flagpole to snap. When it was replaced, the Americans ensured that their flag flew at least a metre higher than the Union Jack. This had confounded the British for a while until it was pointed out that the height of the flagpole was irrelevant. It had been the custom for centuries for trading and naval ships visiting Muscat to paint the names of their vessels in large letters on the steep, jagged rocks surrounding the town. As a result, on both sides of the forbidding 200-metre cliffs were inscribed in large white letters scores of ships' names, including HMS *Surprise*, HMS *Hardinge* and HMS *Seahorse* (which called at Muscat in 1775 when Mr Midshipman Horatio Nelson commanded the name-painting party). Sultan Said bin Taimur called the cliffs his 'marine autograph book'. The crew of one British ship, HMS *Runnymede*, had the idea of painting a coloured Union flag next to the vessel's name. This Union Jack was still clearly recognisable and, as it stood well over 100 metres above sea level, it gave the British ambassador great satisfaction to point it out to his American colleagues. Britannia still ruled in the question of flag ascendency.

Ollie's last social engagement was dinner at the *Al Falaj* hotel to meet Colonel Said Salem. Mac arrived with the Colonel, a cheerful Omani with a respectable midriff over which he wore an enormous gold *khunja* – clearly the larger and more elaborate the *khunja*, the more important the wearer. The Colonel told us that His Majesty was very pleased with Ollie's report and would give serious thought to a new zoological garden. He had been asked to thank Mr Graham-Jones for his very practical help with the garden at Seeb and His Majesty hoped he would soon return to Oman. Ollie beamed with delight and Said Salem presented him with a solid gold Rolex inscribed with the Sultan's crest – 'as a small token of His Majesty's gratitude'. We all applauded and a bemused Ollie got to his feet and gave a short speech to say what a privilege it had been to visit such a wonderful country and he hoped he had managed to contribute in some small way.

It was a touching end to a successful trip. The next day I took my adviser to the airport for his trip back to the UK, the Royal Veterinary College and his final year students. I thanked him for dropping everything to help me out, but I was certain he had loved every minute of his brief two-day stay. Having seen Ollie off, I drove next door to SOAF to catch my Viscount back to Salalah, BATT and the Dhofari animals.

As I flew south, I mulled over the prospect of being Palace Veterinary Officer. If I was offered it, would I take it? I was still only twenty-five and barely out of college. In any case, I was only halfway through my army Commission. Fate would have to take its course.

Chapter 15

White City

I never did discover why the bleak settlement in the Eastern Dhofar *jebal* called *Medinat al Haq*, or 'town of truth', some 25 kilometres north-east of Salalah, was known to the military as White City. One of the SOAF guys told me it was named after a Captain White who was the first pilot to land there successfully when it became a settlement after Operation Jaguar in 1971. What was undisputed was that White City was of considerable strategic importance and had been a strong operational base during the war, largely because the powerful *Bait Ma'asheni* tribe was prominent in that part of the *jebal*.

The Sultan's mother was a *Bait Ma'asheni*. Princess Mizoon was the daughter of Sheikh Ahmed Ali, and was chosen by Sultan Said bin Taimur as his second wife in about 1940. Tony Jeapes tells how at the time of the betrothal the *Bait Ma'asheni* did not think Mizoon's marriage settlement was enough and removed the lovely young bride into the depths of the *jebal*. Another tribe gave chase, caught the raiding party and returned the Sultan's betrothed to Salalah.

When I visited White City with Hafeedth, I found it to be a place of transition and full of activity with a company of Royal Engineers and some civilian workmen busily drilling wells, erecting wire fencing, replacing prefabricated huts with brick CAT buildings, and generally working to transform it into a permanent settlement. White City and the other key location to the south-east, Tawi Atair, were often completely cut off during the monsoon but it was military policy that both should be fortified and occupied throughout the year to prevent the *adoo* regaining a foothold.

As always on the *jebal*, there was a need for water but although the engineers had drilled 200 metres, they had so far failed to find a source. One small borehole existed but was rapidly drying up so an alternative supply was urgently needed. Tom, the BATT troop leader at White City, took me down to see the cattle trough. Water that had once flowed freely was down to a trickle, and although there were a few inches of water it was covered in green algae which also coated the floor and sides of the trough. Water was tactical. If there was no water, there would be no animals, and if no animals came the tribesmen would pass by and there would little value

141

in having a permanent settlement, however important it might be strategically. So the sappers continued to drill.

The sun was beginning to set as we stood by the deserted trough. I suddenly heard a rumbling sound, faint at first then growing in intensity and accompanied by a distinct vibration. Tom backed away looking behind him as I turned to see a hundred thirsty goats cantering towards us at a cracking pace. They split either side of me and dived for the slimy water, drinking greedily. Some jumped right into the trough in their eagerness to get a drink. The old, the lame and the heavily pregnant animals brought up the rear. *Jebali* goats were prized as the best-tasting and hardiest of animals and commanded premium prices both in Salalah and on the hill, where a ready market was available in supplying the *firqats*. No wonder the local people wanted water for them.

A few moments later a woman appeared. She was dressed in black and her face was covered with the typical *jebali* women's stiff facial mask with slits for her eyes. She carried a camel stick and an aluminium bowl and, totally ignoring us, followed her goats to the trough where she joined them, quenching her own thirst by scooping water into her battered bowl from the murky green depths.

Sunset was watering time. As we stood there, two further herds, each forty or fifty goats, thundered up pushing and prodding for space at the trough as the herds mixed in a confusion of bleating and shoving. The woman who had arrived first was angry at the arrival of two other herds and waded into the midst of the newcomers, lashing out with her stick and shouting coarsely at the other women, who responded equally robustly as if tribal rivalries also extended to goat herding. Eventually, animals and humans drank their fill and the women settled for an uneasy peace with only the occasional insult barked half-heartedly across the scrub. The goats began to wander away and the women called to them, and to my surprise they all regrouped into their own herds before gradually disappearing into the valleys for the night.

It would take more than a couple of hours to refill the now empty trough and I could see why DDD had given the hugely expensive drilling operation such a priority status.

Hafeedth and I were to stay two days at White City and the BATT camp briefly became our home. There were several tents and a *basha* solidly built into the side of a ridge and reinforced by sandbags. Tom's team was made up of a typical four-man unit. The idea behind this formation is that each man brings different skills in support of the team. One team member was often 'the medic' and would lead on medical problems, although in fact all four would have far more than a basic knowledge of first aid. The BATT Medics often worked in difficult conditions, treating a variety of ailments and diseases, and even delivering babies. Medical assistance was part of

142

the original strategy for Operation Storm, along with veterinary and agricultural development and the whole psychological thrust to persuade the Dhofaris to back the Sultan. The BATT medical services played a pivotal role in the battle to neutralise the PFLOAG influence.

There was a tiny hut with a white door on which was painted a red crescent, a symbol of medical care in the Islamic world and the equivalent of the Red Cross in the West. Inside, the BATT Medic, whose name was Sean, saw his patients. In White City, as elsewhere, the Qara people once they had come over to the Sultan's side trusted the BATT Medics but had little time for the semi-trained medical assistants, mostly from Egypt or India, who were being sent to replace them. It was something of a dilemma for BATT, whose time in Oman was finite, for if the Medic refused to help and insisted the patient saw the assistant, relations with the locals could deteriorate fast. It required a delicate balance that could be further complicated by my arrival as the animal *tabeeb*.

Sean was a young, well-educated soldier in his mid-twenties and could not be more unlike the popular view of an SAS stereotype. He might have been a schoolteacher or an aspiring city executive. Over endless cups of tea we discussed medical and veterinary treatments we had given in Dhofar, as well as his thoughts on the war. He had cultivated a respect for the *adoo* who, he cautioned, were well-trained, well-armed and fiercely determined, particularly when under pressure like they were now as the tide was turning. But despite the many successes of the Sultan's forces, the *adoo* still exerted a powerful influence over sizeable numbers of the *jebali* people. He then added a word of warning:

'The *adoo* are formidable shots,' he said, 'and any soldier on the hill should never let his attention slip. Snipers are out there and blend into the scenery. Always be on your guard and never trust your eyes. When they tell you there's no hostile intent, remember there just may be.'

Another tip from Sean was always to shake out my boots and clothes before putting them on. Scorpions and spiders had a nasty habit of creeping into shady, cosy places at night and generally resented the arrival of a large foot.

We sat and ate our rations contentedly as the red sun set over the hill. The food vaguely resembled risotto and made a change from soup or dehydrated mashed potato and corned beef. Hafeedth and I were to sleep in a tent next to the medical hut. This was a relief, as the sandbagged *basha* looked hot and uncomfortable. The *basha* was also infested with a variety of animal life, including several large rats, which the BATT boys seemed to get used to. I was less adaptable. I dumped my kit in the tent and thought it would be wise before it got too dark to unpack some of the gear ready for the next day of veterinary clinics.

Hafeedth had gone off to talk to some local *firqats* as we wanted to recruit a young *jebali* to train as a veterinary assistant with a view to establishing a permanent staff member on the hill. As White City was known to be fairly friendly with plenty of *Bait Ma'asheni* around, Mike Butler thought it might be a good place to find someone who wanted a career. The value of having a *jebali* on the team could be considerable.

The stars were beginning to appear as I stooped down to open the tent flap. As I stepped inside, there was a sudden furious swirling of fur and teeth and claws as, quick as lightning, an animal that looked like an angry dog spun round to face me from the far corner of the tent. My heart thumped like a drum roll in my chest and I was stunned into momentary paralysis by this unidentified creature, which seemed to be all jaws, tail and glittering eyes. The pause lasted only a fraction of a second as the animal, baring its teeth in a ferocious grimace, saw freedom beyond the tent flap and dived straight for me. I leaped aside and he was through the opening in a flash and away into the *jebal*.

'What in Christ's name was that?' I asked Sean, who had followed up behind me.

'God knows,' said Sean. 'Hyena or fox maybe. Friendly-looking chap, wasn't he?'

It all happened so quickly and in the dark I didn't really get a good look at it. Later I wondered if it might possibly have been an Arabian ratel, also known as the honey badger, an aggressive mammal that was reputed to inhabit the Qara hills. They are said to attack anything that threatens them, and if it happens to be male, they have a disturbing tendency of directing their powerful jaws directly at his balls. They eat anything from fruit to lizards, as well as small mammals and birds. They will even dig up carcasses, including human remains, of which there was no shortage on the *jebal*. Understandably, they have very few enemies, apart from other ratels. There was more than the *adoo* to watch out for on this green hill of Arabia.

The morning after my experience in the tent, Sean asked me to take a look at the foot of a young British sapper who had sliced it open on a tin can near the BATT *basha*. He was a robust and cheerful soldier, eighteen or nineteen years old, and not particularly perturbed about his injury. Sean had already cleaned up the wound and the bleeding had largely stopped.

'It's quite deep,' Sean said, 'but the edges are neat enough so I won't stitch it; some strips will keep it closed and I'll dress it.' Turning to me, he asked, 'What do you think about tetanus?'

Tetanus is a nasty disease caused by bacteria that form spores outside the body. These spores can live for years and can be found almost anywhere – in the soil, on thorns or in droppings. Once the bacteria get into the body they release powerful toxins that attack the nerves causing stiffness, spasms and eventually, if not treated, respiratory failure and death. The jaw is often affected early, which gives the disease its nickname 'lockjaw'. Soldiers were routinely vaccinated against tetanus but, as anti-body levels wane with time, it was often a good idea in the case of wounds and injuries to give a shot of tetanus antitoxin.

'Well,' I said, 'the tetanus bug loves warm countries and I reckon the risk is above average here. Have you got any antitoxin?'

'Yes,' replied Sean, 'there's some in the fridge but I've never used it before. I'll fetch it.'

He went off to the hut and I looked at the sapper's foot, which Sean had cleaned up well. I asked the soldier if he had recently had a tetanus injection and with predictable teenage squaddie awareness he replied, 'Aven't a clue, Sir.'

Sean came back, opening the pack and reading the insert that gives details of administration, dose, precautions to be taken and so on. He swabbed the soldier's bum and gave him the intramuscular injection. Then he skilfully bandaged up the foot and the sapper hobbled back to his unit. Ten minutes later he was back. He looked flushed and was shaking.

'I feel really ill,' he said. Sean told him to lie down in the Medical hut. I went with them.

The boy couldn't stop scratching himself. 'I've come over all itchy, Sir,' he said, beginning to look worried. He was sweating profusely, was very flushed and was beginning to wheeze. It didn't look too good.

'Anaphylactic response,' I said to Sean. 'He must have been allergic to the antitoxin.'

Sean kept his cool. 'OK mate, you're not going to die,' he said to the young soldier. 'Stay calm and we'll soon get you sorted.'

Sean took me outside. 'What do you reckon we do about this?' he asked.

'Give him a shot of adrenaline,' I said, 'and follow up with an anti-histamine and a corticosteroid. Most allergic reactions are self-limiting.' I added quietly, 'Let's get some oxygen too.' However, there wasn't any oxygen.

Sean started to fix the injections and I took off the boy's shirt. He was covered in a lumpy rash and the itchiness was driving him mad. It was as if he had rolled naked in a patch of stinging nettles.

'Have you ever had anything like this before?' I asked.

'No Sir,' he sobbed, scratching his rash furiously and with his tear-stained eyes rolling around the tent.

'Sean will give you something to help and let's see if we can ease this rash. You've reacted to the anti-tetanus jab but it'll be over soon,' I promised.

Symptoms can often be made worse by fear, so it was important to keep the sapper as composed as possible. As Sean gave the injections, I ripped open some pads and applied cool water and wet towels to his red body, which seemed to bring some relief.

The patient began to relax as he realised he was not dying and the adrenaline began to have some effect.

'What do you think about casevacing him?' asked Sean.

'Well, the rash will wear off quite quickly but he's in a state. He'd be happier down at FST. Shall I tell Tom?'

'Yeah, let's go for it,' said Sean.

I found Tom and told him what had happened. A casevac meant calling in a helicopter at short notice to remove a wounded or sick soldier. He got on the radio at once.

I then went over to the small RE unit camp to find the troop commander, a young captain of about my own age. He had no idea what had happened since the sapper reported sick with a bleeding foot an hour earlier. Having detailed another soldier to get the lad's kit together, he came back with me to see the patient who was now calm but pale and the itching was beginning to subside. The thought of a trip to Salalah may have helped. Sean decided to go with him just in case there was a relapse and within half an hour we heard the sound of a Huey. Soon Sean and patient were on their way to the FST.

Hafeedth and I stayed at White City for another night and Hafeedth successfully recruited a seventeen-year-old *jebali* assistant, Ahmed bin Salim Al Jaboob, to work with us. He was proud of his protégé and took him completely under his wing. Hafeedth had been Number 2 Dresser for so long he relished having someone he could be responsible for. Sadly, it didn't last as Ahmed's nomadic instincts proved to be too compelling and after only two days at *Bir Bint Ahmed* he disappeared, presumably back up the hill.

A few days after returning from White City, I called to see the sapper at his unit HQ in *Umm al Gwarrif*. He had been discharged a few hours after admission to FST and was completely back to normal apart from the dressing on his foot. He looked a bit bashful.

'Sorry I got meself in a bit of a state up there Sir,' he said. 'I was in a right tizzy.'

I told him I would have been just the same and I thought he had behaved impeccably.

'Just always remember,' I said, 'you're allergic to tetanus antitoxin. And don't ever let a vet recommend treatment for you again.'

'No Sir,' he responded with a smile. 'And thanks.'

A few days later, on Friday 12 April 1974 to be precise, BATT was shaken by the death of Simon Garthwaite at the hands of the *adoo*. He was twenty-six, and although we had only met a few times at *Umm al Gwarrif* and *Tawi Atair*, I liked him immensely. He was gently-spoken, friendly and, as Tony Geraghty recalls, his magnetism was considerable. It needed to be, as he worked closely with the *firqat*, in particular the *Firqat al Umri* who were based in the area between Tawi Atair and Mirbat. Simon was the second Royal Irish Ranger to be killed in action with the SAS in Oman – the Fijian Sergeant Talaiasi Labalaba BEM had died two years before in the famous defence of Mirbat.

Paddy King-Fretts told those of us at evening prayers what he understood had happened to Simon on that fateful Friday. I was stunned by the news and everyone was deeply upset. The Squadron was still mourning the loss of Lance Corporal 'Curly' Kent, who was killed in action on the hill just before I arrived. We all dispersed silently and thoughtfully after the briefing, each to seek his own reflective solace. I went to my room in the RAF Mess and lay on my bed for hours, watching the fan rotate.

The citation on the webpages of the Royal Irish Rangers in 2011, thirty-seven years later, sums up what may have happened:

Captain Simon Garthwaite, 22nd Special Air Service, was the officer in charge of the British Army Training Team attached to Firqat Al Umri in The Oman. On 12th April 1974 a force consisting of elements of the Muscat Regiment, Sultans Armed Forces, Firqat, and elements of the British Army Training Team were deployed on a wadi clearing operation. The operation commenced once the Muscat Regiment's picquets were in place and the Firqat under Capt Garthwaite commenced their search. Contact was made with a group of the enemy in 5 or 6 well-prepared positions in the wadi bottom. They were armed with SKS and AK47 rifles and at least one light machine gun. In the initial contact the Firqat leader, his Sergeant Major and a Corporal were killed outright. Captain Garthwaite was seen to charge forward onto the area of the heaviest fire to give cover to the remaining members of the Firqat who were withdrawing. He was last seen firing his M79 grenade launcher and engaging the enemy at point blank range. The position was retaken in the follow up and it was evident that, although wounded, Captain Garthwaite had continued to fire his weapon until he himself was killed. For this action in complete disregard for his own safety, Captain Simon Garthwaite was awarded a posthumous Mention in Dispatches.[1]

---

1. See: www.royalirishrangers.co.uk/role.html

Chapter 16

Court and Social

The social event of the Salalah calendar was the annual party thrown by the Manager of the British Bank of the Middle East, Norman Jackson. A large man of ample girth, 'Norman the Bank' was probably only in his early thirties, but he was one of those individuals who has been middle-aged since childhood. A product of Manchester Grammar School and a confirmed bachelor, Norman, who looked and talked like the great character actor Robert Morley, had been in Oman for years and the April BBME party was something everyone looked forward to before the onset of the annual monsoon, or *khareef*.

I had met Norman a handful of times, but was surprised to get an invitation to 'A Roman Orgy', with a line to say that fancy dress would be welcomed. It was to be held at Norman's house, which was next to the Bank, beside the old Palace, just inside the walls of the town. Mike Butler was away, so I offered to escort his wife Robin. Invitations were coveted among the British serving and SAF contract officers and there were plenty of mutterings in the various Salalah Messes from among those who had and who had not received one. SAS would be well represented as Peter de la Billière was paying a brief visit accompanied by the Colonel Commandant, The Right Honourable The Viscount Head GCMG CBE MC, a former Minister of Defence. Invitations for the two VIP visitors had been readily issued.

Lord Head had supported the SAS from its very beginning and was said to have been a close friend of the Regiment's founder, David Stirling. I was scheduled to see him officially the following day and Paddy had asked me to show him *Bir Bint Ahmed* and the Royal Stables. Fortunately, the Muscat Regiment would be providing transport, so the statesman could be spared the BATT Vet Land Rover. It did seem a bit odd to be meeting him first at a Roman Orgy.

When Robin and I arrived at the party, there was already a large number of cars parked outside – Range Rovers, Mercedes, Datsuns and an assortment of military vehicles. The guests, British and Omani, entered Norman's *bait* through a side door and stepped into a courtyard, which had been lit by a striking chain of coloured lanterns suspended from the walls. Large bunches of plump Lebanese grapes and other Bacchanalian decorations hung about the yard, making the atmosphere as enchanting as any Roman orgy could possibly be.

Magnificent in a rich blue toga with a laurel wreath crowning his large head, Norman greeted his guests at the entrance. As we entered he extended a regal hand to me and kissed Robin effusively on both cheeks before wafting us into the courtyard to join the other guests. Many had come in fancy dress; there were gladiators from the Muscat Regiment, centurions from the RAF, gentile slaves from the housewife sector and even a scribe from *KJ* Regiment. A cowboy had also turned up but nobody minded. There were representatives from all the divisions of the British community – commercial, military and political, as well as Dhofari merchants and businessmen.

Alcohol flowed – cocktails, wines, beers – demonstrating Norman's negotiating skills. Expatriate residents were allocated a monthly alcohol allowance which they could spend at Spinneys the Salalah Cold Store, the one Western shop in Dhofar (apart from the NAAFI), housed in a building that looked like a Nissen hut. The licence had to be produced and endorsed by the shop whenever a purchase was made. Norman had evidently over-come these constraints but, as most of the major merchants (and the Palace) banked with BBME, he could hardly have been better placed.

I spotted Paddy King-Fretts with some senior SAF officers over in a corner. They were not in Roman dress and were talking rather stiffly with a man in his late sixties, whom I took to be Lord Head. It looked as if it could be rather heavy going. Paddy caught my eye and waved for me to come over. I made a face as if to say 'Who, me?' and shook my head deferentially. This produced a response that lip-reading told me could be roughly translated as 'Please come here right now.' Robin vanished into the middle of a party of merry centurions so, sighing, I sidled up to the VIP group, grabbing a rather un-Roman whisky on the way.

Peter de la Billière was having a cheery time with some of the *KJ* men, but when he saw me he peeled off to shake me by the hand and say hello. This was gratifying for a junior officer, but he always seemed to find time for his men, even loosely attached ones like me. He also had a considerable curiosity and was keenly interested in the work of the BATT Vet. I was happy to fill him in on my varied duties thus far.

Paddy came over. 'Ah, Lord Head,' he said, grasping my elbow and steering me towards his guest in a determined way, 'I'd like you to meet our Veterinary Officer, Andrew Higgins.'

Lord Head farmed in Wiltshire and appeared to have a genuine aware-ness of the work of DDD and my role on the *jebal*. Soon we were joined by the CO and we had started to discuss the significance of the water troughs at strategic locations when my arm was suddenly clutched in a vice-like grip. I turned to Lord Head, who had gone a deathly white colour. His glass slipped from his fingers and fell with a crash.

'Oh dear,' said the Colonel Commandant, 'I'm most dreadfully sorry. I feel rather weak.' And with that he slid to the floor in a complete collapse. At that precise moment there was a loud shout from the entrance.

'Where's Caesar?' came the cry in unison from the three army Medical Officers posted to the Field Surgical Team, as they made their dramatic entrance, dressed as Roman senators, clutching their togas, made from green surgical drapes, and brandishing home-made swords. A loud cheer went up from the partygoers.

By now, I was kneeling over Lord Head's prostrate body looking for a pulse, with Paddy beside me loosening the Colonel Commandant's tie. Somebody then noticed us in the corner. The laughter died rapidly and, as heads turned, the party chatter was replaced by murmurings of sympathy and curiosity. After their spectacular entrance, the doctors lowered their swords and came over with more professional demeanours.

'I think he has just fainted,' I said.

'Carry him through to my bedroom,' boomed Norman, who was hovering nearby.

We put the unconscious peer on Caesar's bed and I willingly left him in the care of the RAMC senators.

'For once the medics arrived on time!' someone said as Norman and I went back into the courtyard. This broke the ice and soon the general party buzz resumed. Before long, the word went round that the SAS Colonel Commandant had recovered and had been taken back to the Mess. He had been exhausted after the long flight, followed by the double challenge of the Dhofar heat and Norman's powerful cocktails. The next day, when I saw Lord Head at the farm, he apologised for his undignified exit, adding that he thought he must be in the next world when he had come round to find three Roman senators tending him.

A couple of days after the party, the Sultan and Royal Court returned to Salalah and once again the Province moved up a couple of gears. With His Majesty came the black servants, of course, and with them their Harrods dogs. By now, the puppies of January were growing into strapping and energetic pre-pubescent adolescents and I was pleased to find that they were looking well and, importantly, happy. They seemed to be loved and well-kept by their masters.

One morning, during my rounds of the dogs, I found Loqman in a distraught state. His Dalmatian, Mac, had been chasing an alley cat along the balcony of the old family house. The dog had misjudged his footing and fallen 3 or 4 metres to the ground. Now he was dolefully holding up his right front leg, whining with the pain of his injury.

I knelt down, and with Loqman holding him tightly and affectionately, I gently examined the leg. There was no doubt, it was broken. The force of the impact as the dog had landed with his front legs extended had caused a chunk of bone to sheer off the end of the humerus at the elbow. Mac looked up at me with large, wet eyes. This needed surgery, but *Bir Bint Ahmed* was a livestock farm and, although it had a small laboratory and rooms for minor procedures and autopsies, it was not geared up for small animal orthopaedics, and there wasn't even an X-ray machine. The only realistic option I could think of was to ask FST if we could use theirs. The RAMC Colonels had always been helpful when I ran out of dressings or drugs and were necessarily well geared up for radiography, anaesthesia and surgery. I gave the dog a sedative and a painkiller and told Loqman to keep him very quiet until I got back. I sped off to the RAF Camp and went straight to the FST office.

The FST resembled MASH in the TV series set in a US Mobile Army Surgical Hospital in a forward line medical treatment centre during the Korean War in the 1950s. The wards were in wooden huts, mostly cooled by fans but a few rooms had air-conditioners. The anaesthesia unit and operating theatre were also in a hut, but the rest of the hospital was in brown or camouflage canvas tents. There was an emergency treatment tent, which could be brought into use rapidly following a major incident. Next to it was the X-ray tent and a laboratory tent. The Colonels and the dedicated RAMC orderlies ran a tight and highly professional operation; and their presence was extremely reassuring to all British military personnel in Dhofar who knew they would receive the best possible treatment speedily, efficiently and effectively. It was said that the SAS only agreed to be deployed in Dhofar on the understanding that a field surgical team would always be available. FST could also be used by the British expatriate community in Salalah when operational demands permitted.

The OC was an orthopaedic surgeon. He was in his early forties, well-built and with the sense of humour one would expect of a man who could enter a party wearing a toga and yelling for blood. He was only too willing to take on the challenge of operating on one of the royal dogs and, as the day was quiet, he suggested bringing Mac in at once and he would rally his troops. That was just what I wanted to hear. I drove to Loqman's house and we returned in his new Mercedes, with me cradling the dog on my knee. After the formalities of introducing the courtier to the FST team, we discussed the fracture.

'I hope you realise,' one of the surgeons said to me, 'that this theatre was completely re-sterilised yesterday. Do you see any irony in having a dog as its first patient?'

'Just think of the Rolex!' I winked at him.

I anaesthetised the dog and we took X-rays of the elbow. I looked at the plates with the surgeon; there was a clear and definite fracture.

'Hmm,' he said, 'the anatomy's a bit different but it's a bit like a paediatric fracture. Should hold with a screw. Let's get on with it.'

As the two surgeons scrubbed up, I passed a tube down Mac's wind-pipe, which was then joined up to the anaesthetic machine. Loqman watched anxiously from the side of the hut.

It was unreal. Three army colonels and a vet operating on an anaes-thetised Dalmatian undergoing orthopaedic surgery in a field surgical unit on a sandy plain in South-East Arabia. The Sultan himself couldn't have had better attention. With the occasional question about the anatomy of the canine elbow, the surgeon made his incision and with a glance or two at the X-ray plate on the illuminated screen on the wall, he soon identified the fracture, inserted a screw and sutured the wound. We took another X-ray and saw the stainless steel screw clearly visible securing the severed condyle back in its rightful place.

Mac was lifted off the operating table and, with a couple of post-operative injections to prevent swelling and infection, I loaded the sleeping patient into the back of the Mercedes and Loqman drove us gently home. I carried the still sleeping dog into Loqman's house and into his bedroom where we settled him on a large, scented cushion on the floor. Loqman had tears of gratitude in his eyes. I told him to keep Mac very quiet and to stay with him and nurse him carefully until he came round, and I would be back later in the day to check how he was.

When I returned, I also brought the before and after X-rays to show Loqman. He asked to keep them as he knew His Majesty would be inter-ested. I am sure he was, as a rumour soon went around that HM planned to visit FST. Yet sadly it never happened and the Colonels never got the Rolexes they so deserved for their vital contribution to Operation Storm.

Dealing with the Sultan's animals involved more than treating horses and dogs. Just outside the village of Awqad Bait Fadil, between Salalah and Raysut, was a small, ancient tower about a kilometre from the road. I had noticed the tower as I drove to and from the harbour, and concluded that it was a watchtower that at one time must have been sited on the boundary of Salalah's perimeter fence. One day, as we were returning from the quarantine station, I noticed a number of cattle and goats clustering around the base of the tower. Something was not quite right about these animals, but they were too far away for me to make out what the problem was, so I decided to go over and take a look. We spun off the road and bounced along a bumpy track until we reached the tower.

As we approached I could see that the animals were starving. The land was a barren salt flat with no water, grazing or shade to be seen. A dozen or so desperately thin *jebali* cattle and thirty or so emaciated goats stared at us as we drove to a halt by the tower. Six or seven of the goats were exhausted and lay on their sides panting as their wasted bodies tried to lose some of the heat which was soaking into them from the day's strong hot sun.

Hafeedth disappeared into the tower and reappeared with a young boy, who was yawning having been woken up from a morning snooze. He was about fourteen and smiled at us. Saleh and Hafeedth began the interrogation and eventually the story emerged.

It transpired that the boy's father was in charge of the animals but he was not there at present. The cattle and goats were in a bad condition because the food lorry, which was supposed to come every day with fresh alfalfa, hadn't been for over a week. A water bowser also used to come but had not appeared for several days. The boy's father had strict orders to keep the animals here by the tower. He had gone to Salalah every day for the last few days to try to get someone to listen to him about the problems. I told Saleh to ask the boy who was the owner of the animals. Why, His Majesty of course, came the reply.

With a bit more prompting from Saleh, the boy described how, at Oman's last National Day, several Qara tribes had made gifts to the Sultan of cattle and goats. What we were looking at was the remains of one of these gifts. It looked as though the herdsman had simply been unable to penetrate through to anyone with the authority to listen and take the necessary action. The food would come, *Inshalla*, said the boy.

I drove to the old Palace and managed to get in at once to see the President of the Royal Court, the affable but powerful Lieutenant Colonel Said Salem Al Wuhaibi, whom I had met in Muscat with Ollie Graham-Jones. I explained the dilemma at Awqad Bait Fadil. The Colonel listened carefully, getting distinctly upset as I told him the full extent of the situation. Finally there was an exasperated outburst in Arabic, that caused several clerks to look nervously towards their boss. He was very annoyed; the reputation of the Sultan was at stake. Colonel Said Salem rose from behind his large desk and announced we would go at once and look at the animals.

With moustache bristling and stomach quivering beneath his perfectly ironed snow-white dishdash, the Colonel, fastening his *khunja* about his waist as he went, cut a swathe through those before him as we swept out to his large white Mercedes, which was parked in the courtyard. He sat behind the wheel and we sped off to Awqad. Saleh followed at a safe distance in the Land Rover. As we drove, the Colonel explained with expansive gestures that the man who was detailed to provide the food and water for the animals was regularly drawing a substantial allowance. His Majesty would be very angry.

153

The wrath did not abate when we arrived at the tower. He shouted angrily at the poor boy, who tried to reply but was probably scared out of his wits by the sudden appearance of the President of the Royal Court, one of the most influential men in Oman. I pointed out that two of the goats were dying and I felt it would be humane to kill them. The Colonel agreed but said the rest would be provided with good food and water within an hour. He shook his fist at nobody in particular, muttered about speaking at once to His Majesty and drove off in a cloud of dust.

Within an hour of Colonel Said Salem's visit, fresh food arrived in abundance, and clean water was delivered, somewhat unexpectedly by the Salalah Fire Brigade. Soon a new herdsman had taken over and the collection rapidly became known at *Bir Bint Ahmed* as 'the Royal Farm'. Within a month the herd began to look exceptionally fit and well. Saleh and Hafeedth made suitable noises of approbation. Colonel Said Salem also kept a watching brief on progress. It was hardly a prestigious herd but I was proud of it, and believed that the improvement, thanks to the Colonel's prompt action, had genuinely contributed to the official perception of animal welfare.

One morning I got a call to visit the Sultan's mother's farm at Shabiat on the eastern outskirts of the town. I was surprised that I had not been asked to go there before, but Saleh explained that this was because of Princess Mizoon's brother, Sheikh Isa, a fiery *jebali* of the powerful *Bait Ma'asheni* tribe, who had responsibility for the farm. Tactfully, Saleh described how one of my predecessors, not knowing who Sheikh Isa was, had upset him by criticising the state of the farm. The Sheikh had felt he was being insulted in front of his farm workers, and the loss of face would be hard to forgive. According to Saleh, the BATT Vet had been ordered off the farm and told his services were not required. My prospective visit sounded far from encouraging.

I remembered Scott telling me that he had treated Bibi's Persian cat for ear mites from time to time at *Bir Bint Ahmed*, but had never been to Shabiat. He said that the Palace, including the Sultan, got all their fresh milk from the farm as the *jebali* cows' milk was particularly favoured by His Majesty.

Saleh and I drove apprehensively to Shabiat early in the morning. The farm was tucked away some distance inland from the road, and a couple of elderly *askars* sat at the gate nursing ancient Lee Enfields. The farm was a jumble of wire, dust, *burmails* and lean-to shacks. Housed in the main enclosure were about a hundred or so *jebali* cattle, picking their way through the yard with alfalfa scattered on the ground for them to eat. The cows looked fit enough and had a healthy gloss on their coats. Saleh explained that each evening the cattle were brought in for milking and

154

were then crammed into a tiny shed for the night. There was no ventilation, and the scope for the spread of diseases such as tuberculosis was self-evident.

However, Saleh made me see it in perspective. 'On *jebal*,' he said, '*jebali* man put cows into cave, smaller than this.'

'Yes,' I said, 'but these are the Palace cows and surely we can do better than this?'

'Sheikh Isa no want change,' Saleh replied, adding, 'he *Bait Ma'asheni*,' as if that explained everything.

Three *jebali* women squatted in the yard scooping up the night's droppings, each using two small squares of plywood as shovels to put the dung on a couple of smouldering fires in the centre of the yard. Several cows stood with their heads above the fire in the midst of the pungent smoke, cunningly keeping away the flies and mosquitoes.

All of a sudden there was a roar, a screech of brakes and a large, pale-blue Mercedes pulled up beside us. This was Sheikh Isa. I braced myself. Apart from his smart dishdash, new-looking *khunja* and gold Rolex watch that was too big for his thin wrist, he looked a typical *jebali*, with his dark, thin face, meagre beard, straggly hair and slight features such as might be seen anywhere on the *jebal*. But he also had an undoubted air of authority as befitted a close relative of the Ruler.

'*Salaam alay koom*,' he muttered with no particular friendliness, but he did extend his hand.

'*Way alay koom salaam*,' I replied, as we briefly touched palms.

Sheikh Isa turned to Saleh and explained in Arabic that he had called us to see some camels. Feeling very conscious that no vet had been near the farm since the comments about the state of the place, I was rather relieved that I was here to see clinical patients. He led us to a nearby enclosure, where five or six restless camels were penned together. They all had mange, or *djarab*, and I could see their discomfort as they rubbed ceaselessly against fence posts and against each other trying to relieve the intense itching caused by the mites, *Sarcoptes scabiei cameli*, which burrow into the skin and make tunnels in which to lay their eggs. When the eggs hatch into larvae, these too burrow in the skin so the disease gradually spreads outwards. The Sheikh's animals were still in the acute stage of the disease and obviously very scratchy. They were also highly infectious and I was relieved to see there were no other camels around the farm.

I told the Sheikh I could do something to help but it would take time. One by one, I had each camel led out of the pen. We filled a knapsack sprayer with water and mixed in a sachet of *Gamatox*, a powerful ecto-parasiticide. We used a full 10 litres of wash for each camel and I explained that the treatment would only work if the acaricide got everywhere on the skin – under the armpits, around the tail, head, ears – wherever the mites

155

could hide. Crusty bits of skin had to be brushed vigorously using a stiff broom dipped in the chemical. The camels didn't seem to mind the brush – it must have eased the itching.

It took about three hours to treat all of the camels. The pale-blue Mercedes went off soon after we started and returned just as we were finishing. I told Sheikh Isa that he must find a new enclosure to house the camels so they did not get re-infested from the fence posts and I would send Saleh back in ten days' time to treat them again. In the meantime, I advised him to feed lots of fresh alfalfa. I gave the camels each a shot of a long-acting corticosteroid to reduce the inflammation and irritation, and some multivitamins to help them get over their debility. The Sheikh nodded curtly as Saleh translated all this, then barked some orders at his men, got back into his Mercedes and vanished in a cloud of dust.

'Nice to feel appreciated,' I said to Saleh as I rinsed the *Gamatox* off my hands and arms and washed the dust from my face.

'*Inshalla* camels now OK,' said Saleh prophetically.

'*Inshalla*,' I replied, spitting the foul-tasting *Gamatox* out of my mouth and lighting a cigarette to take away the taste.

Ten days' later, I dropped Saleh and Ali at the farm for the repeat treatment. Sheikh Isa was not there but the camels were transformed. Their hair was growing again, they looked bright in the eye, there was no sign of itchiness and they were happily eating from a trough full of freshly-cut alfalfa. They looked up with dromedarian curiosity as we arrived, and it seemed as if these lovely creatures knew we had played a part in easing their distress.

Our success with the mange transformed relations, as a few days after the second spraying, one of Bibi's servants came to *Bir Bint Ahmed* and asked me to visit a cow. I was delighted at this hint of new confidence and we sped quickly to Shabiat. Sheikh Isa was there with his Baluchi cowmen. Everyone looked concerned as they took us over to the patient who was lying on her side in the shade with her head turned towards her flank. Her eyes were dull and staring, and her muzzle was dry.

I was upset but not surprised to see that all over her neck and sides were fresh marks of the *wussum*, or hot iron, where she had been branded and a mixture of dung and dust had been smeared over the burns. Education was going to be an uphill struggle, but I felt this might be the very case to prove the value of more conventional veterinary medicine.

I asked the Sheikh when the cow had calved. Saleh translated and was told it had been two days before. She had been taken ill soon afterwards, staggering and stumbling before collapsing onto her sternum where she had remained. I nodded gravely. The cow had milk fever, a disease that follows calving and the onset of lactation. As the calf takes more and more milk, the mother loses more and more calcium. If her food is deficient in calcium, her own body stores become depleted and cannot be replaced from the diet. As a result, parts of the body start to go wrong. The muscles become weak and unsteady, the appetite goes and the cow slowly becomes duller and comatose and will die if not treated. Happily, there is a remedy and although she looked at death's door, I knew I could save her.

I went to the Land Rover and got out bottles of calcium borogluconate, glucose and other essential minerals such as phosphorus and magnesium. I attached a sterile rubber flutter valve to the first bottle of calcium, placed a large bore needle into the cow's jugular vein and began to infuse the life-saving liquids. She made no objection at all, which for a *jebali* beast was a sure indication that she wasn't feeling too good.

Saleh was holding the cow's head and I told him to tell Sheikh Isa to watch the cow's bone-dry muzzle. They all stared at the nose and slowly, almost imperceptibly, like dew appearing on a clear spring morning, drop-lets of moisture could be seen forming on the parched tissues as the fluids got into the bloodstream and started to exert their vital effects. I gave the glucose and minerals, injected a second bottle of calcium under the skin and finished off with some multivitamins.

I said nothing but went to pack up my things in the car. Saleh left the tiny cow and helped me. The Sheikh and the others stood and watched as life came back into her eyes; she lifted her head from her side once or twice, then allowed it to sink back. Then she raised it again, shook it and gave a big sigh. I crossed my fingers. After a few minutes, she suddenly heaved herself onto her brisket, lifted her hind legs under her and, shakily, stood up, feet apart and began to focus her eyes as she slowly started to take in her surroundings again. My audience was stunned. Here was a dying animal restored before their very eyes.

'Right,' I said to Saleh. 'Tell the Sheikh to give her lots of good fresh fodder, then dates, dried fish, and plenty of water. Feed the calf separately for the time being and we'll be back this afternoon.'

Whistling cheerfully, I drove back to *Bir Bint Ahmed* feeling extremely pleased with myself. When we returned in the evening, we were greeted as heroes by the staff. Apart from the burn marks down her sides, which would heal in time, one would never have known the cow had been ill. She had passed some dung and was eating well. We put the calf back on her mother's distended udder and after a few tentative nuzzles, nature took over. I told the head man to ensure the cow had lots of food to feed both herself and her calf. The same applied to other pregnant cows in the herd – prevention before calving would prevent a repetition.

Veterinary care had won the day and the BATT Vet was once again allowed at Shabiat. We became regular visitors, treating goats and sheep as well as the cattle and camels.

157

One day at the farm I thought I had stumbled across an ancient tribal rite when I saw a *jebali* man with his face pressed to the vagina of a cow, which was being held by the Baluchi workers. His cheeks were extended and it was clear he was blowing with all his might.

'Milk no come,' said Hafeedth matter-of-factly.

Milk was a very important commodity in Dhofar, and on the whole the men milked the cows and the women looked after the goats. A fall in milk production was often ascribed to the 'evil eye' and treated by ancient traditional remedies. I tried to work out what the man was doing and it sort of made sense: when a cow gives birth, the calf presses on the walls of the birth canal which releases a hormone called oxytocin that helps to make the walls of the uterus squeeze to help the calf out. It also stimulates milk release ready for the newborn calf to drink. Blowing hard into the vagina also stretches the walls, so oxytocin is released into the bloodstream and out comes the milk. The *jebali* people were very close to their cattle and they were undoubtedly remarkable husbandrymen – but how on earth had they worked that one out?

Chapter 17

The Animals Come First

Mike Butler had personally supervised the finishing touches to the new bull-pens he had designed and sited at strategic locations throughout the Province. He had also arranged to buy some young pedigree Sahiwal and Boran bulls through an agent in Nairobi. He called me into his office one morning to say he wanted me to go to Kenya to check the bulls, examine the paperwork and bring them back to Salalah. As Connor McGilligan was scheduled to arrive the following week to take up his duties as Provincial Veterinary Officer, he said I could leave for Nairobi once we had completed a few days' handover and Connor had settled in.

'You'll find the Kenya Livestock Agency will do all the organising,' Mike added. 'They are highly efficient.'

Mike had already spoken to Paddy King-Fretts and when I talked it through with him later Paddy could see no reason why I should not go and sent off a request to MOD for approval. The Squadron was due to change over during the time I would be in Kenya and so it was a good time to be away.

The imminent arrival of exotic bulls from East Africa meant some serious planning. First of all, there would need to be suitable quarantine facilities for them. Then, despite assurances about the capabilities and reliability of the company supplying the bulls, I had to ensure the animals had all the necessary vaccinations before coming into Oman and would not bring any exotic diseases with them. I decided to telex my contact in Beirut, Dr Wooldridge, for guidance. I would also need to choose what drugs and emergency supplies to take with me for a week at sea with ten strapping bulls.

I told Saleh about the plans and gave him what little background I had about my successor. Mike said that Connor had spent time in Africa, and I saw from the *RCVS Register* that he had qualified as a veterinary surgeon at the National University of Ireland in 1957 and so was probably about forty. Saleh was unfazed. I suppose he had seen a series of RAVC officers come and go at six-monthly intervals for three years, and this would be just one more change.

In any case, Saleh had his own preoccupations. He had managed to secure a loan from the Dhofar authorities to set up his own business and had invested in a small roadside shop in a new single-storey unit just outside the town. It was in an area that looked decidedly uncommercial and bleak, but was due for modernisation and redevelopment. Behind the building was half an acre of land, which Saleh had also shrewdly acquired to build a new house for his family. He still diligently attended to his veterinary duties each day, but as soon as one o'clock came round he was away to manage his shop and stock it with general goods ranging from chewing gum to shoelaces, tinned tomatoes to fly-spray. A couple of white plastic tables and chairs were positioned strategically outside the door so Saleh was well-placed to offer coffee and exchange gossip and goodwill with his friends and passers-by. Business was particularly brisk on two nights each week, when the nearby open-air cinema showed Hindi films to packed houses of Indian, Pakistani and Dhofari customers. Sometimes, when an exceptionally good film was showing, an over-excited *jebali* would fire off a volley of rifle shots into the air to wild ecstatic cheering from the all-male audience. Once, at Raven's Roost on the *jebal*, a cowboy western was shown and when the cattle rustlers got to work the indignant *firqats* fired at the screen. The screen was a concrete wall and the audience had to hit the deck as bullets ricocheted in every direction. Or so the story goes.

I called to see Saleh's shop soon after it opened, and he proudly walked me around the outline of the house that would be built, painfully slowly, brickload by brickload as and when the profits from his new enterprise allowed. Nevertheless, he was a patient man who had lived through some terrible times and he had a very deep and unwavering faith in God and fate. He was also a loyal new-Omani with a quiet devotion to his Sultan and an unspoken gratitude for the radically improved standards of living and quality of life now available to him and his family.

Hafeedth meanwhile had announced that he was about to be married and a subtle change came over him. His passionate and rather serious character had manifested itself in some endearing ways, such as his distinctive suits in bright psychedelic colours. Since his engagement, his dress had toned down a bit and he had also become a bit more introspective, although he retained a zealous and intense determination to educate his fellow Dhofaris to look after their animals properly and to shun the hateful *wussum*. His youthfulness and energy augured well for the future of the Dhofar Veterinary Department in which I felt he would be a rising star.

One morning, Hafeedth told me there was to be a special gathering of the women of his extended family as part of the celebratory preparations for his nuptials. So during a scheduled visit to the Quarantine Station at Raysut, he excused himself and wandered off to buy lunch. It took him twenty minutes to wade through the mass of goats as he critically viewed

160

suitable candidates. I watched from behind a well-placed *burmail* as he barely once raised his eyes from the wary animals that surrounded him. Then it was apparent that he had made up his mind as his eyes became fixed on a particular target.

Hafeedth's gaze did not waver as he made his way stealthily, almost cat-like, through the bleating throng, following his prey with the skill and doggedness of a deer-stalker. I could tell that the goat perceived danger with that strange sixth sense that animals and humans often seem to possess when they are the focus of hostile intent. Slowly, steadily, Hafeedth made his way to the victim. The goat bleated a few times and tried to escape to anonymity among the other goats, but the way was barred by sheer numbers and the *burmail* corners of the enclosure. With a swift pounce, Hafeedth caught him by the horns. The goat wriggled a few times trying to shake free of the firm grip that held him tight, then it gave up, allowing itself to be dragged, wide-eyed, to the side of the enclosure.

Saleh helped Hafeedth to lift the goat over the *burmails* to be led to its execution by the barbed-wire fence where the blood-stained wooden gibbet had been built. By law, live animals could not be removed before they had completed the statutory quarantine period, although they could be bought for food if killed on site. Hafeedth paid the foreman and borrowed his knife. Saleh held the goat and hitched up his dishdash. The struggling beast was placed on its side, Hafeedth put one foot on its neck, stretched back its head and with a swift, deft stroke, slit the carotid arteries and jugular veins and sliced back as far as the vertebral column. With a pathetic series of fast twitches of its little tail, the animal was dead; but it was a swift and humane death.

Thoughtfully Hafeedth piled *burusti* leaves in the back of the Land Rover before heaving in the carcass with a satisfied grin on his face. I dropped them at Hafeedth's house and wished him a festive time and delicious meal.

When I wasn't on the hill, I spent a lot of time at *Bir Bint Ahmed*. Somehow reading signals and writing reports was more bearable when relaxing on the grass under the trees, breathing in the fragrances of the gardens, with the glorious bougainvillea all around me and the sounds of the doves and the gentle splashing of the water as it flowed through the garden's *falaj* system.

The *falaj* was an ancient system of irrigation, which had been introduced to Oman by the Persians in pre-Islamic times. Some *falajes* were open channels, others ran beneath the ground, often for several kilometres, and, a bit like London's Victorian sewers, must have required vast amounts of labour to build. The canals provided water to towns and villages, as well as to gardens such as that at *Bir Bint Ahmed*. The prosperity of a village or settlement often depended on the upkeep and sustainability of its *falajes*. Villagers collectively paid the equivalent of water rates to maintain the supplies and this allowed access to so many minutes' water each day for their crops and animals. *Bir Bint Ahmed*'s channels were fairly small, perhaps 30 centimetres wide and about the same deep, running from a well to supply the water troughs and the modest plots of alfalfa and vegetables that were grown on the farm. *Falajes* were masterpieces of engineering and as inspiring an example of practical plumbing as the aqueducts of ancient Rome.

Saturday morning was the first day of the Moslem working week in Dhofar and, like Monday morning in the UK, was usually busy. Hafeedth and I were on our Saturday rounds when we called at the house of the mother of one of the black servants. She was a traditionally-built woman, with classic African features and wore colourful orange, red and green drapes over her generous body. She had a coarse voice and emotion led her to shout at Hafeedth as she explained her problem. She had one of Mike Butler's Friesian-*Jebali* cross cows, which she kept for milk in her small courtyard. It seemed that the cow had been hit by a car on the road the previous day.

The woman knew her Koran, or at least that part of *Sharia* law that demands an eye for an eye and a tooth for a tooth with a fixed scale of blood-money payments. It seemed she was all for hauling the unfortunate car driver before the local *Qadi*, or *Sharia* judge, and she wanted me to be her witness.

The drawback to her case was that the cow was actually doing fine. Perhaps a bit sore and walking a little stiffly, but nothing serious that would not be right in a few days. She would not accept that diagnosis, however, and became louder and more vociferous as she realised my decision had gone against her. Hafeedth endeavoured to placate her but eventually gave up and, fascinated, we watched and listened to her as she ranted furiously that the cow was irreparably damaged and was dying. This was hard to reconcile with the placid bovine ruminating quietly in the corner of the yard. She told us she had already reported the matter to the police and the *Sharia* court. I shrugged and asked Hafeedth what to do. He advised calling in at the police station so he could explain to them that there was nothing wrong with the cow. He then made the mistake of telling the woman this was the plan. Tin cans, stones and anything she could lay her hands on were suddenly hurled at us like cannonballs as we made a rapid exit through the solid wooden door, ducking and weaving and slamming it firmly behind us as the tirade continued. Dealing with the ladies of Dhofar was an art.

It was the end of a long, hot and tiring morning when Saleh came in to say there was a very sick goat to see in the town.

'Can't they bring it here?' I asked wearily.

162

'*Wali* goat,' replied Saleh impassively and I saw that even he realised an early lunch had vanished with the wind. This was a priority call.

'OK,' I sighed. I got up and we drove to one of the largest old houses in Salalah. We went into the yard and found the goat, lying on its side with its hind legs rigidly extended back behind it. The eyes were staring and the breathing laboured. This goat, I could see, was a goner. I was puzzled, however, why they had even bothered to call me in and not just slit its throat and eaten it for lunch, which is what usually happened with expiring goats.

Saleh got the story from a woman relative of the *Wali* who was minding the goat. Our success at treating the cow with milk fever at Bibi's farm at Shabiat had got around. The *tabeeb* had raised a dying animal from the dead by a single injection. The goat, she added, had also just given birth to two kids. In fact, she was probably suffering from a similar problem to the cow, but sadly had been left too long. Mercifully there were no *wussum* burns, but I had to get Saleh to explain that things did not look good.

'*Inshalla, Inshalla*,' came the predictable reply.

The goat was an oldish beast, which had clearly had several kids over the years. Her swollen, deformed and unbalanced udder sagged with the weight of milk. We lifted her gently onto her sternum but she made no attempt to hold her head up. With little hope in my heart, I put a needle into her jugular vein ready to infuse some calcium solution, but as the first few millilitres began to flow, the poor goat let out a wretched last bleat and sagged in final collapse. Saleh was fast on the ball and yelled to the woman to bring a knife. He rapidly slit the throat and blood flowed and then oozed onto the ground. By killing the goat ritually before the heart stopped beating, it would be permissible to eat the flesh. He smiled at the woman who thanked him for his quick action. Her expression told us it had been an old goat anyway and its death was no great loss, but I felt that my reputation as a miracle-worker had been short-lived.

Goats are multipurpose animals that produce milk, meat, skins and hair for humans, but all these products require proper nutrition. As the goat is an inquisitive and indiscriminate feeder, it can and does survive (where no other ruminant would) on diets that are very high in fibre, which in Salalah included cardboard, paper, clothing rags and cement bags, together with any herbage to be found and every bit of cast-off human food such as decomposing vegetables. Protein was sometimes supplied by sardines, of which there was no shortage in this fishing town, and it was common to see these herbivorous animals chomping away on rotting sardines and swallowing them, bones and all.

Sometimes even the hardy goat's digestive system rebelled. When they eat stuff that is rotten or overripe, they tend to get bloat. The gut micro-organisms (that help the animal to digest tough fibrous food) go into

163

overdrive and the stomach inflates like a balloon due to the rapid increases in fermentation. Scott Moffat had warned me that there was a particular risk from *khobz* or chapattis, which were produced in epidemic numbers to meet the dietary demands of the burgeoning Indian and Pakistani workers. Sometimes the rumen would swell up so much that it would bulge out from the flanks and the gas pressure was so great the animals couldn't even burp or fart to get rid of it. The vet's ultimate weapon was to pierce the rumen through the flank with a large-bore needle and watch as an impressive jet of methane hissed out. Stories abounded about ill-fated farmers who happened to be holding a lighted cigarette near the gas as it emerged from a cow with bloat, producing an impressive blowtorch effect. I tended not to smoke when inserting needles into my goats.

Late one afternoon, I was on my own at *Bir Bint Ahmed* wrestling with some paperwork from RAVC HQ in Droitwich, when an anxious old *Bedouin* called. Our mutual command of the other's language was limited but the old chap managed to communicate to me that he had a *wagid takleef*, or big problem, with his camel. He was a gentle fellow and seemed so helpless and worried that I agreed to come at once. He had walked or cadged a lift to *Bir Bint Ahmed* and it was fortuitous I happened to be there. He climbed into the Land Rover beside me and we set off. The camel was on the far side of Salalah, near the perimeter wire on the road to Taqah. As we drove, I struggled with my Beaconsfield Arabic and I think he told me that the animal had been far away and it had taken him three days to get to Salalah to find me. I really hoped I would be able to help.

Camels are stoical animals with a surprisingly high pain threshold that must have been a valuable asset in the days when armies used camels in battle. The brave actions of the British army's camel-mounted troops in the nineteenth and early part of the twentieth centuries bear testimony to man's exploitation of animals. The camels would lie patiently in the front line, protecting their soldiers and barely flinching as shots were fired across their backs, often staying their ground when hit. Their contribution to the Afghan wars and the Indian Mutiny as well as to campaigns in the Crimea, Abyssinia, Egypt, Sudan and in World War I was legendary. During the second Afghan War, over 70,000 camels were slain. On the Embankment in London, outside the Ministry of Defence, is a little-known statue recognising the unsung valour of the Camel Corps. In the first decade of the twenty-first century I was proud to be a trustee of the Animals in War Memorial, a superb monument in London's Park Lane that is a powerful and moving tribute to all of the animals that served, suffered and died alongside the British, Commonwealth and Allied forces in the wars and conflicts of the twentieth century.[1]

1. See: www.animalsinwar.org.uk

In 1974 camels were still being used by the *adoo* in Dhofar and camel trains provided an important resupply route into the operational area from the west, particularly during the monsoon when stores were replenished under cover of the mist and low cloud. Unfortunately, it was not unusual for these trains to be taken out by ground or air attack on the *jebal*. Brigadier John Akehurst, the Dhofar Brigade Commander, was clearly uneasy about this necessity; he wrote that camels were important targets, but killing them not only raised the question of cruelty but also distressed the Strikemaster pilots who were tasked with these missions. The policy was not without risk too, as the capricious but animal-focused *jebalis* could be so angry if a friendly herd was hit that all chances of continuing dialogue could evaporate. Nevertheless Akehurst argued that camels often represented the only means the enemy had of transporting weapons and munitions to some parts of the hill, and he believed the civilians would turn against the faction whose use of the animals brought this slaughter upon them.

The camel can go several days without water, but the belief is apocryphal that liquid water is stored in the hump which is largely made up of fat and is a food reserve. The military value of the camel is obvious where transport is required across desert terrains, and camels have been critically important in many campaigns. They are also integral to numerous *Bedouin* cultures as they provide a large part of a man's mobile wealth in addition to power; food and skins for tents and clothes. It is not surprising that the prophet Mohammed taught that God has created no animal better than the camel. It is said that at the third blast of the trumpet on the day of Resurrection and Judgement, the truly faithful will be borne to heaven on winged camels, as white as milk, with saddles of fine gold.

The camel on the Taqah road was not quite so seraphic. In fact it was a wonder that it had managed to travel as far as it had. The journey must have been laboriously slow and painful. For an Omani camel, she was quite big-boned, and well-proportioned. Her body was in good condition and I could see that she had been well cared for. Her owner, who had led her from goodness knows where, stroked her affectionately and reassuringly as soon as we arrived; but she could hardly put her left hind foot to the ground. Below the hock it was swollen with an ugly mass of purple and red blotches along the length. Several open wounds on the leg had become fly-blown and were suppurating. The owner tried to demonstrate the camel's incapacity by encouraging her to take a few steps. I did not need any convincing.

There was no need to hobble her; she wasn't going anywhere in a hurry. The camel looked at me with big, curious, trusting eyes as I leaned forward to feel very gently the surface of the inflamed limb. It was hot to the touch, so at least it was not gangrenous. I got some water and antiseptic from the Land Rover and tried soothingly to clean the leg. She did not object, only gurgled gently, indifferently passing a few hard pelleted droppings and occasionally turning her long elegant neck to observe questioningly what I was doing. Anything could have caused this infection. It might have started with something as small as a bite from a scorpion or a vicious horsefly, or she could have become tangled in wire or thorn bush; it might even have been the result of *wussum* with dung rubbed into the burn. Without Saleh or Hafeedth to translate, I would not learn more from this worried owner.

I dressed the wounds as best I could and treated them with insecticide powder to kill the maggots and discourage more flies from laying their eggs. I then administered massive doses of antibiotics and an anti-inflammatory drug, as ever having to guess what the weight of an adult camel might be. I could see that despite her uncomplaining fortitude she was very uncomfortable, so I decided also to give her some painkiller into her jugular vein. The camel's veins are about 4 centimetres in diameter and impossible to miss. I was rewarded by seeing her visibly relax as the drug took effect. She began at once to pick at the alfalfa that remained largely untouched at her feet.

I returned to the camel every day for the next week. The man was always there, sometimes alone, sometimes with others. The leg began to improve and lost its angry colour. The swelling went down and the heat left it as the bacteria were killed off and healthy tissues began to replace those that were dead and infected. As the wounds healed, the camel began gradually to put weight on the leg. On the seventh day I knew we had won. She was lying on her brisket chewing the cud as we drove up, but as we approached her she slowly and steadily put her hind legs behind her, rose up on her knees and stood up. Yes, she was very stiff, but it was as if she wanted to say: 'Look! I *can* lie down and get up again.'

The owner was overjoyed. He hugged me warmly and repeatedly thanked God. He would not let me go without a present. I tried to demur as he was clearly very poor, but Saleh whispered to me, 'Is OK, is OK', as the man fussed and rummaged among his possessions. He produced a clear polythene bag, opened it and encouraged me to sniff the contents. It was a dry mixture of frankincense that was sweet-smelling and exotic. There were small beads of the hardened yellow sap among shreds of desiccated plant material and dried but odourless camel dung. Saleh thoughtfully produced an empty Elastoplast tin and the man filled it with the fragrant mixture and pressed it into my hands, grasping them with both of his in a gesture of real appreciation. It was incredibly touching.

I did not see the camel again – but I did burn some of the incense in my room at the Mess. It was very special and the room filled with a beautiful and exquisite fragrance. This simple and precious gift was the most special thank-you present I received in Dhofar.

166

Chapter 18

The Coming of the Irish

It was now May. In June the south-west monsoon would hit Dhofar and for four months a grey, hazy drizzle would fall and the sunshine and blue skies would be hidden for days or weeks at a time by the *khareef*. The temperature would remain fairly steady at about 27 degrees Centigrade and it would be very humid. It was strange how the monsoon hit only about 130 square kilometres of Dhofar's 1,500 square kilometres, turning large parts of the *jebal* lush and green, perfect for agriculture and cattle-rearing. Beyond the *jebal*, however, north of Midway, the air would remain clear, with the sun shining as fiercely as ever and aircraft continued to operate, which was not always possible in the mists that would shroud Salalah.

Connor McGilligan arrived in Salalah when I was up the hill attending to some sick SAF donkeys. By 1974, there was only a small troop of donkeys remaining in Dhofar with their Baluchi handlers. Pack animals were little used now as their roles had been largely superseded by the Skyvan and the Huey, but donkeys and mules had both played an important role in the early stages of the Dhofar war when troops were loaded with water, provisions and ammunition to supply forward positions. Donkeys were well suited to the terrain – sure-footed and easy to keep, and a fit, mature mule could carry up to 100 kilograms of supplies for six or seven hours each day. They were also used by the *adoo* as part of their resupply chain.

Mike Butler invited me to come and meet Connor over a drink on his second evening in Salalah. My successor was a middle-aged, well-built man with a neat beard. He had a lilting Irish voice and, as he had also served in the RAVC, we immediately found we knew people in common. Having had considerable experience working overseas in developing countries, Connor seemed to be an obvious choice for Provincial Veterinary Officer, Dhofar, and I could see at once why Mike had chosen him. Connor told me that he planned to settle in first, and then arrange for his wife and family to join him. He had been allocated a house near to the Butlers and had spent the day trying to unpack after a tedious journey from the UK.

Connor proved a ready listener and I tried to explain something of the problems I had faced in Dhofar. He was surprised there was such a strong military presence and that part of the Province was still considered a war zone. It was because of such concerns that I had felt that it was premature to withdraw the BATT Vet. There was more than enough work for two veterinarians, and whereas a civilian could focus on developing a properly regulated animal health service and helping to introduce and implement appropriate laws and regulations essential for effective disease control measures, an army vet could be deployed to look after the continuing needs of the *jebali* people. Despite encouraging signs, the war was not yet over and I believed it was still necessary to maintain the 'Hearts and Minds' work for at least another six to twelve months. More and more tribesmen were coming to trust, accept and use the DDD and CAT facilities – water, food, education, health and animal care. Connor as a civilian Provincial VO would have more than enough on his plate based in Salalah. But it had been decided that expenditure on a BATT Vet had gone on long enough. After all, my own appointment had been very much an afterthought as Scott Moffat was meant to be the last RAVC attachment.

It was stimulating to have a fellow professional to talk to again and I thoroughly enjoyed introducing Connor to the challenges he would face. I collected him each morning in the BATT Land Rover as his new DDD vehicle had still to be delivered. We drove around Salalah and he got on well with Saleh and the others. He was interested in the quarantine station at Raysut and the plans for a new, purpose-built centre were already on the table for discussion. I took him along the beach to Taqah to meet Taqah Ahmed, but I felt he was not particularly comfortable to be accompanied by an armed SAS escort.

Although Mike had made clear the new VO would not take on the work of the Royal Stables, he agreed Connor should accompany me on a quick visit to Muscat as part of his induction. The emasculators had finally arrived from Cyprus so I could at last castrate the stallions for John Clarke. The instrument had been sent by Scott, who was now commanding the Army Dog Training Unit in Episkopi. A note from Scott had come with the instruments wishing me luck and emphasising in rather unnecessarily large letters, underlined three times in red ink, that the emasculators were 'on loan'. The RAVC Stores in Aldershot had also sent the immobilising agent I had requested some weeks previously, so we were all set and made plans to leave for Muscat the following day.

John Clarke was in Salalah as the Sultan was in town and riding daily. As John's wife, Clody, had returned to Switzerland to look after her ill father, John kindly said Connor and I could use his flat and car and signalled Tony Brunton to say we were coming. The trip worked like clockwork. John's driver met us at Seeb airport and, after a quick tour of the capital, we were soon settled comfortably in John's apartment, agreeably drinking his gin. His houseboy cooked for us and made the beds and we felt very much at home.

At six o'clock the next morning we arrived at the Royal Stables in Wutayyah as I wanted to get on with the surgery before the flies were too active. As ever, it was a very peaceful time of day and cool enough to wear a pullover. The sand was moist with overnight dew, and the air felt clean, fresh and new. Horses stamped in their stalls impatient for their morning feed, while others snorted contemptuously or watched inquisitively as I carried my kit past them to set up an improvised operating theatre in a small paddock at the rear of the horse lines.

Everything was still and quiet as we waited for the first horse. It was helpful to have Connor there and we agreed to operate alternately; one would anaesthetise and the other castrate, after which we would change about. I was relieved to have my *Immobilon*. This was a relatively new drug containing etorphine, a highly potent opioid sometimes called 'elephant juice', as zoo and wildlife vets had found it particularly useful for immobilising large animals. It was ideal for the conditions in which I had to operate. It worked very quickly, the horse laid down within thirty seconds and was out of action for thirty to forty minutes; plenty of time for a castration. A specific antagonist, aptly called *Revivon*, was then given and the horse soon stood up, none the worse for wear – apart from the loss of a couple of testicles.

Immobilon had to be handled with care as it was extremely powerful and potentially dangerous to humans; veterinarians had died by accidentally injecting themselves when giving the drug to an animal. It was reassuring to have a colleague around ready to administer the antidote in case of emergency. However, that day the drug worked well and there were no accidents. The first stallion went down and we rolled him over on his side. I attached a rope to the uppermost hind leg and a couple of *syces* drew it forward out of the way of the operating site. Then I carefully cleaned the skin, scrubbed my own hands and arms and made the incision. The well-travelled emasculators did their job cleanly and efficiently.

I tried telling Tony to get the *syces* to count to ninety after I injected the *Revivon*, but he said none of them could make it to ninety. Nevertheless the first horse, now a gelding, came round spot on ninety seconds after the injection of *Revivon*, to a spontaneous round of applause from the fascinated huddle of *syces* who were riveted to the action. Connor castrated the second stallion and we soon got into a rhythm as we worked our way through the list.

Vets should never be vindictive towards any of their patients, but I did take particular pleasure in removing the balls from the ill-tempered

169

stallion that had nearly killed me when I tried the standing castration technique. This time he was knocked out and well under my control.

By ten o'clock we had finished and were eating breakfast. I thought this would be a good time to take Connor to see the new stables at Seeb that were rapidly approaching completion. They looked stunning. The main building was designed like a series of *Bedouin* tents with a white concrete roof spanning the boxes and overhanging walkways along the sides to provide shade. The open, airy boxes were large and spacious with carefully designed mangers, water troughs and doors. Bored, housed horses can sometimes adopt repetitive or stereotypic behaviour, and vices such as crib-biting or wind-sucking, but cautious planning, such as letting horses have plenty to look at, can help to minimise these dangers.

John and Tony had worked hard to produce a superb and exciting unit. It was very nearly finished and the site was alive with painters, plumbers, plasterers, electricians, gardeners, carpenters and their mates. Traditional design had not been a limiting factor in the creation of this royal equestrian megastructure by the sea. What a contrast from the idyllic and tranquil lines of palm-leaf *burusti* at Wutayyah and Salalah. John would no longer run the stables from a trestle table under the acacia trees but have a large, carpeted, air-conditioned Director's Office. The tack would be kept in a spacious room and even the empty feed and fodder stores had been carefully planned and thoughtfully laid out. There was a sumptuous suite for the Sultan to rest and change and to entertain his guests.

Nearby was the housing complex for the *syces*. Most of these boys came from poor homes in India or Pakistan and were in Oman to earn foreign currency to send home, often as the sole means of maintaining an extended family. Few, if any, were likely to have experienced the comfort of living in brand-new accommodation with electricity, showers and flushing lavatories, surrounded by landscaped and cultivated lawns and gardens. The position of *syce* at the Royal Stables would be a coveted job.

We also had a look around the Royal Zoological Collection where the animals and birds seemed to have settled well into their hastily erected but effective enclosures. The mortality rate had fallen dramatically and the surviving population appeared to have adapted and stabilised. We spent an enjoyable couple of hours in those lovely surroundings. I was keen to share with Connor this pleasant and peaceful side to veterinary duties in Oman. Eventually we were interrupted by John's driver, who informed us that it was time to take us to the airport for the afternoon SOAF flight back to Salalah.

The days grew nearer for my departure to Kenya to collect the bulls, in what had predictably become known as Operation Noah. I spent more time at *Umm al Gwarrif* and less at *Bir Bint Ahmed* as I reckoned Connor needed to get his feet under the desk without me breathing down his neck.

A new supply system had to be set up – my stores had always come through Aldershot and were flown out by the RAF; Connor had to find a way of getting his vaccines and drugs to Salalah safely, reliably and suitably chilled. The whole Veterinary Office needed reorganising; it was one thing for an army vet to run a unit on a six-month secondment, quite another to set down the foundations for an efficient Provincial Veterinary Office on a permanent basis. Connor would need to agree budgets, find clerical assistance and administrative support, look for more clinical staff and develop an effective chain of command to DDD. He would also have to deal with the Kenyan bulls once I delivered them. In addition, the Arizona cattle were due to be flown in shortly for the new American FMC farm.

I hoped Connor would decide to keep Saleh and Hafeedth and the rest of the team, but this would be his decision, and I noticed a sudden increase in alertness and willingness generally among all the staff as they came to the same conclusion.

I made a few excursions to the *jebal* but without Connor, who had no desire to spend time among the sandbags, rats and compo rations. I set down my thoughts in a Report to the Director AVRS and talked them through with Paddy King-Fretts. 'A' Squadron's tour was almost finished and he was in the middle of wrapping up ready to hand over to the incoming 'D' Squadron, but he gave me time and was sympathetic to my submission that if there was no veterinary cover on the *jebal* there could be a serious setback to one of the established and successful core objectives of Operation Storm.

The next morning Paddy told me he had spoken to the Brigade Commander and we were to go and see him. We were both wearing OGs and mine had certainly seen better days, but I managed to stand fairly reasonably to attention when the Brigade Major, Peter Packham, showed us into the office of the commander of Dhofar Brigade, Brigadier Jack Fletcher. He had been a very successful appointment and was popular throughout Dhofar, but was shortly to hand over to Brigadier John Akehurst. I had got to know Brigadier Jack and his wife Mary through visits to their villa in the expat compound on the beach to treat Mary's budgerigars.

The Brigadier sat us down and picked up the copy of my short report that Paddy had given him. I explained my concern and questioned whether it was right to expect a civilian vet to work in a combat zone. The war was not over yet, and I said I was worried that with no cover there was a danger of losing the momentum on the hill. I stressed the huge workload that faced a new Chief Veterinary Officer setting up a veterinary Department within DDD. Paddy supported me by saying he believed the SAS would continue the RAVC attachment for as long as the regiment was operational in Dhofar, as the Hearts and Minds campaign was key to the success of Operation Storm. The Brigadier listened and made notes. He promised nothing but said he would take soundings and discuss my concern with the GOC and SAF Commander, General Tim Creasey.

'What do you think?' I asked Paddy as we left the office.

'He's a shrewd bugger,' said Paddy. 'He'll talk to the General alright but it will probably get down to politics and the wishes of DDD to run their own show. Also, don't forget it is the Sultan who pays, so if the *Wali* says it's time the position is civilianised, which well he may, that will be that.'

Meanwhile DDD was having a few problems getting me to Kenya. Robin Butler apologetically explained she could only get me from Muscat to Nairobi via Bombay or London. She had opted for Bombay. As I was travelling on behalf of DDD (and therefore as a civilian) I was on the Gulf Air flight from Salalah to Muscat rather than the SOAF Viscount. After an overnight stay at the *Al Falaj* hotel in Muscat, I would then continue to Bombay where I was to spend a second night before flying on to Nairobi. Happily, as the route between Muscat and Bombay was always heavily booked, I had been given a first-class seat, which was cheering compensation for what promised to be a tedious journey.

Robin told me I would be met at Nairobi Airport by Don Henderson, the Managing Director of the Kenya Livestock Agency. She had received a confirmatory telex from him to say everything had been arranged and he was looking forward to meeting me. She gave me the contact details both of Henderson and the Oman Government's Agent in Bombay and £300 in travellers' cheques. Robin made sure I knew her telex and phone numbers and the frequency of Jeremy Raybould's Maritime Radio ready for my return by sea. In addition, Paddy King-Fretts had secured the name and telephone number of the British Military Attaché in Nairobi and asked Hereford to notify the High Commission that I was coming, so I felt I was prepared for most emergencies.

On the morning of my departure, a *shemaal* was blowing. This powerful north wind often blew up suddenly and unexpectedly in the weeks leading up to the monsoon, whipping dust and sand high into the air and making life unpleasant for anyone out of doors. The temperature was over 30 degrees Centigrade so it was uncomfortable driving with the Land Rover windows shut. If they were opened, dust flew into the car and the swirling mass of fine particles got everywhere. Visibility fell too and it felt in every way the desert sandstorm. The *shemaal* had blown up overnight and when I woke in the morning the whole of my room in the Mess was covered in a layer of sand which had blown under the door and got everywhere – in clothes, hair, nose and throat. The gusts of wind were so strong that crops and trees could be badly damaged and probably explained why so many of the Salalah palms grew at peculiar angles. As I drove my rocking Land Rover to *Umm al Gwarrif*, I could see trees leaning in the force of the wind with their long, elegant fronds blowing like tresses behind a fast-moving Porsche. Less exotically, flights were liable to be cancelled or postponed as aircraft could often not take off or land in a *shemaal*. I prepared myself for a long delay.

Paddy King-Fretts and 'A' Squadron were leaving Salalah the next day. When I reached BATT HQ, I found Paddy seated at his desk surrounded by the orderly chaos of a handover. There was another officer sitting with him who was introduced as Dave, OC of 'D' Squadron and Paddy's replacement. Paddy walked with me to the Land Rover and we wished each other well. It had been a privilege to serve with him in BFPO 66.

Within hours the *shemaal* blew itself out and although the little Gulf Air Fokker Friendship was four hours late arriving in Salalah, I was pleased to get away. Connor kindly took me to the airport. As he held out his hand to say goodbye, he said, 'You may find I've had a change of heart before you get back. I'm not so sure this job is for me.' With that we parted.

The Fokker slowly grumbled its way to Muscat, taking even longer than the Viscount. I was pleased to find Mike Foster-Turner on the flight with me. Working for Taylor Woodrow, Mike had a smart car and driver waiting for him at Seeb airport, so I hitched a lift into Ruwi and was left at the door of the *Al Falaj*. I went in with little enthusiasm, but there was no choice other than to spend the night there. Mac Maclean was in Muscat but about to leave for London with a member of the Royal Family who needed hospital treatment, Tony Brunton was in Salalah with John Clarke, and Chuck Pringle was out of the country.

I checked in but, unlike the booking for Ollie Graham-Jones, mine did not have the Palace backing, only that of the Dhofar Development Department. I suppose I was lucky to get a room at all, and I was not surprised to find I had to share. My room-mate was already in the room when I opened the door. He was a Japanese businessman, who tried to be friendly as he retrieved his underpants and socks from my pillow and the rest of his kit from various places on the floor. He had not been expecting a room-mate. I went to Reception where I asked for the Manager. No, he was very sorry, but I had the only available bed in the entire hotel.

By now I knew perfectly well that they always kept a couple of rooms back in case of emergencies so I asked for a phone and put in a call to Mac who, fortunately, was still in his flat, and I explained my predicament. He sounded amused at my plight, but told me to put on the Manager. Soon my things were removed and I was shown into a single room. I rang Mac again to thank him for saving me from a difficult night and wished him a good trip to the UK.

The following morning, I caught the first flight to Bombay and, with the one and a half hour time difference, I arrived at lunchtime. As I had a connecting flight in the early hours of the following morning, the airline had arranged to put me up at a city hotel. This was my second visit to Bombay and the old, outdated airport was still as I remembered it as a student: a dark, steamy, anonymous furnace, at once exotic, exasperating, demanding, infuriating and crammed with thousands of the city's noisy, jostling citizens.

My arrival was complicated by the need to retrieve my veterinary chest. Travelling first-class helped, and the friendly staff at the Seeb check-in desk had arranged for the container to be placed in a priority hold so I could collect it easily at the other end. The Indian Customs, however, had other ideas. With a bureaucracy inherited from the British, compounded by corruption and heat, I spent two hot, sweaty hours in the offices of various airport officials as I waited for someone to make a decision about the medicines. I suppose it was understandable that they did not want me wandering into Bombay with a variety of emergency drugs and equipment. Eventually we compromised and it was arranged that the chest would be placed in a Customs refrigerator and passed directly to Air India who would put it on the Nairobi flight next day. I could collect my drugs in Kenya.

I staggered out of the airport and into the searing heat and dust of pre-monsoon Maharashtra. The poverty of Bombay was intense, and the paradox the city presented was bewildering. It teemed with life and death and something in between. At every traffic light the taxi stopped and the car was surrounded by beggars and cripples of all descriptions: scrawny women with fly-covered, gummy-eyed babies in their arms; men with gross mutilations and deformities; scruffy, wild-looking children; others with blank eyes already infected with trachoma, pleading, imploring and craving help; some sham, some desperate. I guiltily wound up the window.

The manicured gardens of the five-star hotel were in dramatic contrast to the airport and I was ushered solicitously into the foyer by a splendid Sikh with a magnificent moustache and beard, wearing a red coat and spotless turban. After an efficient and courteous check-in, a bell-boy took my meagre possessions in a gleaming lift to a splendid air-conditioned room, bulging with all the amenities I could possibly hope for and several I would never need. When I was finally left alone in peace, I looked out of the window and gazed upon one of the city's many shanty towns. A congealed ramshackle mass of wood, cardboard, corrugated steel, rags and mud. A whole universe separated the struggles of the people who lived here from the struggles of the *jebali* refugees in Dhofar. Poverty is manifest in many ways – material, doctrinal and spiritual.

Bombay is the largest port in India as well as the country's financial centre. The name came from the Portuguese, *Bom Bahia*, meaning Fair Bay, as the seven islands that originally made it up must once have been. My visit was a powerful experience: the hot, sticky air seemed to carry on its droplets a million sensations of fruits and spices, sweetness and putridity, petrol and animals, dust and decay, sweat and blood, life and death. Yet the city had an extraordinary vibrancy and exhilaration if you could accept the wealth and prosperity alongside the deprivation and urban poor.

The next morning, from my first-class seat on the Air India Boeing 707 bound for Nairobi, I looked down at Bombay feeling confused and impotent. Like a Sybaritic deity, I sipped my glass of beautifully-chilled champagne and ordered breakfast.

Chapter 19

A Load of Bull

I stayed for about a week in Nairobi. For the first few days, I travelled around the highlands surrounding the capital with Don Henderson, who was not only a helpful and knowledgeable livestock dealer but also a highly-experienced auctioneer. The plan was for me to start by visiting the farms from where our bulls were coming, so I could reassure myself about their health status. This suited me well, and provided an opportunity to see something of the country.

Henderson had booked me into the exclusive Muthaiga Country Club, a relic of empire some 5 kilometres from Nairobi's city centre. The Club had been built in 1913, originally for the coffee-growers who settled along the Nairobi-Kiambu road, and it was fixed in an Edwardian time-warp. The African servants, many in their fifties and sixties, were still called 'Boy' by the older members and their terrifying wives, and the polishing, cleaning and tidying in the reception rooms was to a standard no less than would be found in Boodles or Buck's Club.

Copies of *The Times*, *Country Life* and *The Field* were laid out as in a Harley Street waiting room and I would not have been surprised if the newspapers had been ironed. Afternoon tea arrived at four o'clock for the elegantly dressed matrons, who sat in wicker chairs and talked about servants and shopping and shortages as they sipped Earl Grey from china cups and nibbled their scones with laps protected by strategically positioned and immaculately starched double damask napkins. Outside, elderly men in *Daz*-white shirts and shorts, long socks and plimsolls quietly played bowls on a green that must have remained unchanged for sixty years.

My bedroom could have been based on any fairly smart country house in England around 1900. The brass bedstead was solid and dependable, and the bed beautifully made up with crisp linen sheets and bolsters, and shrouded in an elegantly arranged mosquito net. A couple of rugs lay on the dark-dyed wooden floor, on which sat a Victorian chest of drawers, desk and chair, all made from gloomy mahogany. A lighter touch was

176

provided by a chintzy dressing table with lace covers on which had been placed a small vase of fresh flowers. A ceiling fan lazily turned the air. The scene was completed by a washstand with bowl, stiffly laundered handtowels and a large jug full of cold, clean water for washing face and hands. A 100-year-old wash stand that was still in daily use was quite a find in 1974.

I had nearly come to Kenya without a jacket and tie. I was transporting cattle across Africa and the Indian Ocean, for heaven's sake. At the last minute I had shoved them in my bag just in case. It was just as well. Without them I would not have been allowed into the Club. As it was, my eligibility for entry to this focus of privilege was my commission. Officers in the British army or navy were granted immediate temporary membership but, for reasons undeclared, this did not extend to the Royal Air Force.

The Muthaiga Club probably had its heyday in the 1930s and was described by Jane Fox in *White Mischief* as 'a place beyond the reach of society's official censure'. It was not difficult to conjure up images of bright young things and carefree aristocrats making merry in this exclusive sanctuary, under the knowing and world-weary eyes of the experienced African retainers. Some of the staff I met told me they had been employed by the Club for decades and they were fiercely loyal to its traditions. Some were even noticeably cool towards the few black businessmen, who after independence in 1963 had joined the Club.

Despite the stuffiness and colonial anachronisms, the Muthaiga Club had a relaxing charm. The gardens, with their ficus trees, colourful flowers, striking scents, exotic birds and soothing chorus of cicadas, blended with the distant sounds of tennis racquets hitting balls or the satisfying thwack of golf clubs.

Don drove me around the White Highlands to half a dozen or so cattle farms. One day we went west, past the Veterinary School and Research Centre at Kabete that I had visited two years previously as President of the International Veterinary Students' Association. Then north to Kikuyu, and on through Naivasha to Nakuru, a bustling town in the centre of a rich farming area. Here, on the cusp of the Great Rift Valley, is Lake Nakuru, home to a million migrating pink flamingos. Another day, we travelled east to Thika then up through Fort Hall to Nyeri, with its stunning views of the snow-capped Mount Kenya, an extinct volcano towering 5,000 metres above the hills, forests and plains of the Aberdares. Nyeri was at the forefront of the struggle for independence in the 1950s and also has the grave of Lord Baden-Powell, founder of the Scouts. A small shrine exists for the world's scouting pilgrims, discreetly marked on the road to Treetops, the Lodge where Princess Elizabeth learned of the death of her father, George VI, and that she was to be Queen.

177

Further north, on the equator, sits Nanyuki, an important farming centre. Here we called at a rural cattle market where Don was auctioneer. He and I were the only white men, but there were a couple of Indian clerks who busied themselves with the paperwork and administration. Farmers had come from miles around and were seated stolidly on stepped wooden benches surrounding a small ring. The cattle were assembled in a large pen and were urged in single file along a narrow, wooden race for branding with a red-hot iron. The passageway was so small that the animals could not turn, but bucked and squirmed and moaned as the blistering metal burnt their hair and seared into their hides giving each a unique number and their owners or purchasers some protection against fraud. Singly or in pairs they came into the ring and Don swiftly and efficiently conducted the bidding in Swahili. I watched the farmers as they joked with each other, grumbled over prices, reluctantly bid or sold, smoked and scratched. They were no different from farmers at markets the world over.

The ranches that housed the bulls destined for Oman were impressive and vast by UK standards, often covering thousands of acres. The white farmers, however, were a mixed bunch. Some were caricatures of old colonials, confident of their place on the stepladder of their society. Others were more enlightened and progressive, trying to help their workers through structured education programmes, better housing and family support. We were buying two bulls from one such young farmer, who had just inherited his farm. He told us that, following his father's death, the farm was now to be nationalised. This had come as a bitter blow to this enthusiastic and ambitious man, who thought that keeping a united farm would be of far more help to the struggling Kenyan economy than the fragmented subsistence farming system that was likely to take its place.

The mid-1970s were not an easy time for white farmers. The Kenya government under Jomo Kenyatta, the London School of Economics educated Kikuyu President and former Mau Mau leader, had embarked on an Africanisation policy. This involved the compulsory purchase of generally profitable white-owned farms, and dividing them up into smallholdings to be allocated or rented to black Kenyans. As part of its overseas aid programme to Kenya, the British government provided some compensation.

Mike Butler had specified that he wanted three Borans and six Sahiwals. Although I suppose in theory I had some discretion over the selection of the bulls, my familiarity with the two breeds was nil, and as the farms presented their stock so professionally I happily left all decision-making to Don and restricted my interests to veterinary matters. Don set about educating me. The Boran, he said, was primarily a meat animal, which fitted well with Mike Butler's plans to cross the *jebali* cows with the bulls to produce bigger and more muscular offspring that would command good meat prices in Salalah. The breed had been developed in Kenya from the cattle of the Boran peoples of Southern Ethiopia. The bulls were handsome, short-haired, greyish, zebu-type animals, with big beefy quarters and a thoracic hump to dissipate heat and (as with the camel) store fat which metabolises to food and water in times of drought or food shortages. An additional benefit was the Boran's resistance to ticks and parasites, scourges of livestock production in developing countries.

The Sahiwal on the other hand, said Don, was a highly successful dairy cow and in each lactation could produce a couple of thousand litres of milk for human consumption at the same time as suckling a calf. It originated in the arid Punjab, where it was kept in large herds by cowherders called *junglies*. A fine-looking, reddish-brown breed with large, soft, floppy ears, I felt the Sahiwal should also prove helpful to the *jebali* people of Dhofar, who were big milk-drinkers. Like the Boran, the Sahiwal also had a large thoracic hump and a high degree of resistance to diseases. We finally settled on the nine bulls. Six were between one and two years of age but three of the Sahiwals were just under a year old. The big Borans had rings in their noses to help manage them.

They were all in tip-top condition, but I needed to visit the District Veterinary Officers responsible for each farm as they had to sign the paperwork including the health and export certificates. Kenya's veterinary services were well-organised and the bureaucracy necessary for the deal was easily completed. We then had to decide what would be needed for the voyage. Henderson said he would arrange shipment of cattle and consumables by rail to Mombasa within a week to tie up with the scheduled sailing date of our cargo ship, the 5,200-tonne MV *Southern Trader*.

After that, there was not much else to do other than relax at the Muthaiga Club. I looked up some old friends from the Kabete Veterinary School who decided I needed to experience some of the nightspots of Nairobi. I was also taken to a formal veterinary dinner at a city hotel and listened to a lengthy speech from the Minister of Agriculture. As we happened to be sitting on the next table to the Minister's, I even got my photograph on the front page of the *Daily Nation*, having been snapped as part of the background.

I did have one preoccupation. Apart from my veterinary chest, which had arrived with me from Bombay and included some barbiturates, I had no effective means of killing large animals. Disasters did happen, and on rough sea voyages it was not beyond the realms of possibility that I could find myself with a bull with a fractured limb, or other condition that demanded prompt euthanasia. It had not occurred to me to bring my pistol from Dhofar (and I doubt whether the Indian Customs Officers would

179

have been impressed if I had). So I decided to call on Colonel Begbie, the Defence Adviser at the British High Commission.

Begbie was a genial man, thoroughly enjoying his final posting. He was based in the High Commission, which disappointingly was located in a high-security office block in the centre of Nairobi. Following the anti-British feeling that peaked during the years of the Mau Mau and the fight for independence, it was understandable that diplomats needed to barricade themselves behind such defences, but it was depressing nonetheless. I was taken along a maze of corridors and told by a thin, officious, middle-aged English woman in a flowery dress to wait outside a heavily reinforced door. Next to the door was a two-way mirror, the forerunner of the closed circuit television camera. I was collected by a uniformed sergeant and, as we moved through the door, we faced a pair of tough metal gates that would not have looked out of place at Broadmoor. The doors of the cage were operated by another tight-lipped, unsmiling woman positioned on the inside. I followed the NCO down more passages, through yet more security doors and eventually we arrived in Begbie's office.

The Colonel was reading the *Daily Telegraph* and seated at a large desk. His office was that of a military man, with regimental shields on the walls alongside prints of Waterloo and Omdurman and there was a model of a field gun on a small table. Paddy King-Fretts' signal to advise of my arrival in Kenya had smoothed the way, and my request for help to buy a firearm was met with total equanimity and within twenty-four hours, the police had issued me with a Kenya government firearms licence.

Led by Begbie, I went in search of a suitable weapon in the gun shops of Nairobi. I looked at old and new captive bolts, which are humane killers that do not fire bullets but push a metal bolt perhaps 10 or 12 centimetres long into the brain of the animal and then withdraw it. A wise old veterinary surgeon once told me never to use a captive bolt pistol unless I had a spare one, for if the animal moved at a crucial moment the bolt might bend, rendering the gun useless. You could then be stuck with an injured or dying animal but with no means of finishing it off. Not helpful in a Force 8 gale and 15-foot waves on the Indian Ocean.

An elderly Scottish gunsmith called McNab proudly produced from the depths of his shop an ancient and dusty 0.310 Greener humane killer. This old-fashioned weapon had a 9-inch barrel and bell-shaped muzzle that fired a free bullet when a wooden mallet was tapped firmly against the firing pin. Both hands were needed to fire the Greener, so it was pretty useless if you were on your own with a distressed animal. It also took an age to unscrew, remove the spent cartridge and reload in cases where a second shot may be needed. Eventually I decided to buy a 9-millimetre Browning automatic pistol as I was familiar with it and had used it to shoot horses. I also bought twenty rounds of ammunition, which with hindsight

seems extremely pessimistic. Begbie sorted out the necessary Export Certi-
fication and the weapon was stored in his safe until I left for Mombasa. He
helpfully telephoned East African Airways to advise them that I would be
travelling with a firearm; he must have been a superb networker, as I was
able to check in with ease, sign a few forms, and the gun and ammunition
were taken off in a sealed package to travel in the cockpit to Mombasa
where I retrieved them without difficulty.

Don Henderson suggested I flew to Mombasa ahead of him to establish
contact with the shipping company and, if possible, see the *Southern Trader*
to discuss the crating and loading of the bulls. He would stay in Nairobi to
ensure the animals were successfully gathered together and, accompanied
by some African handlers from the farms, loaded onto a freight train and
despatched along the 450-kilometre single-track railway that linked the
two cities. Once the train had departed, Don would fly down to join me.

As Kenya's main port with ready access to the Indian Ocean, Mombasa,
which in earlier times had been ruled by Oman, was a thriving city of half a
million inhabitants. It was much dirtier than Nairobi with a stimulating
blend of cultures from Africa, Arabia, Asia and Europe. Old Mombasa is
built on an island linked by a causeway to the mainland. The old harbour,
with its labyrinth of ancient narrow paths and houses and exotic smells,
handled the dhows and small cargo vessels but there was also a vast
modern port with deep-water berths, busy with the to-ing and fro-ing of
container ships, tankers, liners and large vessels supplying not only Kenya
but also Uganda, Ethiopia and Southern Sudan.

From my room in the Nyali Beach Hotel, among the palm-fringed, up-
market outskirts of the town and on the creek leading to the new harbour,
I watched a seemingly endless succession of ships passing only a few
hundred metres from my bedroom window, as they cruised slowly in or
out of the port.

I telephoned the shipping company and learned that the *Southern Trader*
was two days late arriving from her previous voyage and so our own
sailing date would be set back. I sent a telex to Henderson and the telex
operator gamely tried to get a line through also to Robin Butler at DDD.
It took her about twelve hours to make the connection to Salalah but as
soon as she got through she rang me in my room. I came down at once in
case there was any reply or decision needed. Telexes always took a few
minutes to transmit and print out and I was pleased to discover Robin was
on line at the other end. I could picture her typing away on the bulky grey
machine in the DDD office. There was no problem about the sailing
but the text spewing out at my end went on to advise: 'MCGILLIGAN
RESIGNED. PLEASE CONTACT DR ROY ANSELL WHO WAS RUNNER
UP ON SHORTLIST AND LIVES NAIROBI STOP ASCERTAIN HIS

CONTINUING INTEREST IN POSITION OF DDD VO.' A telephone number followed.

I was sad that Connor had called it a day. Much as I liked him, I felt he knew early on that the job was not what he wanted or anticipated. I telephoned Roy Ansell and explained the position and what I was doing in Mombasa. He said he would fly down to join me the following day. He came with his wife, Elizabeth, who was also a vet. Roy was about fifty and had considerable experience in the Arabian Gulf, having worked in R'as Al Khaymah, a tiny state in the United Arab Emirates, where he had helped to develop a national dairy project. It was from this farm that Mike Butler had obtained the original two Friesian bulls for *Bir Bint Ahmed* used for the pioneering work to upgrade the *jebali* cattle.

Roy suggested travelling with me on the ship to Salalah. This would enable him to see Dhofar, meet Mike, and discuss things with Connor if he was still there. I sent a telex off to DDD and a positive reply soon came back. The Ansells flew back to Nairobi and I told Roy I would phone him as soon as we got a departure time for *Southern Trader*.

The bulls and Don Henderson arrived next day. The animals inside their spacious cattle trucks were shunted into a siding at Mombasa station, a delightful red brick relic with its memorable faded lettering over one entrance declaring 'Upper Class passengers only'. Our bulls were scheduled to remain in their trucks only for one or two days, but in fact it was over a week before we could unload them and get them on board the ship. The *Southern Trader* had finally berthed, but now there was a dock strike, which meant the vessel could neither offload its cargo of consumables nor load up our bulls. Henderson decided to fly back to Nairobi until the strike was settled. He left two cow-hands and plenty of feed. I was quite happy at the prospect of relaxing in the Nyali Beach Hotel and exploring Mombasa, but first I went to find the ship.

The *Southern Trader* was lounging patiently in the unusually still harbour. It was not a handsome vessel, nor was it particularly big. At first sight it did not inspire confidence as it was flying the Liberian flag, was in need of repainting and the deck seemed haphazardly crammed with all shapes and sizes of crates waiting to be unloaded. It was built a bit like a small oil tanker with the bridge and living accommodation aft. The deck stretched for'ard with, at equal distances along its length, two rigging masts which were the ship's own cranes for use in ports with no lifting devices of their own. I relaxed a bit when I found that the Master and First Mate were British and there was a young, chirpy German Chief Engineer who over the next couple of days took me on an exploration of some of Mombasa's nautical nightspots.

Colonel Begbie had sent down with Don a signal that had arrived for me from my military chiefs in MOD. They noted McGilligan's decision to quit but the Director AVRS, Brigadier Hector Wilkins, was clearly unimpressed with my suggestion that my tour should be extended until a replacement was found. The message was short and sharp and told me my orders were to leave Oman as soon as practicable. However, first I had to get back there with my load of bulls.

Eventually, the dock strike was settled and the *Southern Trader* was able to unload its deteriorating perishable cargo and load up for its next voyage. I contacted Henderson and Ansell, who both flew down the next day. Meanwhile the cattle in their trucks were shunted down to the quayside. We watched as the ship completed loading the rest of its freight, made up of cement for the Gulf, potatoes for Somalia, and lubrication oil for Aden. The ship, which was based in Mombasa, would call first at Salalah, then Kuwait before returning back via Aden and Berbera. In total, they expected to be away about six weeks.

The crates that would house the bulls on board ship were made of tough hardwood fencing and were put together individually and carefully under Henderson's expert eye. First, three sides of each crate were bolted together, then the crate was loaded by crane onto a flat lorry, which was backed up to the cattle wagon so that the open side of the crate nestled up against the door of the railway truck. The crate had a robust floor and slatted sides so the bulls would be able to see out. It was a clever design. We persuaded the first two reluctant Sahiwals to leave their cattle truck and enter the crate. As soon as they were in, Don's men fastened the fourth side to the crate. Steel bars were slipped under the loading palette and chains swiftly attached. A Kenyan crane operator shouted to the stevedores, and with a lurch and a sway and a prayer the perplexed bulls became airborne. Soon the crate was dangling 20 metres above the ground, gently rotating to and fro on its chains. The crane driver gently moved his load until it was hanging above the deck of the ship. Then, guided by the First Mate and helped by some of the crew, the crate was lowered down and landed with a thump near the bows, where it was rapidly and securely fastened in place on the deck.

Four crates and nine bulls were loaded with incredible speed. Two crates were positioned aft, then there was a consignment of fifty large drums of lubrication oil, beyond which the other two crates were secured in the bows. The fodder and bedding were next loaded and stowed under canvas sheeting by the two aft crates. We fixed canvas shelters over the top of each crate, making effective sunshades and providing some sort of protection against the weather and sea. The bulls coped remarkably well with the loading, and the handlers and I tipped sawdust into the crates, fed and watered the animals and left them contentedly chewing.

The Mate showed me my cabin. It was on the main deck and although small was reasonably comfortable and clean in a salty, maritime sort of way, with centimetre-thick layers of white gloss paint lining the walls. I could look out to sea through a small, rusting porthole, unlike poor Roy who, as a late booking, was given a cabin below decks. I hoped he had a good sea stomach. The Mate said the Master, Captain Green, was to take the ship out to anchor to make way for another vessel and as we would leave on the early morning tide, Roy and I must be on board by 0700 hours.

We had a small party that evening at the Nyali Beach. I signed all the remaining papers and said goodbye to Don Henderson with a promise to telex him as soon as we arrived safely in Salalah. Early next morning Roy and I were delivered by a small launch to the *Southern Trader*. We clambered aboard, struggling with our belongings. I was relieved to find the bulls were perfectly content. The Master said they had all had a quiet night with no complaints and most of them were lying down for much of the time. One tedious Boran had somehow managed to turn round in his crate so he had his back to the direction of travel and now had his companion's rump for company. Well, they would have to stay that way.

We made ourselves as comfortable as possible in our cramped quarters and then I set to work. I suddenly missed Don's two men and realised the deck was a fair length for carting buckets of water, sacks of sawdust and bales of hay. As I worked, the anchor was weighed and MV *Southern Trader* gently steamed out of port, passing the Nyali Beach Hotel, colonial waterside houses and a nightclub or two that I preferred to forget.

The Mate pointed out what he called a ghost ship, moored about a mile offshore. It was surrounded by marker buoys and had been there for several years. According to folklore, her Master had misread his chart coming into Mombasa and run aground on what was a notorious coral reef. The cargo had been wheat, and when the Kenyan navy sent a recovery vessel to try to refloat the ship, they put some men on board to check the hold. By then, as the ship had been holed, the corn was wet and was rapidly fermenting and decomposing. When the hatches were opened, the escape of noxious gas had killed three sailors. This had given rise to so much local superstition that nobody else would go near what was now known as 'the evil ship'. So it stayed where it was, at least providing a good clear warning of the location of the reef.

Soon we were out at sea. The sun shone, the sea was calm, and with a Goanese cook conjuring up masterpieces in his tiny galley, it was possible to enjoy the whole experience. Apart from the feeding and watering routine three times a day, I spent much of the time on the bridge chatting or lounging comfortably on the bulls' bedding stored on the deck, gazing at the sea and the clear blue sky, which for the first few days was spotted only with shreds of cloud. It was particularly lovely in the early morning when it was cool and fresh and I would stroll along the deck throwing back into the waves the bodies of dozens of shiny silver flying fish which had landed on the deck during the night. By day, we would be accompanied by dolphins leaping elegantly through the water keeping easy pace with our 18 knots.

The Master said if we had left it a couple more weeks, we would have run into the monsoon when the weather could turn very nasty. I got a foretaste of what he meant as we approached the Socotra Archipelago, a series of four undeveloped islands, which, until the 1967 withdrawal, had been home to a remote British garrison. The islands now belonged to the PDRY and there was said to be a strong Russian presence on the main island.

As we approached the isolated islands, the wind got up, the sky darkened and the sea became rough. I was anxious about the crates and with the crew's help checked and tightened all the securing ropes, but the crates stayed firmly anchored to the rolling deck although the bulls got uneasy at having to shift their weight constantly with the swell. I also found it tricky tottering along the swaying deck with buckets of feed and water, lurching from oil-drum to oil-drum with little between me and the sea. We rolled past Socotra, and on the fifth day out of Mombasa we approached Yemeni waters.

When we were only a day from Salalah, the Master said it was time to contact DDD on the radio. I dug out the frequency and from the bridge tuned in. At once I heard Robin Butler's familiar voice: 'Dhofar Development Department to Raysut Harbour. Are you receiving me, Jeremy? Over.'

The message was repeated as I listened in my floating farm somewhere in the Arabian Sea, 500 kilometres from Raysut. The message was repeated. Dhofar's phone lines were so erratic that if Robin needed to contact Jeremy the radio was often easier. Yet there seemed to be nobody in Jeremy's office and the radio fell silent. It seemed like a good time to call up.

'Dhofar Development Department, Dhofar Development Department, Dhofar Development Department. This is Southern Trader, Southern Trader, Southern Trader. How do you read me? Over.'

There was a pause, then Robin's voice came clearly over the ether. There was a distinct note of surprise in her voice. She had been expecting Jeremy Raybould.

'Hello Southern Trader. This is Dhofar Development Department. Where on earth are you? You're not expected for two days yet! Over.'

'Hi Robin. Andrew here. We've made good time and our ETA is 0900 tomorrow morning. Bulls have travelled well and so far no one has been seasick. Everything OK at your end? Over.'

'Yes. Everything's fine and we are ready for the bulls. Roger to your ETA. Is Roy Ansell with you? Over.'

'Affirmative. Is Connor still in Dhofar? Over.'

185

'Yes. Roger to that. He and Mike will be at the dock to welcome you. Over.'

'Thanks. See you tomorrow. Dhofar Development Department from Southern Trader. Out.'

It was a misty, dull morning when we eased our way into Omani waters. It was really quite eerie as we approached the coast and landmarks slowly emerged from the gloom. We raised the Omani flag and the Master radioed Jeremy to ask for a pilot. Jeremy replied that he would be right out to join us and the engines slowed almost to a stop. We drifted softly until we heard Jeremy's launch coming through the sea mists of the *khareef*. Connor McGilligan was with him and they both climbed on board.

Jeremy set about guiding the helmsman and getting *Southern Trader* into port. Having introduced Connor to Roy, I set about preparing myself and the bulls for landing. It was odd, I thought, that Dhofar had survived all those years without a veterinary surgeon and suddenly there were three of us arriving together on a cargo ship along with nine bulls.

We soon moored. I was stunned at the ease with which Jeremy got 5,000 tonnes of metal precisely where he wanted them alongside a quay full of expectant onlookers. Robin was there with her two sons and in no time the boys had run up the gangplank to explore. Saleh and Hafeedth had brought a posse of helpers in case we needed manpower. The formalities of immigration and customs were totally forgotten in the excitement and we could easily have offloaded supplies for PFLOAG without anyone really noticing.

For the second time I suffered agonies as the crates with their valuable living cargo were unloaded. This time my concern was that the wooden floors of the crates, now sodden with urine and faeces as well as sea spray, would still safely carry the weight of their beefy passengers. One sagged a bit ominously but, with the ubiquitous Raybould at the controls of the crane, we soon had the bulls off the ship and onto waiting army lorries. Then they were off to their quarantine area on the hill overlooking the port. They settled well and, three weeks later, Mike Butler transferred them to their various locations around the Province, where they served out their days.

Connor had agreed to accept a University appointment in Dublin. Roy Ansell continued his discussions with Mike to take over from Connor as Provincial Veterinary Officer for Dhofar before flying back to Kenya to sort out his affairs. MOD signalled BATT to say I was to be posted in two weeks' time to the Veterinary and Remount HQ in Droitwich. And the MV *Southern Trader* resumed its lonely voyage, delivering its potatoes, cement and lubrication oil.

Chapter 20

A Sleepless Night

While Roy Ansell was negotiating terms with Mike Butler, and with Connor McGilligan still sitting in the office in *Bir Bint Ahmed*, I wanted to pay one further visit to the *jebal*. I talked it through with the new 'D' Squadron OC and we decided Raven's Roost was the place to go. This BATT camp was said to have been named after an SAS troop commander, Peter Raven, who had successfully taken and held the position many years previously. Another claim was that WO Steve Raven of the Intelligence Corps had spent many weeks locating *adoo* bases and stores while perched high on a plateau on this northernmost part of the *jebal* overlooking the *Negd*.

To reach Raven's Roost, I caught a Skyvan to Midway which meant driving back towards Salalah along the Midway road. I was met at the arid and dusty airstrip by a couple of BATT troopers and a 5-tonne Bedford lorry, which was armour-plated against mines. The lorry was piled high with stores and six *firqats* were perched on top. I climbed up to join them and the truck lurched off to link up with two others and a Land Rover escort.

We drove south along the rutted, roughly graded road towards the northern foothills of the *jebal*. After 15 kilometres or so of dry, desert landscape, we began to climb. The twisting track wound its way through a series of rocky basins surrounded by forbidding cliffs, jutting harshly skywards towards the hot midday sun. It would not have been difficult to ambush the convoy. Lofty promontories dwarfed our trucks as we threaded our way into the *jebal*.

Since the time of Sultan Said bin Taimur, the Midway Road had been regularly targeted, effectively preventing Dhofar from developing trade routes overland through the Empty Quarter to Muscat and the Gulf. Sultan Qaboos had decided that this obstacle must be overcome, and a tarmac road had been planned, initially to run between Salalah and Midway, but later to extend further on to the north. However, to get civilian contractors to work on this vital artery, it was first necessary to secure the route.

An Iranian Battle Group of some 1,200 men had been sent by the Shah specifically to take and defend the Midway Road. In a successful pincer movement, the Iranians had moved in from the north and south and built a series of fortified positions along the length of the road. So far, the exercise had worked well, despite the Iranians' trigger-happy inexperience and their American-trained approaches to military life.

Suddenly the gradient became so steep that the truck ground to a halt while our driver engaged his lowest gear. We then set off again with the engine protesting vigorously and noisily at the effort it was being asked to make. We crawled reluctantly up the hill at an excruciatingly slow pace, spewing sand and grit behind us in a choking blur. Halfway up the escarpment was a devil's elbow where the road turned through 90 degrees with no relenting of incline. The sturdy engine roared and the wheels spun on the dirt surface as we inched our way round the bend less than a metre from the edge of an unprotected and awesome precipice.

The *firqats* fell silent and held tightly to the edge of the lorry, placing their trust in Allah and the skill of our BATT driver. I gazed philosophic-ally down into the abyss, where I could see the shells of vehicles that had failed to negotiate the bend successfully. Soon the view was obliterated by the billowing dust thrown up by the spinning tyres and I calculated how best to throw myself to safety if we skidded backwards or suddenly met another vehicle coming in the other direction. Yet, with agonising slow-ness, we eventually reached the top of the hill and the tension eased among the hardened *firqats* who, unlike me, had probably made the journey many times before.

Soon, the first of the sand-bagged defences of the Iranians came into view. My heart skipped a beat and my hand tightened on my Armalite as two men suddenly appeared and started running towards us waving rifles. They turned out to be Iranian soldiers wanting a lift to the Roost. We stopped and they cheerily climbed on board. No conversation was possible as they only spoke Farsi, which was as incomprehensible to the *jebali*-speaking *firqats* as it was to me.

Raven's Roost was marked by large whitewashed stones laid out to form a prominent 'RR' near the helicopter landing site at the entrance to the camp. The BATT location was in a dip surrounded by steep imposing hills with Iranian picquets visible on the top. The story was told how one dark and misty night two picquets on opposing hills had mistaken each other for *adoo*, and prolonged crossfire had taken place with several men wounded. The BATT team, roused from their slumbers in the valley below, had watched in bewilderment as the intensity of the attacks increased and tracer bullets flew ever more frequently over their heads. They had restored sanity by firing several green Verey lights into the sky and even-tually managing to get an English-speaking Iranian officer on the radio.

'D' Squadron's four-man unit was settling in to the Roost and seemed pleased to have a visit from the vet as it helped to cement relations with the local *jebalis*. After a quick lunch, we went to look at the well that was being dug nearby. It was a deep one, already at 150 metres and still drilling, but the signs were good that this would be a productive source of water. I was driven to a small *jebali* camp and, after the usual introductions, was asked to look at some sick goats. The cattle were away grazing, but the word would get around that I was at the camp for a couple of days and any other problems could be dealt with in the morning.

The women tending the goats were young and pretty and their heads were uncovered but as we came into view the *batula*, or face veil, was wrapped around their faces. The word *batula* may come from the Arabic for virgin. It all was part of the Islamic tradition of dressing and behaving modestly.

It looked as though there was a celebration imminent. Several girls were sitting in a circle painting each others' hands and feet with *henna*. *Henna* comes from a flowering shrub called *Lawsonia inermis,* named after an eighteenth-century Scottish physician, Isaac Lawson. The leaves are harvested, dried and powdered, and then made into a reddish-brown paste which is used to make intricate and ornate designs on the palms of the hands, soles of the feet, and faces of girls and women. The dye lasts for weeks and is used to mark big occasions in a family such as a betrothal or marriage or the ritual circumcision of youths. Men, especially those who have been on the *hadj*, or pilgrimage to Mecca (one of the Five Pillars of Islam), sometimes stain their beards with *henna*. Today, I learned, a wedding was approaching. *Jebali* youths often married at fifteen or sixteen, and the girls were sometimes a couple of years younger than that. A particularly beautiful or well-bred bride might cost a father fifty cows, a huge expense for these subsistence pastoralists.

I was billeted in a tent which was used as the pharmacy, but the ongoing nervousness of the Iranians prevented any decent length of sleep as every so often a burst of automatic fire would startle me awake. Shadows on the hill must have frightened the soldiers on guard duty. I rammed cotton wool in my ears and covered my head with my combat jacket and eventually fell asleep. Then, at two o'clock in the morning, I was woken for my 'stag duty'. The 'D' Squadron team assured me that on the *jebal* BATT visitors traditionally took the worst stags between midnight and 0400 hours – the graveyard watch. A likely tale. I yawned, opened my eyes and turned over; the BATT guy I was taking over from gave me a cup of tea ('Have a whet, mate'), which was very welcome at that time of the morning after two hours' sleep and I told him so.

'Bit of tracer fire to watch,' he chuckled. 'But apart from the mad Persians, it's all quiet. Pete's on next; wake him if you see anything.'

With that he turned to his *basha* and I was left alone, sitting on a large rock watching the stars and clutching my Armalite. It was a long two hours and it can be chilly on the *jebal* in the middle of the night. I was kept alert by the occasional volleys and sometimes answering fire from picquets on the surrounding hills. From time to time I got up and wandered about the Camp, careful not to go too far from Pete's *basha*, wondering like the neighbouring Iranians whether an *adoo* might just have crept up to that bush over there and have me at that very moment in his infrared sights. A rustling just outside the silent Camp's perimeter had me down on one knee with eyes and ears straining until I heard the forlorn bleat of a lost goat hunting for the rest of the flock, which were probably in a nearby cave with their *jebali* owners. We had a brief conversation, but I was not interesting enough, and the nervous animal trotted off to look for better company.

It turned out the goat had a lucky escape. During my visit I removed bullets from a camel and a goat. There was no doubt in the minds of the animals' owners that they had been shot by Iranian soldiers, maybe deliberately out of boredom or during some night panic attack. With the high value of their animals it was understandable that the owners were angry. If an animal died through enemy action, the Sultan had agreed to pay compensation but injuries, particularly when caused by our own side, were just inconvenient. It did nothing to enhance the hill people's opinions of their Iranian defenders.

After two busy veterinary days, I left Raven's Roost and the *jebal* for the last time in an RAF Wessex helicopter. I climbed in next to the Loadmaster and we took off. At the controls was Flight Lieutenant Alek Tarwid, a charismatic Polish pilot who, it was said, simply did not know the meaning of the word 'impossible'. As we were chugging towards Salalah, I heard on the headphones Alek acknowledge an order from ground control to make for Mirbat to collect a sick woman.

'Good job ve have ze vet on board,' came the comment from the cockpit.

Mirbat is on the central strip of the Dhofar coast between Taqah and Sudh, and about 70 kilometres from Salalah. Its name was said to come from *marabat al khail* or, literally, the place for tethering horses, as the village was once famed for breeding Arabian horses which were exported along with frankincense all around the world. Mirbat was an attractive town from the air, with a large traditional Omani fortress on the sea and a spectacular coastline running back through some irrigated fields to the impressive peaks of *Jebal Samhan* behind. The village was old and the large, stone-built merchants' houses mingled with the usual hotchpotch of half-built homes, piles of rubbish and general air of underdevelopment. There were several fishing boats and I could see the nets spread out and the silver blankets of sardines laid on the beach to dry in the sun.

The inevitable crowd gathered as the mighty Wessex descended, throwing up a far greater sandstorm than the humbler Huey. The watchers were undeterred. Alek turned off the engines. An old Land Rover came scurrying up to us, scattering the crowd. It was the *Wali*.

'I vill leave zis to you,' came the voice from above as the Loadmaster slid open the door.

I sighed and got out, wishing Saleh or Hafeedth had been with me to translate. The *Wali* was a nervous-looking man with an ingrained worried look. He came up to the aircraft as I leapt down to greet him.

'*Salaam alay koom.*'

'*Way alay koom salaam.*'

'*Kayf haalak?*'

'*Al hamdu l'Illah. Wa inta kayf haalic?*'

'*Al hamdu l'Illah.*'

'*Al hamdu l'Illah.*'

'*Ahlan. Ahlan. T'fuddl.*'

I thanked the Sheikh for his welcome as best I could but explained that we were in something of a hurry to get back to Salalah. The *Wali* spoke rapidly to one of his companions, who in turn shouted over the crowd. The sick woman was carried through the parting onlookers, lying on a conventional bed, carried by four men. Women fluttered around her, one clutching a large bundle of belongings, another mopping her brow and everyone shouting instructions to everyone else. A man, probably her husband, brought up the rear. He was clearly prepared for the journey as he was dressed in a clean dishdash and wore a rather worn but treasured *khunja* at his navel. He was carrying his gun, an ancient Lee Enfield .303.

'How are you going to get the bed in?' I mischievously asked the Loadmaster.

'That bloody thing's not coming in my aircraft,' he muttered darkly.

I decided the time had come to be gallant and to try to exercise some leadership skills. I waded into the crowd and tried my Arabic on the *Wali*. The woman seemed to have some sort of abdominal crisis but I could not understand exactly what. I realised the task was to get her loaded into the Wessex as comfortably as we could. This seemed to be generally understood and the bed was lifted to the door of the helicopter. I persuaded the Loadmaster to open his door a bit wider and the men somehow lifted the poor woman up, until eventually she could be gently eased off the bed and into the Wessex. We then hoisted in a woman companion who wrapped the patient in the bedding as best she could.

The bed was still alongside the door and acted as an effective barricade to keep the large and pressing crowd at a sensible distance. The husband jumped on the bed and climbed in to join his wife and the woman. Then the bed was carried away. At this point there was a rush for the door and a dozen or so men all tried to get inside the helicopter. The Loadmaster tried to slide the door shut but somehow ended up rolling over the sick woman.

The Arabic shouts and the Loadmaster's English expletives were now matched by some strong Polish ones from somewhere above us as Alek got out of his seat to see what was going on. I stood astride the woman to try to protect her from being crushed.

The *Wali* was embarrassed by the riot and with a lot of shouting and effort he got something approaching order. Everyone, it seemed, had a very good reason for wanting a lift to Salalah: there were sick relatives to see, camels to buy, favours to ask. The reasons were endless. There hadn't been a helicopter for two days, and as there was plenty of room they couldn't understand why they were being turned away. Alek was livid at having his aircraft invaded and compromise was not an option. He would take the sick woman, her companion and husband. And that would be all. With a lot of complaining and some very black looks, the extra passengers were persuaded to disembark.

I had no time to say goodbye to the *Wali* as the Loadmaster, having recovered his composure, slammed the door shut.

'Let's get the hell out of here.'

The co-pilot started the engines as Alek, still muttering unknown opin-ions in his native language, clambered back into his seat. As the aircraft lifted, the crowd below was dowsed in sand and debris with *jalabiyas* billowing and headdresses flapping frantically in the rotorwash. Our passengers had their eyes shut in terror. The patient meanwhile con-tinued to groan and I gently mopped her brow and tried to reassure her. The Loadmaster stared vacantly out of his little window, occasionally shaking his head as if baffled by it all.

When we arrived back at RAF Salalah, the Wessex circled the airport for a time. This was unusual but the Loadmaster had not offered me a set of headphones on the return trip so I had little idea why we were being held nor what the uneasy expression on his face might mean as he listened to the exchanges between Alek and the co-pilot and the control tower. Suddenly, we stopped moving forward and hovered about 10 metres above the ground. The Loadmaster hooked his safety harness on to a clip above the door, slid it open and leaned right out, apparently searching the belly of the aircraft. He was reporting back to the pilots. I sat quietly and watched.

Next, Alek flew the helicopter to the end of the runway, turned and we sped along it as if we were a fixed-wing aircraft, less than a metre from the ground. Under less alarming circumstances and with no ill passenger on board, I would have assumed this was a bit of harmless fun – but it was more than that. Every 100 metres or so, Alek would let the Wessex down so the main wheels of the undercarriage hit the runway. The *jebalis* seemed unmoved by these tactics but it may have been their first trip in a

Wessex and they probably thought it was a normal landing. At least they were almost on the ground again.

As we raced along the runway, the Loadmaster kept leaning out of the door, now peering towards the rear of the aircraft. Then he yelled something to the pilots and smiled. We lifted off the ground a little higher and then landed perfectly normally on a helipad outside Brigade Headquarters.

'What was all that about?' I asked as the engines slowed.

'Bloody rear wheel got stuck. He had to bounce it down,' he added, jerking his head up at Alek's feet. 'We don't want wheels getting stuck too often, costs a lot to fix the tail of a Wessex.'

Around the time that 'D' Squadron arrived in Dhofar, the Secret status surrounding the presence of British Special Forces in Oman suddenly seemed to evaporate. That the SAS was deployed in Dhofar had been mooted from time to time in the UK press, and questions had been asked in Parliament, but it had all been remarkably low-key. Now the newspapers had decided there was a story to be told and lengthy articles appeared, confirming the presence of 22 SAS as active participants in the Dhofar Campaign. It became known that BFPO 66 was in fact an oasis outpost of South-East Arabia called Salalah.

In any case, life was becoming safer. Salalah was confirmed as secure. Thanks to the Iranians, the road to Midway was virtually secure and a new tarmac road was being built. The territory east of the Midway Road was rapidly being cleared of *adoo*, whose main area of operation was now largely confined to the land west of the Hornbeam Line and the 80 or so kilometres to the PDRY border. Underground water reservoirs were being found in significant quantities at key locations and, based on the wells, Martin Robb's CAD was rapidly establishing reliable services for the *jebalis* – food, schools, mosques, medicine and veterinary care for animals. The infrastructure was improving rapidly, schools and hospitals developed and self-confidence was palpably growing. Mike Butler's large Kenyan bulls were covering the tiny, if rather surprised *jebali* cows, and livestock production was happening. The Hearts and Minds campaign had played a major part in winning the war: the Dhofaris could now practise their religion and were no longer threatened with communism and its inherent atheism; education was open to all without Marxist indoctrination; water was available and there was an increasing ability for the *jebali* pastoralists to herd their animals freely across tribal areas. It was a remarkable period in Dhofar's history and I was lucky to be there.

Chapter 21

Ma's as-salaama

As the last few days of my posting approached, my emotions were confused. There was a mixture of sadness to be leaving the Dhofar community, military and civilian, and frustration about what to do about my future. I was in a strange state of limbo, uncertain whether there was a job for me within the Palace structure. John Clarke and Tony Brunton had both encouraged me to join them, not least for purely practical reasons as the new DDD Veterinary Officer would not be dropping everything to hop on a plane to Muscat. Certainly the Royal Stables did need a vet and one with both an interest in horses and an enthusiasm for the unusual type of work offered in Oman. Clarke told me he had spoken to Mac Maclean and to Colonel Said Salem. The bush telegraph operated efficiently and I was soon told by everyone I met that I was going to be offered the job. Yet despite this, I had heard nothing.

It would be a unique opportunity, but I was still in two minds. An offer would pose a dilemma as I was only halfway through my short service commission. It was highly unusual for someone to resign his commission. In addition, I loved the army and as the RAVC was desperately short of young officers I had no wish to cause problems for my Director, Brigadier Hector Wilkins, who had been so supportive and trusting in selecting me for the Oman posting, and for whom I had a lot of respect. Wilkins himself knew about the region. In 1940 he was posted to British Forces in Persia and Iraq and in 1942 he oversaw the veterinary care of 3,000 mules as they were marched from Aleppo in Syria to Kirkuk in Iraq, a distance of 400 miles. Remarkably only four animals died.

I reminded myself not to be hasty as my commission offered a guaranteed salary and a tax-free gratuity at the end of the three years. However, Wilkins was about to be replaced by Brigadier Harry Orr, who had strongly hinted that my next posting would be as Veterinary Officer to the King's Troop Royal Horse Artillery in St. John's Wood in London and this was a job I coveted. The alternative prospect of pioneering the veterinary services for the Royal Stables in a politically unstable region might not be so secure but it would certainly be exciting and, if I was paid as a contract officer, would be lucrative too.

I packed my trunk and delivered it to the cargo section at RAF Salalah. It would go on the first available flight to the UK and would be waiting for me at Brize Norton. The previous couple of weeks had been full of farewells and I felt so indebted to everyone that on my last Friday I threw a party at the RAF Mess which was a lot of fun although I spent most of the time parrying questions about my future.

I was scheduled to catch the shuttle to Masirah on Monday morning and, following Scott Moffat's lead, I had arranged to check the RAF dogs there before getting the VC10 home. Then, on Saturday, Robin Butler received a message from Maclean to say he would be very grateful if I would fly to Muscat the following day to see him. If I stayed overnight in Muscat I could catch a flight to Masirah on Monday morning in time for my VC10 connection. I agreed and Robin signalled Maclean to confirm and asked him to book the Masirah flight. Using all her skill, she somehow got me a seat on Sunday's overcrowded SOAF Viscount to Muscat.

And so, unexpectedly, Saturday became the time to say goodbye, and my scheduled circuit for Sunday was abandoned as I scurried round trying to catch as many people as possible. The hardest part was leaving Saleh and Hafeedth, with whom I had worked so closely for six intense months. However, having seen five other BATT Vets come and go, and with Roy Ansell about to return shortly from Kenya, they were far more philosophical than I was.

'*Inshalla* you come back,' smiled Saleh as we shook hands at *Bir Bint Ahmed*.

'I hope your house will be finished and your business does really well,' I told him. He gave a big smile.

Hafeedth, now a married man, had jettisoned his lime-green suits and these days was more conventionally dressed in an ordinary dishdash. He gave every indication that he was enjoying marriage and I knew that before long he would have a family and would be embarking on house-building and a business like Saleh. I wished him all the very best and asked him to keep a special eye on the *jebal* locations for me. We had shared some fun experiences on the hill.

At BATT, I handed in my kit and signed off my material association with the SAS as I passed over my Bergen, webbing and the unused vials of morphine that had been around my neck for half a year. 'D' Squadron were well settled in by now and, as the OC was up on the *jebal*, I left him a farewell note. The Ops Officer signalled MOD with my revised flight times. In the BATT bar, the PSYOPS team of Ben Higson and his NCOs gave me a leaving present of two ash-trays made from the heavy bases of the brass casings of 25-pounder shells, which were marked with their year of manufacture – 1973. To each, a silver Omani coin had been fastened to the hub of

195

the firing pin. We shared a few beers to mark the departure of the last BATT Vet and the success of the campaign over the previous three years.

That evening, I returned to the Kennel Club for a final drink with the dog-handlers. This time, I managed to stay upright and everyone was very friendly. In future they would contact Roy Ansell whenever they needed veterinary cover. Mike Butler would probably even invoice them for the work.

Dhofar was evolving, and military management would soon be replaced with civil administrations. And the phenomenal pace that had accelerated so fast during the first six months of 1974 would speed up immeasurably once the war was officially over. Things had to move on and although it was the end of an era I recognised in my heart that the BATT veterinary support had never been more than a transitory but hopefully constructive part of the Hearts and Minds campaign of the historic Operation Storm.

The next morning, Mac Maclean met me at Seeb airport. I was staying again at Kalbuh. Although Chuck Pringle was away, he had insisted I use his house as my own. What a way to spend my last night in Arabia – in the heights of Costain luxury.

As we drove into Muscat, Maclean finally broached the subject.

'John Clarke tells me that we need a vet for the Royal Stables,' he began. 'I've spoken to Colonel Said who runs the Diwan. I have also spoken by phone to Ollie Graham-Jones, who tells me he knows just the right person for the job.'

He paused. I kept my eyes fixed on the road in front.

'If you were offered the post,' Maclean went on, 'would you be interested?'

I sighed deeply. 'Mac,' I said slowly, 'of course I would like it. But ...' I faded.

Maclean interrupted. 'Your salary would be that of a contract captain in the Sultan's Armed Forces. About £6,000 a year, tax-free of course. Plus accommodation, Palace vehicle, flights to and from the UK and so on. What about it?'

'The trouble is ...' I began again hesitantly, and then stopped. Now I had received an offer, I realised I had to make a decision. Did I want it or not? It sounds strange but I mentally flipped a coin. It came down heads.

'Let's go for it, Mac. I have absolutely no idea what the army will say but I can at least ask.'

He smiled enigmatically. 'I think your new Brigadier may already know something about it.' He glanced across at me:

'The RAVC knows perfectly well that for three years BATT Vets have looked after His Majesty's animals as part of their tasks here,' he said.

'Yes, it may have been a relatively minor part in strategic terms, but the decision-makers know that the veterinary help has played a significant role in building up relations with the Sultan. His Majesty has been enormously appreciative of all your efforts and those of your colleagues. It has been drawn to the attention of your Director that the new arrangements DDD has with their new vet requires him to confine his activities to his duties as Provincial Veterinary Officer. It seems he will have a big task ahead of him and His Majesty agrees he should not be detracted from it by having to look after the Palace animals.'

He turned off the road towards the SAF HQ at *Bait al Falaj*.

'We are going now to see General Tim Creasey. Have you met him?'

I gulped. Young Captains rarely called on General Officers Commanding.

'Er, no,' I said. 'I have met his wife and daughters riding though. Er, why are we going to see the General?'

'To solicit his support for your transfer,' Mac replied. 'So much simpler if your Director gets the story through the military net that we need you here. It will help facilitate things.'

Maclean, the ex-Petty Officer and former Secretary to the Managing Director of PDO, was a smooth operator. He had worked this plan out carefully and put it into operation with skill and attention to detail. He must have gambled that I would say yes.

'Does HM know about this?' I asked.

'Of course. I can tell you it has his full support. He will talk to the General about it when they meet tomorrow.'

We stopped outside the General's house. I wondered why we were there and not at his HQ office at *Bait al Falaj*. The General's daughter Pauline opened the door.

'It's Mr Maclean, Daddy,' she said over her shoulder.

'Come in, come in,' boomed a voice and the towering figure of General Tim appeared at his daughter's side.

This was the first time I had met a General. And this one had the reputation of tolerating fools badly. I felt I would be best advised to sit quietly and say little.

Maclean had obviously already explained the background to Creasey and I sensed that the shrewd General needed to see my reaction and to assess for himself whether I was suitable for the job. He seemed to take it for granted that I wanted it. He asked me predictable direct questions about my commission, age, aspirations and family commitments.

'I think the best approach,' he said finally, 'would be to arrange for you to be transferred to the Reserve. You would become a Regular

Army Reserve Officer and there would then be no reason why you could not accept a post as a contract officer in Oman.'

He turned to Mac. 'Would he be in SAF under my command?'

'No. We would have him either on the Palace staff or possibly within the RGR if that helped,' said Maclean. The General nodded and stood up.

'I'll give it some thought. Where are you posted to next?' He turned to me as I scrambled to my feet.

'Droitwich,' I said.

'I thought that's where the army has its medals section?'

'Yes,' I replied. 'Medals and vets.'

'Well you won't have far to go to collect your Dhofar medal,' quipped the General. 'Best of luck and have a good flight home.' He added to Maclean, 'I'll be in touch.'

As Mac drove me to Muscat for lunch, I thanked him for his interest and help.

'There's still some way to go but I think we're winning,' he said, adding, 'Colonel Said is coming to the flat this evening. We'll talk more about it then.'

There was a message waiting at the flat. It was from John Clarke asking me to visit the new stables at Seeb to look at some horses before I left. By now it was late May and the midday sun was very hot. As there was no hint that it was an emergency, I decided to wait to go to the stables until late afternoon. Mac lent me his Palace car for the one-hour drive back out to Seeb. His driver was off duty, so I drove myself feeling highly conspicuous, especially as the Palace plates got me several waves as I drove along the airport road.

The horses had settled in to their new stables. The open-plan design had worked well for airflow, but summer in Seeb was very hot and humid and, although it was only May, John had already found it necessary to fit ceiling fans above each box. As the complex was big and labour-intensive, he had recruited a lot more *syces* as well as clerks, gardeners, drivers and sweepers. The Royal Stables was becoming a big operation. Rasul Bux now had a smart pharmacy and store which he proudly showed me. The whole complex was hugely impressive. The pretty and simple *burusti* lines at Wutayyah had been taken over by the Royal Oman Police, who had set up a Mounted Division. John and Tony were both having new houses built on the site and, by the look of them, they would be worth waiting for.

It was a heat-related problem that John wanted to discuss with me. Unlike previous summers in Wutayyah, this year several of the horses had erupted with numerous small lumps mostly over their backs. These did not cause much problem except where they developed in the saddle area, which meant the animals either could not be ridden or only with thick blankets or *numnahs*. The condition reminded me of the lumpy goats in Salalah that had puzzled me so much when I first arrived and I came to think that, once again, this was probably an allergy to midge bites.

The horses were not really bothered by the swellings; there was no apparent irritation or hair loss and, except where they rubbed against a saddle, the lumps just looked unattractive. I took a biopsy from one horse to have a nodule looked at in England, where they could double-check my diagnosis. I gave the horses some long-acting steroids to reduce any inflammation and told John to apply insect repellent twice a day. Insects are often most active for fairly short periods of the year and I hoped that once the weather got really hot, their activity might decline and the lumps resolve.

The Sultan's herd of thirty racing camels had also been transferred to the new Stables. They were grazing peaceably under a clump of date palms and Tony drove me over to look at them. They were fine-looking animals. Camel races were popular in the villages of northern Oman and regional events were held, culminating in the big National Day races. Sultan Qaboos took a mild interest in his camels but one of his uncles was very keen and kept a close eye on the pedigree, breeding and training of the Royal string. Somehow I was persuaded to climb on the back of one of the older females, who obligingly went down on her brisket to make it easy to get on. I would have preferred a saddle. The idea, I thought, was simply to take a photograph but Tony knew perfectly well what he was doing when he told the handler to take me for a walk. The camel jerked forward and then back as she stood up. I felt a very long way above the ground but surprisingly comfortable as we ambled around the grove. After our short ride, the handler tapped the camel's foreleg to make her go down again to let me off. There must be a definite technique for maintaining balance, I thought as I picked myself up from the sand to hoots of laughter.

Many further changes were planned at Seeb. The Sultan was so pleased with his new stables he had decided there would now be a racecourse around it, with Tony as the Racing Manager. Polo was to be introduced, and John was to arrange for a polo field and Club to be set up. Ideas were also being considered for a stud farm for Omani Arabian horses leading to the establishment of a Royal Oman Stud Book. So much had happened in such a short period of time, but this was typical of the pace of development in this dynamic country.

'Oh, and by the way,' said John in his sorrowful voice, but with eyes twinkling, 'I told HM we would soon need a veterinary hospital and a vet's house.'

Colonel Said Salem al Wuhaibi arrived at Mac's flat that evening. As far as he was concerned, the matter was settled. I would be working for the Royal Court and would be responsible to him. He told me the pay and conditions of service and asked when I would be returning. I told him I would let him know as soon as I could see the way ahead with MOD. He told Mac to write a formal letter to MOD for him to sign. With that, the Colonel stood up, shook hands and we parted, the deal done.

My last night was spent in Chuck Pringle's relaxing guest room. From the balcony, I gazed pensively over Kalbuh Bay and the shimmering sea as the stars twinkled in the moonlit sky. It was a warm night with a gentle breeze breathing softly landward from the Gulf. It seemed that I had just made a major life decision. I only hoped it was the right one. The next morning, Maclean's driver, Yacoub, took me to the airport for my flight to Masirah and on to Brize Norton at the end of the most exciting six months of my life.

Within a week of my return to the UK, I took up my posting at MOD (AVR) Droitwich. It was early summer and England looked at its best. On my first day, I was called into Brigadier Harry Orr's office. I had thought long and hard about this interview and I told my story as openly and honestly as I could. The new Director listened quietly, showing no trace of reaction. He debriefed me on my tour in Oman, my successes and failures and the handover to a civilian. Then he said:

> Well, it's clear to me that someone will be needed to keep the Sultan's animals fit and healthy. You are well suited for that role. If you want it, you can be transferred from the Active List to the Reserve. It will take about a month to formalise.

So I became a Regular Army Reserve Officer Class I. I wrote to Colonel Said Salem to confirm the position and within a fortnight a contract was returned to me. It was written on stiff Palace paper with the Royal Crest of Sultan Qaboos at the top and began: 'I am commanded by His Majesty to write offering you the post of Veterinary Officer to His Majesty The Sultan's Royal Stables ...' I signed the contract and three months later, in September 1974, I returned to Muscat, not as BATT Vet, but as Palace Vet to the Sultan of Oman.

* * *

On 4 December 1975, Brigadier John Akehurst, Commander Dhofar Brigade, passed a message to Sultan Qaboos. It read: 'I have the honour to inform Your Majesty that Dhofar is now secure for civil development.' The war was over.

Glossary and Abbreviations

ADC – *Aide-de-Camp*.

Adoo – The enemy.

ADU – Army Dog Unit.

Ahlan– Welcome.

AK47 – Kalashnikov 7.62mm semi-automatic assault rifle.

Alfalfa – Also known as lucerne; a fast-growing legume used for animal feed.

Al hamdu l'Illah – Thanks be to God.

Anaphylactic – A widespread and serious allergic reaction.

AP – Anti-personnel (mine).

Arachnid – Class of arthropods that includes spiders and scorpions.

Armalite – A US M16 5.56mm semi-automatic rifle.

Askar – An armed tribesman – a sort of local guard.

ATLO – Air Transport Liaison Officer.

Autonomic – A system of nerves whose actions are automatic.

AVRS – Army Veterinary and Remount Services.

Azhan – The call to prayer (from a mosque).

Bab al-Kabir – The Big Gate.

Bait – House or home.

Bait al Falaj – SAF Headquarters at Ruwi near Muscat.

BAOR – British Army of the Rhine.

Basha – A dugout, usually lined by sandbags.

BATT – British Army Training Team.

Batula – Face veil worn by women.

BBME – British Bank of the Middle East.

Bedouin or *Bedu* – A nomadic desert-dweller.

BEM – British Empire Medal.

Bergen – Rucksack.

BFPO – British Forces Post Office.

Bir Bint Ahmed – DDD's farm in Salalah where the Veterinary Office was located.

BM – Brigade Major.

Burmail – Oil-drum (after the Burma Oil Company).

Burusti – Palm fronds.

C-130 (Charlie-130) – Lockheed Hercules transport aircraft.

Cache – Hiding place (for stores, ammunition etc.).

CAD – Civil Aid Department.

Casevac – Casualty evacuation.

CAT – Civil Action Team.

CLO(D) – Civil Liaison Officer (Dhofar).

CO – Commanding Officer.

Compo – A composite 'hard' ration for use in the field.

CSM – Company Sergeant Major.

CVO – Chief Veterinary Officer.

DAA & QMG – Deputy Assistant Adjutant and Quartermaster General.

DDD – Dhofar Development Department.

DFC – Distinguished Flying Cross.

Dhobi **(wallah)** – Laundry (man).

Dianas – A series of defensive positions along the southern edge of the *jebal* overlooking Salalah.

Diwan – The Office of the Royal Court.

Djarab – Mange.

DLF – Dhofar Liberation Front.

Dystocia – Abnormal or difficult labour.

ETA(D) – Estimated time of arrival (departure).

Expat – Expatriate (foreigners living in another country).

Falaj – Irrigation canal.

FF –Frontier Force.

Firqat – A company of *jebali* (often ex-*adoo* irregulars).

FMD(V) – Foot-and-mouth disease (virus).

FN – Fabrique Nationale, a Belgian firearms manufacturer.

FRS – Fellow of the Royal Society.

FST – Field Surgical Team.

GOC – General Officer Commanding.

GPMG ('gympy') – General Purpose Machine Gun (fully automatic machine gun).

GSP – German short-haired pointer.

Hadj – The Moslem pilgrimage to Mecca.

Halwa – Gelatinous sweet delicacy made from dates or honey.

Hedgehogs – Observation posts around RAF Salalah.

HM – His Majesty (Sultan Qaboos bin Said Al Busaid).

HMS – Her Majesty's Ship.

HMAS – Her Majesty's Australian Ship.

Hornbeam line – A physical barrier 50km west of Salalah, running from Mugsayl on the coast to Oven.

HQ – Headquarters.

Huey – Agusta Bell 205 helicopter.

ID – Identity.

Inglesi – British.

Inshalla – God willing.

Int – Intelligence.

IO – Intelligence Officer.

Jalabiya **(dishdash)** – Long robe traditionally worn by the men.

Jebal – Hill.

Jebal Akhdar – The Green Mountain (in Northern Oman), focus of a major campaign in the late 1950s.

Jebali – Hill people, or used to describe something from the *jebal*.

Juma – Friday. The holy day.

Jungli – Cowboy.

Kayf haalak – How are things?

Khareef – Monsoon mist.

Khobz – Arabic flat bread, like chapattis.

Khunja – Omani dagger with curved blade, often having an ornate silver sheath.

KJ – *Kateebat Janoobiya* (Southern Regiment).
Longhi – A skirt-like garment worn by men.
M79 – US 40mm grenade-launcher.
Ma'a as-salaama – Goodbye.
Maglis – A place where guests are received.
MASH – US Mobile Army Surgical Hospital.
Moazzhin – The Moslem official who calls the faithful to prayer (from a mosque).
MOD – Ministry of Defence.
MR – Muscat Regiment.
Musar – An Omani turban.
MV – Merchant Vessel.
NAAFI – Navy Army and Air Force Institutes (canteens and shops for service personnel).
Na'am – Yes.
Naib Wali – Assistant governor.
NATO – North Atlantic Treaty Organisation.
NCO – Non-commissioned officers.
Negd – The region between the hills and the desert.
NOC – No Objection Certificate (for entry to a country).
OC – Officer Commanding.
Oedema – Swelling.
OG – Olive green.
Ops – Operations.
PA – Personal Assistant.
PDO – Petroleum Development (Oman). Oman's main oil company (part of Shell).
PDRY – People's Democratic Republic of Yemen.
PFLOAG – Popular Front for the Liberation of the Occupied Arabian Gulf.
Picquet – Position on a hilltop.
PNG – *Persona non grata.*
Post mortem – After death (can refer to an examination of the body).
PSYOPS – Psychological operations.
Qadi – A *Sharia* judge.
Qahwa – Arabic coffee.
QM – Quartermaster.
R & R – Rest and recuperation.
RAEC – Royal Army Education Corps.
RAF – Royal Air Force.
RAMC – Royal Army Medical Corps.
RAVC – Royal Army Veterinary Corps.
RCVS – Royal College of Veterinary Surgeons.
RE – Royal Engineers.
REME – Royal Electrical and Mechanical Engineers.
RG – Royal Guard.
RGR – Royal Guard Regiment (the Sultan's bodyguard).
RPG-7 – Shoulder-fired recoilless anti-tank rocket-propelled grenade-launcher.
RSM – Regimental Sergeant Major.
Rub al Khaya – The Empty Quarter.
RVC – The Royal Veterinary College (University of London).
SAF – Sultan's Armed Forces.
Salaam alay koom – Peace be upon you.
SAM-7 – Shoulder-fired Soviet surface-to-air missile.
SAS – Special Air Service.

Sharia – Islamic court based on the Koran.

Shemaal – Powerful wind common just before the annual monsoon.

Shemagh – Omani headdress worn to keep out sun and sand.

Shukran – Thank you.

SITREP – Situation report.

Skyvan – A small short take-off and landing transport aircraft made by Short and Harland of Belfast.

SLR – Self-loading rifle.

SOAF – Sultan of Oman's Air Force.

SOAN – Sultan of Oman's Navy.

SOP – Standard operating procedure.

Souk – Market.

SSM – Squadron Sergeant Major.

Strikemaster – A British-made light jet bomber aircraft.

Syce – Groom.

Tabeeb (baitary) – Doctor (of animals).

Tagiyah – Small white rounded cap.

TB – Tuberculosis.

T'fuddl – Welcome, come in, help yourself.

TW – Taylor Woodrow.

Umm al Gwarrif (UAG) – Headquarters of Dhofar Brigade.

U/S – Unserviceable.

Verey light – Coloured signalling flare.

VO – Veterinary Officer.

Wadi – Valley.

Wagid takleef – Big problem.

Wa inta kayf haalic? – And how are things with you?

Wali – Governor of a district or Province.

Way alay koom salaam – And peace also be unto you.

WO – Warrant Officer.

Wussum – Branding or applying fire to skin to 'treat' disease.

Yimkin – Maybe, perhaps.

Further Reading

Akehurst, J., *We Won a War. The Campaign in Dhofar 1965–1975* (Michael Russell Publishing Limited, Salisbury, 1982).

De la Billière, P., *Looking for Trouble. SAS to Gulf Command. The Autobiography* (HarperCollins Publishers, London, 1995).

Fiennes, R., *Where Soldiers Fear to Tread* (Hodder and Stoughton, London, 1975).

Gardiner, I., *In the Service of the Sultan* (Pen & Sword, Barnsley, 2006).

Geraghty, T., *Who Dares Wins. The Story of the Special Air Service, 1950–1980* (Lionel Leventhal Limited, London, 1980).

Henderson, E., *This Strange Eventful History. Memoirs of Earlier Days in the UAE and Oman* (Quartet Books, London, 1988).

Jeapes, T., *SAS Secret War* (HarperCollins Publishers, London, 2000).

Jenkins, A., *Built on Teamwork* (William Heinemann, London, 1980).

Morris, J., *Sultan in Oman* (Faber & Faber, London, 1986).

Niven, B.M., *Special Men, Special War. Portraits of the SAS and Dhofar* (Imago Productions (F.E.) Pte. Ltd., Singapore, 1990).

Peyton, W.D., *Old Oman* (Stacey International, London, 1983).

Phillips, W., *Unknown Oman* (Librairie du Liban, Beirut, 1971).

Phillips, W., *Oman – A History* (Librairie du Liban, Beirut, 1971).

Raban, J., *Arabia Through the Looking Glass* (William Collins, Sons & Co. Ltd., London, 1979).

Smiley, D., *Arabian Assignment* (Leo Cooper Limited, London, 1975).

Index

Abdur Rahim, laboratory technician, 12
Adams, President John Quincy, viii
Adoo, enemy, 8, 12, 13, 19, 62, 76, 98, 141,
143, 187–90, 193; and animals, 72, 80, 101,
165, 167; Battle of Mirbat, 27; Garthwaite
killed by, 147
Afghanistan, Psychological operations, ix
Ahmed Ali Fat, *see* 'Taqah Ahmed'
Akehurst, Brigadier John, 17, 171; killing
camels, 165; declares end of war in
Oman, 200
Al-Balid, 44
Alcohol, 11, 18, 136, 149
Al Falaj Hotel, 130, 139, 172–3
Al Jaboob, Ahmed bin Salim, 146
Al Mahysun, Mohammed Awath,
Veterinary Assistant, 55
Al Mashani, Princess Mizoon bint Ahmed,
11, 37, 141, 154
Al Mashani, Sheikh Ahmed Ali, 141
Al Mashani, Sheikh Isa bin Ahmed, 154–7;
author treats his camels, 155–6; treats his
cows, 156–7
Al Mutassim, Major Sayyid, ADC to Sultan
Qaboos, 48, 60
Al Said, see Royal Yacht
Al Said, Sayyid Tariq bin Taimur, 85
Al Shanfari, Said Ahmed Said, 49, 51
Al Theeb, Hafeedth bin Ahmed, Veterinary
Dresser, 13, 16, 49, 51–3, 55, 56, 57, 64,
67–8, 141, 142–4, 146, 153; plans to
marry, 160–1; 162; author bids farewell
to, 195
Al Wuhaibi, Lieutenant Colonel Said
Salem, President of Royal Court, 138–9,
153–4, 200
Al Yafai, Saleh bin Hassan, Veterinary
Dresser, 6, 13, 16, 26, 28, 33, 34, 37–8, 48,
49–50, 51, 53–4, 55, 56, 57–8, 64, 66–9,
78–9; treats author and Higson to a meal,
80; broadcasts on radio, 80; 91–5, 118,

120–1, 124–5, 126–7, 153, 154–7; sets up
shop, 159–60; 162–3, 166; author bids
farewell to, 195
Ali, tea boy, 64, 68–9, 70
American Embassy, Muscat, 139
Animal cargo: author inspects, 52–3
Animals in War Memorial, Park Lane,
London, 164
Ansell, Elizabeth, vi, 182
Ansell, Roy, vi, 186, 195–6; offered
McGilligan's job, 182–3
Arabian Gulf, ix, 1, 6 ,13, 34, 36, 51
Armalite M16 5.56mm rifle, 23, 28, 74, 103,
188, 189
Army Veterinary and Remount Services, *see*
AVRS
Arzat, 27, 44
Askari: Bir bint Ahmed, 12, 38, 55, 81;
quarantine control, 15, 16, 49; Sudh, 27–9;
Salalah, 38–9, 83, 122; Seeb, 114; Shabiat,
154
Augusta Bell 205 helicopter, 25, 146, 167,
190
AVRS, 117, 164, 171, 183
Aydrus, Mohammed, Veterinary Assistant,
55

Bahrain, 135
Bait Al Falaj, Ruwi, 113, 197
Bait Ma'asheni tribe, 141, 144, 154–5
Baluch, or Baluchi, 17, 30, 58, 167
Baluchistan, 17, 110
Basra, Abdu' Sittar, Agriculture Officer,
122–3, 125
Batinah coast, 114
BATT, Land Rover breaks down, 125–6;
medical services,142–3; Team Leader,
75–9, 98–100
BATT Vet, vii, ix, 7, 13, 19, 25, 40, 42, 49,
50, 55, 60, 114, 119, 134, 149, 154, 168,
195–6, 200

BBC World Service, 81
BBME, 90, 148
Beaconsfield, RAEC, 6, 164
Bears, Himalayan black and sloth, 115, 137
Begbie, Colonel, Defence Adviser British High Commission, 180–2
Bibi, *see* Al Mashani, Princess Mizoon bint Ahmed
Bir bint Ahmed: introduction to, 10–14; 55, 64, 92, 106, 121, 148, 151, 161; staff, 55–6, 146; cattle herd, 57; *askari*, 81; bull pens, 125, 182; *falaj*, 162
Bombay (now Mumbai): zoo animals come from, 105, 112, 116; zookeepers, 116; author visits, 172, 174–5
Boran bulls, 159, 178–9
Braik bin Hamoud, Sheikh, *Wali* of Dhofar, 11, 12, 40, 60, 72; DDD and, 35; quarantine regulations, 15, 49; author treats his goat, 163; BATT Vet and, 172
British Army Training Team, *see* BATT
British Bank of the Middle East, *see* BBME
British Embassy, Muscat, 139
British High Commission, Nairobi, 172, 180
Browning 9mm automatic pistol, 23, 64, 72, 74, 99, 180, 187
Brunton, Beatty, 109
Brunton, Tony, Assistant Manager, Royal Stables, vi, 45, 107–9, 112, 128
Bulls: Friesian, 13, 56, 58, 162, 182; Kenyan, 170–1, 176–9, 181, 193; at sea, 182–6; pens, 76–7, 122, 125, 159; treatment for abscess, 58–9
Butler, Michael, 11, 13, 21, 40, 56; entertains author, 62–3; 122, 129, 144, 159, 178, 182
Butler, Robin, PA to Robin Young, 39, 60; entertains author, 62–3; 148, 172, 185
Bux, Rasul, Veterinary Assistant, 46–7, 71

Camel Corps, The Imperial: monument in London, 164
Camels, ix, 8, 28, 65, 72, 77, 165; Sultan Qaboos and, 14, 199; treating, 14, 77, 78, 80, 155, 164–6, 190; *adoo* and, 20, 62, 165; milk, 38, 69; *wussum* and, 67; mange, 155–6
Camel spider, 121
Cameronians (Scottish Rifles), 7
Carter, Surgeon-Major Henry, FRS, 123
Castration, 168–8; cultural problems, 133

Cattle: *Jebali*, ix, 8, 56–7, 66, 100, 154–5, 189; upgrading local stock, 13, 40 ,56, 77, 182; milk, 56–7, 78, 154, 158, 162, 179; Operation Taurus, 72; treating, 76, 78, 98, 152–4; water, 101, 141; exotic US dairy cattle, 120, 171; author saves cattle and goats from starvation, 152–4; milk fever, 156–7; *see also* Bulls
Charles Kendall and Partners, 117, 130
Civil Aid Department, 46, 70
Civil Aid Teams, 8, 46, 76, 79, 101, 141, 168
Civil Liaison Officer (Dhofar), 46, 128
Clarke, Major John, Manager, Royal Stables, vi, 14, 45; involved in *Jebal Akhdar* campaign, 104; 112–13, 128, 132, 134
Clemenger, Major John, vii
'Colin', Skyvan pilot, 42
Communism, ix, 7–8, 193
Coup, 1970, 5; Maclean and, 85
Cracker battery, 10, 82
Creasey, Major General Timothy, Commander Sultan's Armed Forces, vi, 197–8

Dahariz Ahmed, Veterinary Assistant, 55
DDD, 8–9, 21, 33, 35, 56, 171; first visit to offices, 39–41; CAD teams, 46; bulls policy, 77; Saleh and, 80; rubbish disposal, 124; water, 142, 168; delivering Kenya bulls, 181–6
de la Billière, Lieutenant Colonel Peter: Commanding Officer, 22SAS Regiment, Briefed author, 6–7, 99; involved in *Jebal Akhdar* campaign, 104; 148
Desert Regiment, 17
de Silva, Felix, Director General Omani Police, 131
Dhofar Brigade, xii, 17, 25, 74, 89, 90, 165, 171, 200
Dhofar Development Department, *see* DDD
Dogs: author examines HM The Sultan's, 92–5; escape, 94–5; courtiers' dogs, 37, 84; 'Bron', 87, 92; 'Mac', 92, has surgery, 150–2; 'Rashid', 112, 117
Donkeys, 28, treating, 14, 33, 99, 120–1; *adoo* and, 62; SAF, 167
Driving licence: problems with, 130–1
Droitwich, Ministry of Defence: author's posting to, 186
Dubai, 131
Durrant, Major Geoffrey, vii

207

Education in Oman, 56

Empty Quarter, *Rub al Khaya*, 107, 187

Falaj, aqueduct system, 12, 40, 161–2
Field Surgical Team (55-FST), 68, 146;
operate on dog, 151–2; revive Lord Head,
150
Firing, *see wussum*
Firqat, 8, 27, 72, 75–6, 98–103, 142, 144, 147,
188
Fletcher, Brigadier Jack, Dhofar Brigade
Commander, vii, 9, 171
FMC farm, 171
FN, *Fabrique Nationale*: General Purpose
Machine Gun, GPMG, 18; self-loading
rifle 7.62mm SLR, 18, 22
Fokker Friendship, aircraft, 41, 135, 173
Fort Jalali, 111, 139
Fort Mirani, 111
Foster-Turner, Mike, Taylor Woodrow
Manager, 90, 173
Fox, desert, 116, 137, 144
Frankincense, 13, 27, 44, 66, 123, 166, 190
Frontier Force, 17, 58

Garthwaite, Captain Simon, 21, 103; killed
by enemy (*adoo*), 147
Gayler, Gren, Salalah Palace engineer, 85–8,
105–6, 128
Geraghty, Tony, 147
Goats, 8, 142, 158; Sultan's, 14, 152–4;
author treating, 14, 19, 31–3, 37, 48, 66–7,
70, 79, 163–4, 189; prized, 15, 125, 142;
quarantine and, 15, 33, 49, 51, 57, 160;
wussum, 67; Operation Taurus, 72; author
saves goats from starvation, 152–4
Governor: of Dhofar, *see* Braik bin
Hamoud, Sheikh; of Mirbat, 191–2; of
Sudh, 19, 25, 28–34, 119; of Taqah, 55,
123–5
Graham-Jones, Oliver, vi, advises on zoo
animals, 116–17; 130; arrives Muscat,
135–6; inspects zoo animals, 137–8; tours
Muscat with author, 138–9; receives gift
from Sultan, 139
Gulf Air, 41, 172
Gulf of Oman, 36, 132
Gwadar, Pakistan, 17

Hafeedth, *see* Al Theeb, Hafeedth bin
Ahmed

Hamid, Maclean's Indian clerk, 134—5
Harcourt, Major Geoff, CO Royal Guard
Regiment, 47
Harris, Mrs Eileen, 130
Harrods: Pet Department, 37, 43, 84
Head, The Rt Hon The Viscount, former
Minister of Defence, 148; faints at
'Roman orgy', 149–50
'Hearts and Minds', viii, ix; importance in
Dhofar, 8, 9, 80; veterinary work and, x,
9, 25, 106, 168, 171; Operation Storm, 99,
100, 193, 196
Hedgehogs, observation posts, 10
Henderson, Don, Managing Director,
Kenya Livestock Agency, 172, 177–8;
educates author about bulls, 178–9
Henna, 189
Hercules C-130 transport aircraft, 5, 6
Hewson, Commander Brian, Master of the
Royal Yacht, 87, 89
Higson, Captain Ben, PSYOPS officer, 21, 61
Hormuz, Straits of, *see* Straits of Hormuz
Hornbeam line, 62, 193
Horne, Major Tony, viii
Horses: Al-Balid ancient breeding centre,
44; *Reem el Fellah*, 45; shoeing, 46–7;
firing, 66, 71; author treats, 70–2;
snakebite, 121; shoots horse with liver
failure, 132; fails to castrate stallion, 133;
castrates stallions, 169–70; Mirbat famous
for, 190; lumps, 198–9
Hospitals: Salalah, 11, 68–70, 88, 91, 120;
American Mission, 11, 132; field, *see* Field
Surgical Team
Huey, *see* Augusta Bell 205 helicopter
Humane killer: author buys, 180–1
Hussein of Jordan, King, 18
Hyena, 116, 120, 137–8, 144

'Ian', Sergeant (interpreter, Intelligence
Corps), 26, 28, 30–3
Ibri, 114
'Innes, Captain John', 21, 24
Iran, 36; Shah of, 18; Iranian Battle Group,
76, 187–90, 193; Helicopter Squadron,
25–6, 34
Iraq: Psychological operations, ix; Wilkins
and, 194
Isa, His Highness Sheikh, *see* Al Mashani,
Sheikh Isa bin Ahmed
Izki, 114

Jackson, Norman, Manager of BBME, 90; invites author to 'Roman orgy', 148
Jarvis, Major Tony, Civil Liaison Officer (Dhofar), 46, 70–2, 121, 128
Jeapes, Major General Tony: involved in *Jebal Akhdar* campaign, 104; Operation Taurus, 72
Jebal, Dhofar, 5, 12, 14, 35; Hornbeam line, 62, 76; Operation Jaguar, 75; drilling for water, 90, 141, 189; author makes final visit to, 187–90
Jebal Akhdar campaign, 187–90; *adoo* and, *see adoo*, 104, 113; Clarke and, 104; de la Billière and, 104, 148; Smiley and, 105
Jebali people, ix, 8, 189; importance of animals, ix, 8, 14, 31, 40, 77–8, 98, 100, 158, 165; indoctrination, 8; 'hearts and minds', 9, 21, 80, 97–9, 101, 168, 171, 193; Sultan and, 9, 48; refugees, 64–70; veterinary assistant, 144, 146
Jebal Regiment, 17
Jebal Samhan, 190
Jibjat: trip to, 74–80; treats animals at, 77–9; author visits, 98–100

Kalbuh Bay, 131–2, 136, 196, 200
Kateebat Janoobiya (KJ) Regiment, 17
Katyusha 122mm rocket, 5
'Keith', Tawi Team Leader, 103
'Kennel Club', RAF Regiment dog handlers' Mess, 4, 196
Kent, Lance Corporal A., vi, 147
Kenya: author visits, 176–84
'Kev', armourer, 22, 23
Khareef, south-west monsoon, 71, 97, 148, 167, 186
Khuria Muriya islands, 107
King-Fretts, Major Paddy, 'A' Squadron Commander, vi, 21, 24, 61, 72, 82, 96–8, 122, 128, 171–2; leaves Oman, 173
Klotz, Chris, American Peace Corps Volunteer, 40, 120–1

Labalaba, Talaiasi, Sergeant, 147
Landon, Colonel Tim, 8
Lane, Corporal Bronco, 19, 96, 98
Lawson, Dr Isaac, 189
'Lee', Gunner, 101–2
Long Kesh prison camp, 1

Loqman, Palace courtier, 87, 91–2; author treats his dog, 150–2
Lympne, 75

Mac, *see* Maclean, James; dog, 'Mac'
Macaques, 116, 137–8
Maclean, James, ('Mac'), Secretary to Sultan Qaboos vii, 36, 43, 60–1; author visits, 83–90; 112, 114–18, 129–32, 134–6, 138, 196–8
Malik, Abdul, servant to the Sultan, 92–5
Mange, 78, 92, 155–6
Marabou stork, *see* Stork, Marabou
Martini-Henry rifle, 12, 22, 83
Masirah, RAF, 6, 23, 42, 195
Maze prison camp, *see* Long Kesh
McGilligan, Connor, Provincial Veterinary Officer, 129, 159; arrives Salalah, 167; author shows him the ropes, 168; visits Muscat with author, 168–70; 171, 173; resigns, 181; meets the bulls, 186
McLaren, Major Bill, vii
Mecom Oil Company, 76
Medinat al Haq, *see* White City
Midway, also Thumrait, 76, 167, 187; Midway Road, 76, 100, 187, 193
Mines, anti-personnel, 13, 62, 64, 65, 76
Mirbat: battle of, 27, 147; veterinary centre, 55; author calls in, 190; famous for breeding horses, 190
Moffat, Major Scott, vi, vii, 3, 6, 9, 10–16, 18–24, 25–33, 36–43, 44, 45, 47, 48; makes his farewells, 55–6; received by Sultan Qaboos, 59–61; provides help from Cyprus, 168
Mohammed, Mess attendant, 10, 81
Mombasa: author flies to, 181; 182–4
Monsoon, south-west, *see* khareef
Moresby, Sir Fairfax, anti-slavery campaigner, 52
Mughsayl, 62
Mumbai, formerly Bombay, *see* Bombay
Muscat: author first visits, 106; description of, 110–11; police, 130; old palace, 134
Muscat Levy Corps, 110
Muscat Regiment, 17, 95, 122, 147, 148
Mutassim, Major Sayyid Al, *see* Al Mutassim, Major Sayyid
Muthaiga Country Club: author stays at, 176–7
Muttrah, 108–10; author visits souk, 138

Nafis, Palace courtier, 87, 91
Naib Wali, the, of Taqah, 124–5
Nairobi: author flies to, 174–5
Nelson, Midshipman Horatio, 139
Nizwa, 114
Northern Ireland: author posted to, 1–3;
    PSYOPS and, ix
Northern Frontier Regiment, 17

Oman Artillery, 18
Oman Gendarmerie, 18
Operation Jaguar, 75, 141
Operation Storm, vii, ix, 7, 99, 143, 152,
    171–2, 196
Operation Taurus, 72
Orr, Brigadier Harry, vi, 194; debriefs
    author, 200

Packham, Brigade Major Peter, 25, 171
Palace, Royal: Muscat, 110, 113, 134, 194;
    Robat, 12, 36–7, 82, 86, 91, author visits,
    92–5; Salalah, 7, 27, 39, 128, 153, Moffat
    visits, 59–61; Seeb, 105–6, 108, 114, 134;
    animals, 197; vet, 134, 138, 140, 194–200;
    agents, see Charles Kendall and partners;
    engineer, Muscat, see Williams, Alex;
    engineer, Salalah, see Gayler, Gren
PDO, 36, 114, 118; Maclean and, 36, 197
PDRY, ix, 5, 49, 62, 193, Socotra and, 49, 185
People's Democratic Republic of Yemen, see
    PDRY
Petroleum Development (Oman), see PDO
PFLOAG, 5, 7, 35, 91, 143, 186
'Phil', Skyvan pilot, 74–5
Phillips, Dr Wendell, 108
Popular Front for the Liberation of the
    Occupied Arabian Gulf, see PFLOAG
President of the Royal Court, see Al
    Wuhaibi, Lieutenant Colonel Said Salem
Princess Mizoon bint Ahmed, see Al
    Mashani, Princess Mizoon bint Ahmed
Pringle, Chuck, Managing Director, Yahya
    Costain, vi, 131–2, 136, 138, 196, 200
Psychological operations, see PSYOPS
PSYOPS: importance of, viii, ix; Dhofar, 7,
    21, 143; Higson and, 21, 61, 74, 195;
    Northern Ireland, ix

Qaboos bin Said, His Majesty Sultan:
    assumes power, ix, 5, 7–9, 85; 'hearts and
    minds', 8–9, 11, 48; armed forces, 17, 62,

200; allies, 18; government, 35, 56, 85,
    187; court, 37, 43, 82–3, 134; stables, 45,
    104, 128; camels, 199; receives Moffat,
    60–1
Qara hills, 5, 14–5, 28, 100, 144; people, 8,
    65, 76, 143, 153; primitive medicine, 67
Quarantine: quarantine station at Raysut,
    14–15, 49, 160–1; importance of, 15, 33,
    80; importation of sheep and goats from
    East Africa, 50–3, 57–8; cattle from
    Kenya, 159, 186
Quetta, capital of Baluchistan, Pakistan, 17
Quigley, Major Gerry, 2–3

Rabies, 42, 84
RAEC, see Beaconsfield
RAF Regiment, 4, 8, 10, 42
RAF Salalah, 5, 6, 25, 61, 80
Raffay, Doctor, Royal physician, 88
R'as Al Khaymah: bulls sourced from, 13;
    Ansell and, 182
Rashid, Major RGR, Royal physician, 88
Ratel, Arabian, 144
RAVC, vii; Northern Ireland and, 1–2;
    Depot, 3, 5; Graham-Jones and, 117;
    McGilligan and, 129, 167; in Oman, 3,
    159, 168, 171, 194, 196
Raven, Peter, SAS Troop Commander, 187
Raven, Warrant Officer Steve, Intelligence
    Corps, 187
Raven's Roost (BATT camp): author visits,
    187–90
Raybould, Commodore Jeremy,
    Harbourmaster, 49, 50–1, 53, 186
Raysut, port, 11, 50, 71, 87, 185–6; refugee
    camp, 64–9; quarantine station, see
    quarantine
Reem el Fellah, Sultan's favourite horse, 45
Refugee camp: visited by author, 64–9;
    treats pregnant woman, 67–9
Robat Palace, see Palace
Robb, Major Martin, 46, 193
Romans, Reverend Philip and Laura, vi, 7
Royal Army Education Corps, see
    Beaconsfield
Royal Army Veterinary Corps, see RAVC
Royal Engineers: Hornbeam line, 62; water,
    101, 141; sapper with injured foot, 144–6
Royal Guard Regiment, 39, 44, 47, 59, 82,
    94, 198

Royal Irish Rangers: Garthwaite and, 21, 147

Royal Oman Police: traffic, 38, 41, 111, 130–1; immigration, 135–6; Mounted unit, 198

Royal Oman Stud Book, 199

Royal Stables, 44–7; smartened up, 128; author visits new stables, 170; offered position at, 196; author visits horses, 198–9; author accepts post of Veterinary Officer, 200

Royal Veterinary College, University of London, *see* RVC

Royal Yacht, *Al Said*: author visits, 89

Royal Zoo, preparations for, 115–16; author visits, 170

Rub al Khaya, *see* Empty Quarter

Ruwi, 11, 113, 132, 136, 173

RVC, author graduates from, 1; consults, 70; Graham-Jones lecturer at, 116–7, 139

SAF, 10, 17–18, 27, 76; 98, 100; HQ, 113; donkeys, 167

Sahiwal bulls, 159, 178–9

Said bin Taimur, His Majesty Sultan, 5, 14, 17, 36, 111; marine autograph book, 139

Saleh, *see* Al Yafai, Saleh bin Hassan

Salem, Lieutenant Colonel Said Al Wuhaibi, President of Royal Court, *see* Al Wuhaibi, Lieutenant Colonel Said Salem

Sandhurst, RMA, 2, 5, 7, 17

SAS: author's opinion of, ix, 96–8; Bradbury Lines briefing, 6–9; BATT Vets, ix, 3, 21, 75–6, 171; *Jebal Akhdar* campaign, 14, 104–5; Mirbat, battle of, 27; Operation Jaguar, 75; operation at Tawi Atair, 101–3; medical work, 143–6, 151; squadron changes, 193; secret presence in Oman revealed, 193

Sayyid Tariq bin Taimur Al Said, *see* Al Said, Sayyid Tariq bin Taimur

Seeb, palace and stables, 105, 108, 112, 114, 129, 134, 139, 198–9; airport, 106–7, 113, 116, 135, 168, 174, 196

Shabiat, 11, 154–7, 163

Shah of Iran, *see* Iran, Shah of

Shanfari, Said Ahmed Said Al, *see* Al Shanfari, Said Ahmed Said

Sharia court, 18, 111, 162

Sheba, Queen of, 27, 123

Sheep: quarantine, 15, 49, 50, 52–3, 57; treating, 66, 157

Shemaal, 172–3

Shenoon, head 'lad' at Royal Stables, 46–7, 71, 113, 121, 128; Sultan Qaboos and, 45

Skyvan aircraft, 14, 25, 41, 72, 74–5, 79, 101, 167

Slavery, 37, 52

Smiley, Colonel David: *Jebal Akhdar* campaign, 105

Snakebites, 120–1

SOAF, 25, 72, 74, 101, 107

SOAN, 20, 50, 89

Socotra Archipelago, 185

Somalia: importation of sheep and goats from, 15, 50, 51 ,57, 120

Souk (or *suq*): Salalah, 39; author explores, 59–60; Muttrah, 109

South Yemen, *see* PDRY

Southern Trader, Merchant Vessel, transports bulls from Mombasa to Oman, 181–6; author sails on, 184–6

Special Air Service Regiment, *see* SAS

Spinneys, 149

Stork: Marabou, 116, 138; painted, 116

Storm, Operation, *see* Operation Storm

Straits of Hormuz, 36

Strator, Rita, 84

Strikemaster aircraft, 25, 27, 107, 113, 165

Studbook, *see* Royal Oman Stud Book

Sudh: visit to, 27–33; author revisits, 119

Sultan Qaboos bin Said, *see* Qaboos bin Said, His Majesty Sultan

Sultan Said bin Taimur, *see* Said bin Taimur, His Majesty Sultan

Sultan's Armed Forces, *see* SAF

Sultan of Oman's Air Force, *see* SOAF

Sultan of Oman's Navy, *see* SOAN

Sumhuran, 123

Taqah: description of, 123

'Taqah Ahmed' Ali Fat, Veterinary Assistant, 55; author visits, 121–5

Tarwid, Flight Lieutenant Alek, 190–1, 192–3

Tawi Atair: author visits, 101; SAS operation at, 101–3

Taylor, Sir Frank, 90

Taylor Woodrow, author entertained at barbecue, 90–1, 93–4, 173

Templar, General Sir Gerald, viii

Tetanus: risk of, 144–5; soldier reacts to antitoxin, 145–6
Thompson, Major Brian, vii
Thumrait, *see* Midway

Umm al Gwarrif, camp, 17, 18
United Arab Emirates, 11, 36, 114, 182
United States Department of Agriculture, *see* USDA
United States Embassy, Muscat, *see* American Embassy
USDA, 120

Viscount aircraft, 25, 36, 41–2, 44–5, 61, 107, 173

Wali, see Governor
Water: importance of, ix, 8, 27, 62, 72, 77, 82, 101, 189, 193; camel and, 165; *see also falaj*
Wessex helicopter, 25, 190–3
White City: author visits, 141

Wilkins, Brigadier Hector, 183, 194
Williams, Alex, Palace Chief Engineer, 115–16, 136
Wooldridge, Richard, British Animal Health Adviser, Beirut, 119–20, 159
Worby, Wing Commander Ian, 25
Wussum, or firing, 66–7, 71, 80, 156, 160, 166
Wutayyah, old Royal Stables, 14, 108, 112–14; castrations at, 132–4, 169–70; Royal Oman Police and, 198

Yacoub, driver, 114–15
Yahya Costain, 131, 196
Yeandle, Staff Sergeant George, 2, 84
Young, Robin, Director DDD, 35, 39

Zanzibar, 37, 110
Zoo animals: imported into Oman, 105–6; inspection of, 137–8